Look at the SON

The Fruit of Medjugorje

How one woman was led more deeply to
Christ through the heavenly presence of the
Virgin Mary in Medjugorje.

Kimberly Bruce

Look at the SON
The Fruit of Medjugorje
by Kimberly Bruce

Printed in the United States of America

ISBN 9781619044043

The Scripture quotations contained herein are from the New Revised Standard Version Bible, copyright © 1989, Division of Christian Education of the National Council of Churches of Christ in the U.S.A. Used by permission. All rights reserved.

The Roman Catholic Church has not yet made an official ruling on the apparitions of the Blessed Virgin Mary in Medjugorje, still ongoing. This author humbly submits to whatever the Church decides.

www.xulonpress.com

To my husband Paul —
I look forward, my love, with joy
to these next chapters of our journey
together in love.
And to my darling children —
Conor, Anthony and Katerina,
Be Holy

God does plant a dream in our hearts,
but that dream is more awesome in the mind of God
than we can imagine...

And God can speak to us in ordinary and sometimes extraordinary ways everyday if we but look, expect and accept the little incidences and seeming "coincidences" as being from Him. The more we accept them, the more they seem to happen. Or maybe the more we finally see them because our hearts and minds have finally been opened to them. I can picture God in Heaven saying, "Thanks be to Me, they *finally* see — they're 'getting' it!"

-Kimberly Bruce

Table of Contents

Chapter 1

"Look at the Sun!"

I was a faith-filled child. My mother says that I was always very spiritual. People used to call my bedroom "the church" because of the religious statues, pictures and trinkets all neatly adorning it — right alongside Donny Osmond posters! But how could I have known then at such a young age that one day God would use me, by means of a life-changing encounter through the Holy Virgin in Medjugorje, to lead others closer to Him? I look back on my life now and I realize that every piece of the puzzle — the twists, turns, joys and trials of life — was being used by Him to form me into His little servant, His little "emissary" here on earth . . . something He longs to do through your life as well.

Raised Roman Catholic by my parents (although my dad was Lutheran), church was important in our life as a family. When I was quite small I remember going with my parents each Sunday morning to both Catholic mass and to the Lutheran service at my Dad's church. This practice of going to two services every Sunday slowly began to wane after my brother arrived. It got to be a bit too much for my parents to attend both with a growing family. I continued to attend mass with my mother every Sunday, while my dad attended his Lutheran church.

In high school I chose to attend a Catholic school. There my faith really began to blossom like never before. Reading the Bible was required my freshman year in our daily religion class. The Word of God, for the first time, began to amaze me. After doing my reading homework I would show up at the dinner table, Bible in hand, and exclaim, "Listen to this!" as I would read Jesus' words to my mom, dad, brother, and sister. I don't know if it had any impact on them, but I was captivated! By this point my dad had been faithfully attending Catholic mass with us every week for many years, though not having officially converted, which continues to the present.

One thing I knew as early as my teen years was that I wanted to bring people to God. Along with marrying and having a family, that was the deepest desire of my heart. I had a hard time deciding what to major in at college because nothing seemed to line up with this desire. I didn't know exactly *how* I wanted to serve the Kingdom of God or how to even describe this feeling to anyone. If I were to major in theology, what kind of job could I get after college? I did not want to become a teacher in a classroom and I also did not feel called to be a nun.

I spent my first two years of college majoring in nursing because I loved the field of medical science and working in a hospital. I had been a "Candy Striper" as a young teen, volunteering in our local hospital, and my dear mother, the greatest influence in my life, had been a nurse. Despite the joy of what I was learning and love of the college I attended, I decided to leave the school and the pursuit of nursing after two years. Why? The honest answer, which I never told anyone, is that I could no longer get away from the gnawing realization that what I wanted to care for was people's *souls*, not their bodies. Ever present within me was this unspoken, and at times barely conscious, desire to bring people to God. It would continue to haunt me for years to come. I had no role models of those in lay ministry to follow with this desire. I had no direction to pursue, and no real idea how I would carry this out in my life. Everyone else was off pursuing careers in all sorts of fields. No one I knew was out to "bring people to God." Where could I get a job doing that? After much prayer, I chose to switch schools and earned a bachelor's degree in mass communication. The field of public relations and the various communications media intrigued me as ways of connecting people with one another, and I loved to write.

Being a spiritually minded individual, as far as those who claimed to see apparitions of Jesus, saints, angels, or Mary, the mother of Jesus, I had generally believed in them. I knew they happened in the past. Apparitions are in the Bible – Moses and Elijah appeared with Jesus when He was transfigured before the apostles Peter, James, and John. Angels appeared to Mary, Joseph, and to Zachariah, the father of John the Baptist, among others. There have also been apparitions of the Virgin Mary through the centuries which have been approved by the Roman Catholic Church after having undergone intense scrutiny and investigation. I knew also that it was not an impossibility that future apparitions could occur. I believed very strongly in the apparitions of the Virgin Mary in Fatima, Portugal in 1917. I had even read a book about these apparitions as a child and looked upon Lucia, Jacinta, and Francisco, the three children Our Lady had appeared to, as saints. Even so, when I first heard about the supposed apparitions of the Virgin Mary to a group of six young people in Medjugorje, Yugoslavia (present day Bosnia-Herzegovina) beginning in June of 1981 and continuing into the present, I was a bit skeptical. "I don't know…," is what I thought to myself as I watched the nightly television news show *PM Magazine* do a segment on Medjugorje one evening.

To give you a little more background on Medjugorje, the Virgin Mary has been reportedly appearing to four girls and two boys since the youngest, Yakov, was ten and the oldest, Vicka, was sixteen. Mary comes giving messages through these visionaries to bring us to deeper faith in God, to lead us on the path of holiness, and to help unbelievers, "those who do not yet know the love of God," as

Mary calls them, to come to believe. She comes calling us to prayer, conversion, fasting, penance, and peace. "Our Lady," as the Blessed Mother is also referred to, is giving ten secrets to each of the visionaries. Secrets given in her visions are nothing new. When Our Lady appeared in Fatima she gave the visionaries there secrets as well. They referred to the future and were given to the Pope at the time. All of the Fatima secrets have been revealed, with the third and final one being disclosed by Pope John Paul II in 2000.[1]

When an individual Medjugorje visionary has received all ten secrets, Our Lady no longer appears to that visionary on a daily basis. Three of the visionaries, Ivanka, Mirijana, and Yakov, have all ten secrets. They no longer see Mary on a daily basis, but only on a particular day each year, designated by Our Lady, as well as during "particularly difficult times in their lives" when she says they will need her. She has promised to continue to appear to them in this fashion for the rest of their lives. Many years ago the Blessed Virgin began again appearing to Mirijana on the second day of each month in order to pray with her specifically for unbelievers. This has continued to the present. The three remaining visionaries, Vicka, Marija and Ivan have nine of the ten secrets and still see Our Lady daily.

It is during the praying of the Rosary, at the same time every evening, that Mary appears. She says the most powerful prayer, however, is the Holy Mass and she has told the visionaries that if they "had to decide" between seeing her and going to Holy Mass, they were to "go to Holy Mass!" She has also told the visionaries that these are her last apparitions on Earth. On May 2, 1982 she revealed, "I have come to call the world to conversion for the last time. Afterward I will not appear anymore on this earth."[2] The secrets that Mary is giving in Medjugorje also concern the future. They will not begin to be revealed and take place until all the visionaries have received all ten secrets, with the exception of one lone visionary who will continue to receive daily apparitions during this period.

According to the visionaries, the first secrets will be "warnings" for mankind to come back to God. The third secret will be "a permanent and visible sign for all the world to see" left on Mt. Podbrdo, the site of Our Lady's first apparition in Medjugorje. This indestructible sign is to further confirm to the world that the visions are indeed authentic. Some of the secrets given to the visionaries we know nothing about. However, the latter secrets are chastisements for the world for sinfulness and refusal to follow God's laws. Our Lady has told the visionaries that we can lessen and mitigate these chastisements, none-theless, with our prayers. She is a loving mother who has come to call her children to repent, believe in, and follow Our Lord's teachings. Her Immaculate Heart is sad because so many choose not to believe and live only for themselves.

After I saw the segment about Medjugorje on *PM Magazine* in the 1980s, I didn't think about Medjugorje again until 1989 when my boyfriend (and future husband) gave me some articles to read by Wayne Weible, a convert to Catholicism through Medjugorje. Wayne, a Lutheran at the time, knew nothing more about the Virgin Mary than that she was Mary of Nazareth, the mother of Jesus. He popped in a video tape on Medjugorje to watch on his VCR one evening and, unbeknownst to his wife who was sitting with him on the couch, Our Lady spoke to him. She told him that he was her son and that from thereafter, if he chose, he would no longer be in his current line of work as a newspaper owner, but would spend the rest of his life spreading her messages given in Medjugorje. What was the purpose of these Medjugorje apparitions? As I have read many times, they are to bring people to her Son, Jesus, and to tell the world, "that God exists!" I was wowed. I believed. I had only to read the articles about Wayne's own story and, most importantly, hear the words and witness accounts from the visionaries themselves, and I knew — I knew this was from God.

In July of 1990 my husband Paul and I found ourselves on a plane to Medjugorje for the first leg of our honeymoon. We both knew we wanted to go and figured if we didn't make it part of our honeymoon we wouldn't have the money to travel there again anytime soon. While there I experienced the "miracle of the sun" – a common phenomenon in Medjugorje as well as in Fatima. Although people witness the sun dance and spin in Medjugorje as they did during Our Lady's last apparition in Fatima, many in Medjugorje witness other signs as well, in and around the sun. I had just such an experience. Standing outside St. James Church during the apparition one evening, I first witnessed a beautiful sight of several little birds, all the same kind, circling the left bell tower where Our Lady was at that moment in a room appearing to the visionaries Ivan and Marija. The apparition lasted 20 minutes, from 6:40pm until

7:00pm. How do I know? Because at 7:00 pm, the little birds that had been there the entire time circling the bell tower all flew off at the exact same moment.

Then suddenly, from out of nowhere, thousands upon thousands of these same little birds came together to form a huge, thick, long line. They began flying all together from the front of the church at the bell towers, over the length of the church, and heading towards the back where an outdoor pavilion and thousands of pilgrims were. At that moment, I immediately sensed the little birds were forming an escort for the Blessed Mother back to heaven. However, when they reached the back of the outdoor seating area where we were all present, the birds *stopped* and hovered over us for a moment. I then felt Our Lady stopping to lovingly look down upon all of us behind the church. Thus all of her little escorts stopped right along behind her. In the next moment, after I had sensed all this, I heard a peaceful interior command say to me, "Look at the sun!"

I turned to my left and saw the sun. It was huge. There was a blue-gray disc covering almost the entire sun. The only thing I saw of the sun as we normally see it was a bright reddish orange perimeter around its very edge. There were three to four big, blue-gray rays emanating from the sun to its left and right, as if it was being presented to me in the sky. I could stare at the sun and it didn't hurt my eyes. It was very cool in temperature to look at and very peaceful. I looked at it for several minutes, and was unaware of anyone else being able to see what I was seeing. I did not bring it up to anyone except my husband until two days later. I was with a few pilgrims one early evening and we began talking about the apparition the night I saw the "miracle of the sun." One girl said that she had smelled violets during the apparition (there were no flowers around), and we were all commenting on the behavior of the birds that night. I said, "Well…I saw something with the sun…", and a girl named Nancy, who was very knowledgeable about Medjugorje asked, "What did you see?"

I described my vision saying, "I saw a huge blue-gray disc covering almost the entire sun, almost like the moon was in front of the sun, and it was very peaceful and cool [as opposed to warm] to look at."

She looked at me a moment and said, "Do you know what you saw?" I replied, "No, what?" "You saw the Eucharist in the sun." She continued, "Many people see the Eucharist; others see the chalice." *[The Eucharist is the consecrated Host – "communion" that Catholics believe is transubstantiated along with the wine during mass at the recitation of the Eucharistic Prayer by the priest. The bread becomes the actual body of Christ (Matthew 26:26; Mark 14:22), and the wine becomes the blood of Christ (Matthew 26:27-28; Mark 14:23-24). The wine is held in a cup (traditionally called a chalice).]*

At that moment, following Nancy's words, Jesus spoke to my heart saying, "Believe! I AM Real!" I have to emphasize here that I look at my life in two phases: before that moment and after that moment. The words that Our Lord Jesus spoke to me changed my life.

Chapter 2

Body, Blood, Soul and Divinity

I completely believed in Jesus Christ. That was not the issue. Our Lord was trying to address something else with me. Although very Catholic, I was, up until that moment, in great error about a major belief of my faith: *I did not believe in the real presence of Jesus Christ in the Eucharist.* I looked upon the Host which we received in communion at every mass as just a symbol of Jesus Christ. I did not believe that the bread became the true body of Jesus and the wine became the true blood of Jesus. He remains *hidden* under the *appearance* of bread and wine, but as

Catholics we hold as an essential truth that during the consecration at holy mass, Our Lord becomes really present: *body, blood, soul and divinity.* Now I have to tell you, I was not unlike many, and I dare say possibly most Catholics, who believed just as I did. We were in grave error. The Lord was telling me, "Believe! I AM *real"* in the Eucharist! That's why the Eucharist was "presented" to me in the sky. When I heard the command in my heart to, "Look at the sun!" I was really being told to, "Look at the *SON!"* The Son is Jesus, the second person of the Holy Trinity.

I had to take time to process all of this. I had held my own beliefs for twenty-four years, up until that point, and I had to let it sink in. Even though I was not able to yet discuss or debate with anyone on the subject, one thing was for sure, I could no longer deny His presence in the Eucharist.

The very fact of not being able to deny His presence in the Eucharist is what changed my life. Once aware of this, I couldn't stay away from the Eucharist. I found myself going to mass not only on weekends, but on weekdays occasionally as well (with little children in tow.) I sought out Eucharistic Adoration devotional times in any Catholic church where I could find it scheduled. Adoration, as it is often referred to, is when a consecrated Host is placed within a monstrance, which is a stand designed to hold the Host in a window for viewing. It is often quite ornate and made of gold, and it is placed on an altar in church. People come to simply sit in the presence of Jesus, to meditate on the mystery of His presence and to pray. It is wonderful. So many miraculous things have taken place in my own personal life from just going to be with Him. It is healing, consoling, peaceful, enlightening, and can leave the participant filled with joy, gratitude and peace.

I began to grow even stronger in my faith. I grew closer to the Blessed Mother. But what I found even more amazing was that the closer I grew to her, the more she just "dumped me" at Jesus' feet. Our

Lady's only interest is bringing us closer to her Son. I found myself now growing closer to Jesus than I had ever been in my life. Many faithful Protestants think that honoring the Virgin Mary in any way is idolatry and taking away praise that should only be given to Jesus and God the Father. However, God the Father allows the Blessed Mother to bring us to Jesus now just as He allowed her to bring Jesus to us in the first place. He chose her to be the mother of Jesus. He allowed Himself to take on human form and be placed within the tabernacle of her body in order to come to His people. He continues to allow Himself to be brought to us through her. He knows coming to us through the heart of a mother is comforting, protective, and loving. Prayer intercession through the Blessed Mother is extremely powerful. Our Lady, in her messages in Medjugorje, has said, "I can intercede for you." However, she knows her place.

According to the visionaries, when people have prayed to her for healing she has responded, "I cannot heal. Only Jesus can heal. But I can *help you* with my prayers." She is our intercessor. We ask others all the time for *their* intercessory prayers to pray for us when we are sick or going through a difficult situation so why not ask the Queen of Heaven? What is the Fourth Commandment? *Honor Thy Father and Thy Mother.* Jesus honored this and all the commandments. He continues to honor His mother to this day. He will not refuse her. Who wouldn't want that powerful of an intercessor on one's side!

To further emphasize that Our Lady does not desire to overshadow her Son in any way, I have several times heard the story of Fr. Albert Shamon, a priest from New York privileged to be invited into the apparition room during the time of Our Lady's daily apparition. When Our Lady arrived and the visionaries knelt down, all in attendance knelt as well, except for this priest. Try and try as he might, he could not kneel down. Three evenings in a row he was invited into the apparition room. Three evenings in a row he was unable to kneel down. His knees would lock. The third night he asked Our Lady why this was happening. He felt her say, "I do not want My Son to kneel before Me."[3] Father then realized what was happening. Each evening he had been carrying a "pyx" on him, a small container used to carry the Eucharist (Jesus) to those who are sick and infirm and cannot attend mass. The Blessed Mother was aware that Our Lord was literally in the room when no one else was and she refused to let Him kneel before her!

Our Lady's only aim is bringing us to her Son. She has said, "I am a gift to you, because, from day to day, God permits me to be with you and to love each of you with immeasurable love."[4] He "permits" her to be with us. She has said this over and over again. The only reason she has come to earth is because the Almighty has allowed her to come. Why? He is hoping that through her, the loving heart of a mother, we might listen and be converted; we might believe!

Our Lady's way is very gentle. Her touch, via thoughts and signs, has a very different feel. She has a divinely given maternal touch. Anything I've had answered through her intercession has always been so smoothly taken care of in a gentle, serene, quick, and uplifting manner. She expresses her love for us in such a beautiful way. This grace descends from God the Father, through Jesus, and through her to us. Beautiful in appearance as well, when the visionaries have asked her, "Mother, how come you are so beautiful?" She has responded, "I am beautiful because I love."

Another very life affecting experience happened to me on my first trip to Medjugorje. It was my second day there when I decided to go to confession. I knew from reading Wayne Weible's first book, *Medjugorje: The Message*, that going to confession soon after you arrive is very important. Graces pour out on you after you receive absolution from your sins if you have made a good, honest confession. I didn't want to be exempt from those graces on my short five-day stay, so in I went. In those days there was a partition in each confessional separating the penitent from the priest. You would enter and kneel down and speak to the priest from the other side of this partition.

I'll never forget my priest that day. He was a young, newly ordained priest from England. I confessed my sins and after this was finished, he was overcome by something he seemed unable to dismiss as being from the Holy Spirit. Incapable of holding back what was being revealed to him, he told me: "Our Lady has a special purpose for you — just as she has for the children" (meaning the visionaries, as they were still called in those days). Those were words I longed to hear from heaven, the words my soul kept speaking to me about, and I began to weep.

The tears were streaming down my face, and I asked the priest if he would "say a prayer to keep

Satan away from me." I instinctively knew that with such a mission I would need protection. I was already keenly aware of how Satan worked and how cunning he is. In the months leading up to my getting married and going to Medjugorje, Satan had made a rigorous attempt to disrupt my plans. Most everyone who goes to Medjugorje can attest to this. Satan always tries to put a stop to one's plans before one travels in a deliberate effort to disrupt Our Lady's plans for conversions. The priest said to me: "Satan is very much here, even in Medjugorje, because you are the ones trying to steal his kingdom!"

The priest then surprised me by getting up and coming around the partition to where I was — something not done in the confessional unless you are confessing "face-to-face." He stood back diagonally to my left, as I continued to kneel, and he placed his hands above my head and began to pray. In the next moments, I experienced something extraordinary. Three distinct "shields" came down around me. It felt like smooth electricity starting at the top of my head, parting, and simultaneously taking paths left and right down the sides of my head, neck, shoulders, arms, etc. This process repeated itself two more times. Each shield took about a full second to envelope me. I call these shields because I knew that is exactly what they were. I knew this was a gift of protection from God. It was not until a couple of years ago that I was struck with awareness that I had received three shields specifically because they were from the Holy Trinity: one was from the Father, one was from the Son and one was from the Holy Spirit.

After this, the priest just stood back seemingly dumbfounded. I am sure he felt the power emanating through his hands as well, but I was too stunned to ask. I was new to all these miracles. If that had happened today, I would have said loud and clear, "Did you feel *that*?" He seemed at a loss as to what to do next. I believe I thanked him and left the confessional.

I kept this experience and this prophecy about my life to myself, not even sharing it with my husband out of humility and fear that he would not understand it. Two weeks later, however, after spending hours telling family members about Our Lady's messages, I began to sob on our ride home. I loved talking about Our Lady and Medjugorje, but I was physically and emotionally exhausted after spending hours doing this and fully aware of how taxing this mission could be on my life. The realization of what the priest said, and weight of it all, was now becoming evident. And I hadn't even told my husband Paul yet. He pulled the car into a parking lot and said, "Kim! *What* is wrong?" Through tears I told him about what had happened to me in the confessional that day and that I was realizing what my mission would be and what a sacrifice it also may be. I don't think he knew what to think. I was left to contemplate this on my own.

My life changed after I returned from that first trip to Medjugorje. I began praying the rosary more and fasting. Our Lady has said that with prayer and fasting you can stop wars from happening and you can suspend natural laws. That's how powerful prayer and fasting are. The prayer she asks for specifically is the rosary. When you pray the rosary you are, "praying the gospel of Jesus Christ," as I've heard some say. The rosary meditations are taken straight from the gospels in the New Testament. Our Lady says that with the rosary in our hands we can keep Satan away from us. It is that powerful. The rosary is made up of the *Lord's Prayer*, the *Hail Mary*, and the *Glory Be*. *The Apostles' Creed* and the *O My Jesus* prayers are tied to the Joyful, Sorrowful, Luminous, and Glorious mysteries. These mysteries are reflections on major events in the lives of Our Lord and His mother.

The rosary is said using a string of beads called "rosary beads," so it is easy to keep track of which prayer you are on. The rosary can be said using ones fingers, however, so one need not have an actual set of beads in order to be able to say it. It can be said anywhere and at any time.

Our Lady, over and over, has implored us through Medjugorje to "pray with the heart." By this she means to carry on a one-on-one conversation with the Lord. Simply talk to Our Lady and Jesus as if they were right there with you, which they are. Speak to them as if you were talking to your best friend. Prayer with the heart is that simple. There is nothing complicated about it. You can tell them your hopes and dreams, lament with them over the things going on in your life, praise them with love and thanksgiving, etc. Ask them for their love, guidance and direction. Heaven awaits us to speak in this fashion. God truly is our Father; therefore speak to Him as a child speaks to a very loving, all-powerful father. After all, He is the creator of the universe!

During the next several years after I returned from Medjugorje I found myself in what I call the "school of Our Lady." She was beginning to transform me. She didn't leave me orphaned once my newly realized errors about my faith were made known to me. She began to nurture me, instilling more truth and revelations within my soul. She was the source that drew me in by God's grace, however, it was to Jesus to which she was ultimately leading me. Not only did I receive the "miracle of the sun" to correct my erroneous belief about her Son's presence in the Eucharist, but she began to enlighten me with truths about the Catholic faith and the other wrong beliefs I held.

She began to do this not only through my obedient praying of the rosary, but through EWTN, the Eternal Word Television Network. I had never seen EWTN before I went to Medjugorje. Upon returning from our honeymoon, my husband and I took up residence in Warwick, Rhode Island, where, for the first time in my life I was able to view EWTN. In the Berkshires of western Massachusetts, where we were from, EWTN was not yet available on cable television as it is now. In Rhode Island, a very Catholic state, it was on cable. I learned so much from that wonderful spiritual giant, Mother Angelica, a nun and founder of the network. *Thank You, God, for her!*

I also gained so much from the priests and lay people who hosted shows on the network and those who were guests on *Mother Angelica Live.* I continue to gain and grow in the understanding of my Catholic faith through the beautiful light shining forth from that network. Our Lady put me in Rhode Island at that point in my life; of this I am sure, to educate me. During the four years I lived in Rhode Island I was away from family and friends — away from all distractions — so I could be focused on growing in my faith.

My husband had a very demanding job exacting a tremendous amount of time and energy from him during those years and he was not at home much. Our

Lady had me all to herself. During those years we had our first two babies and, as I said, I would often take them with me to mass, Adoration, and even held them in my arms as I knelt in the confessional booth during confession.

Amazing things began to take place in the next few years...

Chapter 3

Heavenly Signposts

As I was led by the Holy Spirit to tell people about Medjugorje, and was growing in faith under the guidance of Our Lady, miraculous signs appeared. Medals from Medjugorje that I would give to people after my witness to them were turning from silver to gold (another common phenomenon associated with Medjugorje). The links on a pair of my own rosary beads began to slowly change from silver to gold as I was changing and growing more obedient to Jesus and Our Lady through prayer and fasting. I frequently smelled roses — a miraculous sign signifying Our Lady's presence — during mass, holy events, while witnessing to others about Medjugorje, and in prayer. I often experienced (and continue to experience) this phenomenon with friends who, likewise, have been transformed through my witness and who are striving to becoming deeper, more faith-filled Catholics.

Once, after taping a silver Medjugorje medal to a note I was sending to a couple, I had met and spoken with about Medjugorje, the medal began turning gold before my eyes. I knew the miracle was for the couple because the medal was no longer mine. I had just finished taping it to the stationery so it was now in place for them. Another time, a blue circle miraculously appeared on a medal I was giving to my hairdresser in Rhode Island. This circle perfectly surrounded the abdomen of Our Lady where the baby Jesus would be. I immediately sensed a significant personal message from the Blessed Mother to my hairdresser. She was the first to notice its presence the moment I gave it to her, and she began to contemplate its meaning.

Our Lady can also speak to us through the witnessing of others' miraculously changed objects. It was Our Lady who utilized such a method in helping to correct me regarding an issue during my first trip to Medjugorje. Everything that we wrongly perceive is miraculously revealed to us in the presence of Our Lady of Medjugorje — even when we have no clue we are in the wrong. That is how these trips there are for me and for most everyone else who makes the sacrifices to go there or is touched by Medjugorje in some way.

A particular belief that I had held for years was about to change thanks to a five day stay in the little village. During our first trip to Medjugorje my husband and I stayed with a wonderful family who had expanded their home to accommodate the ever growing number of pilgrims flocking to the village. Most of the villagers opened up their homes in response to Our Lady asking them through the visionaries to do this for the pilgrims. There were five other pilgrims from the United States staying with us while we were there: a family of four and a single woman named Nancy, who I mentioned earlier. I learned a lot from Nancy and I know Our Lady placed her there on purpose for me.

Through talking to Nancy I found out that she was a "rescuer." I did not know what that was, but soon found out. Rescuers are those devoted, faithful, brave individuals that peaceably stand outside of abortion clinics praying for women planning to enter and trying to talk them out of having abortions. Although I had never had an abortion myself, I was decidedly pro-choice and had been for several years.

Nancy told me that she had had her arms, legs, and many other bones broken from police trying to keep her from these clinics. She had also been thrown in jail numerous times with others for pleading with women against killing their unborn children. She would every now and again return to Medjugorje for a three month stay to regain her strength to "go back out there" on the front lines to prevent abortions. Nancy's rosary bead links, which had previously been silver, had turned to gold, more golden than any rosary bead links I have ever seen miraculously turn color. Then one morning upon waking in the home we were in, she looked out a window and saw the Blessed Mother kneeling on Cross Mountain (Mt. Krizevac) before the crucifix there.

Upon seeing her, Nancy called out to the twelve year old daughter of the family whose home we were staying in, saying, "Gospa! Gospa!" which means "Our Lady! Our Lady!" They both saw her. She appeared to them as a big, white, luminous figure kneeling at the base of the cross, large enough so that they could see her from such a distance and distinct enough to know it was unmistakably her. Our Lady has told the visionaries that she herself kneels in front of that cross every morning and prays to Jesus for the world: "Yes, it is true. Almost every day I am at the foot of the cross. He has suffered on the cross, and by it, He saved the world. Every day I pray to my Son to forgive the sins of the world."[5] There are people, few in number, that have been blessed to see Our Lady there in the morning.

Knowing Nancy had received this grace of seeing Our Lady, and witnessing her golden rosary bead links, I said to myself, "Who is in the right here? *Not me*." That was a very defining moment for me. I could no longer deny that abortion was most assuredly under the "Thou Shall Not Kill" commandment. We did not have the right to kill a human being — no matter if it is in the womb or out. God has a purpose for that soul, for every soul that He creates. We can't encourage or embrace a culture of death as we are doing in our country and all over the world. It's wrong and will only lead to our detriment and ultimate demise as a nation and world community. Now I can't even believe I used to think otherwise. The scales had fallen from my eyes.

Again I was reprimanded, albeit gently. I have to say here, too, that I, being so naïve about my Catholic Christian faith, went so far as to ask Nancy a question one evening about something weighing on my mind. I asked, "What about birth control?" Now, I knew what the Catholic Church taught about it, but I was a rather "lukewarm" Catholic and didn't think it really mattered or should not matter. After all, how could God really not want us to use contraceptives? How would I and all of us deal with *that*? Nancy's response to me (she must have thought what a dimwit "in-the-dark" Catholic I was) was, "Oh, yes! It's wrong!" She said it to me gently (the sign of Our Blessed Mother again ever instructing me), but the poor girl must have been a bit distressed. After all, she was putting her life on the line daily in the fight against abortion, the fruit of the birth control mentality and culture, and I was so naïvely unappreciative of it.

Not long after we were first married I begged the Lord for His help. If He did not want my husband

and me to use birth control then He needed to aid us. We had two children in a relatively short time as our own method of Natural Family Planning wasn't working. This was complicated by two rough, emergency C-sections and difficult recoveries for me. I had never been trained in nor had I ever studied Natural Family Planning. I was just doing guesswork with my reproductive cycles — something you should not do if you've not been formally educated about.

I soon met a fantastic, highly trained Natural Family Planning counselor associated with the Creighton Model Fertility Care System and NaPro Technology — a very sophisticated and highly effective means of monitoring and maintaining a woman's reproductive and gynecological health — and the rest is history. "Ask, and it will be given to you" (Luke 11:9) has always been my favorite Bible quote. He will not leave us "orphaned." If He wants us to live a certain way He will not leave us in the dark. He will provide. What a blessing Natural Family Planning has been for our lives.

Many believe that following God's laws sets limits for their lives and takes away their freedoms. In actuality, it is the reverse. By following our own will we "bind" ourselves; we limit ourselves. When we follow our own desires, disregarding His commandments and precepts, we set ourselves up for disasters of all sorts: physical, emotional, relational, spiritual, and mental. When we do whatever we want, disregarding His will, we will not receive "God's best" for us. We, therefore, forfeit His best plan for our personal lives, for our families, etc. When we make a decision to turn from our disobedience and to stay within the parameters of His will, the result is a magnificent freedom manifesting itself through peace within ourselves, with our fellow man and with nature.

Children are precious to Our Lord Jesus and He loves to use them in His parables. We cannot underestimate their value, purpose, and worth from the moment of their conception. He says, "Let the little children come to me; do not stop them; for it is to such as these that the kingdom of God belongs" (Mark 10:14). At a family picnic a couple of weeks after my first trip to Medjugorje, people swarmed around me like honeybees eager to hear about Our Lady's messages. A ten-year-old girl named Lindsey, the daughter of a very good friend of mine, had been listening though I hardly noticed. I always thought this message was more effective being preached to adults.

Later, my friend said to me, "Did you see how Lindsey was listening to you?" Apparently my talk had made quite an impression upon the young girl. Wow. I did not know and was not aware of how this message affects children. They are more accepting than many adults. No wonder Our Lady has most often chosen children to appear to and speak her messages through. Children don't distort anything they hear. They repeat it verbatim without censoring it, without changing it. Jesus Himself says, "Truly I tell you, whoever does not receive the kingdom of God as a little child will never enter it" (Mark 10:15).

Over the years I have found myself witnessing about Medjugorje in many different places. I have even witnessed to people in stairwells! Once, after giving my neighbor in Rhode Island a Medjugorje medal while we were standing with her ten-year-old son in the stairwell of our apartment building, I smelled roses and immediately said so to them. The ten-year-old boy, who had not uttered a word up until that point, said, "I do, too!" That was a sign for them of the truth of Our Lady's apparitions in Medjugorje, but again, a lesson for me. I had really been addressing the conversation to his mother, but Our Lady was pointing out to me that this message is for children, too, and that children in their innocence can often perceive these messages before adults!

Another time in a cement stairwell that had just been cleaned with extremely strong smelling harsh chemicals at our place of employment, my friend Jerry abruptly stopped and exclaimed, "I smell roses!" I had just been telling him some miraculous details on our way up the stairs about one of my trips to Medjugorje. I laughed and said, "Well, Jerry, you *must* be smelling them because all *I* can smell are the chemicals!"

He looked perplexed and said, "You don't smell them?" I said, "No. It's a sign for you!" letting him know my testimony was true. He was shocked, but welcomed the sign. The fact that he received that sign was a beautiful sign to me from heaven re-affirming my words and reconfirming to me the extraordinary revelations I had had on that particular trip to Medjugorje, lest I had any doubts.

One can be easily tempted to doubt. I am sure there are people who have a hard time believing the things I have experienced. They probably conclude that I "think" I experienced these things, or consider these experiences purely coincidental. While I am pretty good at not letting their feelings influence me, it is a great comfort to have my faith in these experiences reinforced by God through others who suddenly experience these phenomena themselves during my testimonies. I thank the good Lord that this has happened on many occasions.

Recently, while writing this chapter, I was in the car with my sister-in-law, Janie, and my daughter, Katerina. We were heading to a baby shower in New Hampshire for one of our nieces. Katerina had just found out that week that I was writing a book and she was very proud and excited about it. I had told very few people about writing this book at that point because of its subject matter. I was even reluctant to reveal this to many relatives and acquaintances, for fear of their doubt, and I was also trying not to call undue attention to myself at the outset of my new endeavor. I had not yet planned on mentioning my writing to Janie, even though she had been to Medjugorje.

I have always asked the Blessed Mother's intercession in revealing this information to whom *she* wanted when she wanted. Well, this was apparently Janie's day, because from the back seat of my van Katerina blurted out, "Aunt Janie! Did you know my mom's writing a book?" Janie replied, "No, I didn't." Well, then I had to explain. I told Janie how I had felt called by Our Lady to write a book for quite some time. While speaking to her, Janie suddenly exclaimed, "I smell roses!" She continued to smell roses for a bit in the car. A sign to her of the Blessed Mother's call to me to write this book, and a sign to me that I must continue and have no doubts. Twice Janie said to me, "*Why* would you *even doubt*?" She, a person I was afraid to reveal these things to because I thought she would doubt them, was ministering to me about doubt. I thanked the Blessed Mother again for her confirmation to me. I believe I was the one more in need of the sign that day!

The purpose of going to Medjugorje, or to any Marian apparition site for that matter, should be to seek Jesus more fully, not primarily to seek miracles. Praying for a cure for a loved one is one thing, but traveling to Medjugorje just to see the "miracle of the sun" or to smell roses is something else altogether. With agendas such as the latter, one will, more often than not, *not* receive such miracles. Again, our reason for going should be to seek Jesus *more fully* and to grow in faith. Jesus says, "Blessed are those who have *not* seen and yet have come to believe" (emphasis added; John 20:29).

Miracles, if you do happen to receive them, are "signposts" to faith. For me they have always been signs directing me on my path, signs encouraging me when I have proceeded with charity or forgiveness towards someone, or signs letting me know that my thinking or decision in the present moment is heading in the right direction. God speaks to individuals in a multitude of ways. We are all unique and affected in different ways. I know people that have heard audible voices from heaven; I know others who have visibly seen angels and saints. There have often been times when I have not received miracles while others have reported experiencing them.

God's use of the divine is not limited. God's ways of leading us more fully to Himself are not limited. The ways He has manifested Himself to me and His reasons for doing so may not be the ways He chooses to manifest Himself to another. We do not know God's ways. "For as the heavens are higher than the earth, so are my ways higher than your ways," says the Lord in Isaiah 55: 9. Sometimes He awaits a change of heart on our behalf. Sometimes a miracle is not necessary because we already have faith and need no confirmation from heaven. We must simply be at peace whether we receive outward miracles or not and — believe. And remember, "From everyone to whom much has been given, much will be required; and from one to whom much has been entrusted, even more will be demanded" (Luke 12:48).

One of God's divine gifts given to all, irrespective of our personal disposition or holiness, is His mother. Jesus gave Mary to us while still on the cross when He said to His disciple John, "Here is your mother" (John 19:27). Mary and Jesus, mother and Son, were so close. When Our Lord turned to speak to His mother first, however, He did not refer to her as "Mother," but called her "Woman."

He said, "Woman, here is your son" (John 19:26), addressing her as "Woman" just as Eve was addressed in the Old Testament. Mary was to be the "new Eve"— the new mother of creation — the new mother of the now redeemed mankind. Likewise, He was giving a command to John and all of us to honor this particular "woman" as "mother" from now on.

This divine gift given to us of our Blessed Mother exhibits itself in her intercessory prayer for us. The power of her intercession, particularly in the direct presence of her Son in the Eucharist, is enormous. She has told us through the visionaries, "Unceasingly adore the Most Blessed Sacrament of the Altar. I am always present when the faithful are adoring. Special graces are then being received."[6]

One of my more personal stories exhibiting Our Lord's true presence in the Eucharist involves a famous country singer...

Chapter 4

Our Lady's Ambassador

I have been a country music fan for more than twenty years. One of my favorite artists is Collin Raye. In the mid 1990's, I read that Collin was a devout Catholic who made sure he attended mass every week (even on the road), and frequented the Sacrament of Reconciliation (Confession, as it is informally known) as well. This intrigued me. Country music stars, so often from the Bible Belt in the South, are frequently of various Protestant denominations. The fact that Collin was Catholic, and a devout one at that, piqued my interest. On two occasions — one in print and the other on television — I witnessed Collin wearing a large pin of the Blessed Sacrament. This type of pin shows the Holy Eucharist, held by a monstrance, just as it is during Adoration as described in Chapter 2.

I was amazed. No one would know what that pin even was unless they knew of Jesus' true presence in the Eucharist. Anyone else would just think it was a decorative pin. I knew then that Collin was "one of us," one who knew this essential truth, and he was proclaiming the truth by wearing that pin, not that we are in any way an exclusive club. Our Lord gave Himself in the Eucharist through His Church, for all, but those who believe in His true presence often feel alone because so many don't believe. So many Catholics don't even believe this essential element of their faith. When you do come across someone who recognizes this truth, you feel as if you've found a kindred soul in a vast wilderness.

I was beset with the urge that I had to tell Collin to keep wearing that pin. It was so important that he, a celebrity, keep witnessing to this truth in a world in such darkness, a world that has largely forgotten or rejected the truth. I thought of writing to him, but did not have an address. The only way I knew to obtain an address was through his fan club. That wasn't going to do, though. I knew mailing it there might mean it would never reach his hands, and what I felt I had to tell him was too important to be tossed aside.

At that point, I did not even own a Collin Raye CD. I was busy at home raising two small boys, working part-time (I had returned to school, obtained an esthetics [skin care] license and was working as an esthetician), and my husband and I were in the process of adopting our third child, an orphaned little girl from Russia. Extra money was tight and I had never quite gotten around to purchasing one of Collin's CD's. The desire to tell Collin about the importance of wearing that pin never left me, but at the time I had no way of telling him.

Several years later, in 2005, I had some birthday money that I earmarked for a Collin Raye CD. I purchased what would be my first Collin CD and it became a staple in my car's CD player. Several months after its purchase I thought, "I wonder if Collin's playing anywhere nearby?" and I ventured onto his website for the first time to find out. Well, lo and behold, he was coming soon to our area. I told my husband I wanted to go to the concert. Paul, not being much of a country music fan, suggested I ask one of my friends to accompany me. I invited my friend Rita who, as it turns out, had seen Collin before in concert.

The wheels started turning in my head. I began to ask myself, if there was any way to meet Collin and tell him about the pin. I knew the only usual way to meet a country star is through a "Meet and Greet" opportunity before or after a show. To obtain a pass for a "Meet and Greet" you have to be a member of that star's fan club. So I set out to become a member of Collin's fan club. I was a bit embarrassed by this. I hadn't joined a fan club since Donny Osmond's when I was ten. I did not tell Paul about it until he asked me what the cancelled check made out to CRFC (short for Collin Raye Fan Club) was for, thus leaving me to explain! I was now a bona-fide fan club member and found out that there were drawings for members to be picked to meet Collin at his shows. One member per show would be chosen.

I hit my knees before Jesus in the Blessed Sacrament at Adoration that week. I walked in on a Thursday night, at a particular chapel where I make a weekly devotion to Our Lord, and the first words out of my mouth to Him were, "Okay, Lord. If I get to meet Collin, I will bring up the pin!" That was not the way I usually prayed to the Lord. I was making a promise. If He came through on His end of the deal,

I had to follow through on mine. You don't want to make promises to Jesus that you cannot keep. I was unquestionably aware of that, but nevertheless, willing to make this promise. I had had this desire, this calling to do this in my soul for years, and here was my chance. I had to take it.

The following Monday I arrived home from work, still in my uniform, to the phone ringing in my kitchen: When I answered it, the voice on the other end greeted me with, "Is this Kimberly, Kimberly Bruce?" "Yes," I said. The caller then said, "Kimberly, this is the President of the Collin Raye Fan Club. You have been chosen to meet Collin, Friday night, October 7th." The power of Jesus in the Blessed Sacrament! The Lord had set the stage and now had me in place to do what He had put in my heart so long ago. I could bring one friend with me to this meeting. Rita was thrilled when I told her. Incredulous, she asked, "How'd ya' do that?" Her question was a reference to the fact that I never won anything. She, on the other hand, was the one who was always winning something!

The concert was the Friday after I received the call. I was told by the president of the fan club to call the venue beforehand to make sure everything was set with them, and to call her if I had any trouble. The venue didn't know anything about the Meet and Greet. I was getting the sense that *someone* was beginning to meddle and *did not* want my meeting with Collin to take place. After several phone calls to the venue by both the fan club president and myself to rectify the situation, the president called me late one afternoon, while I was standing in a grocery store parking lot, to give me instructions as to what time to meet Collin before the show and where.

Rita and I arrived in plenty of time to be early for the meeting time. The only problem was that there was a huge line of people waiting to enter the venue. We would have to cut the line in order to tell the workers that we had backstage pre-show passes waiting for us. When we finally approached the ticket takers they, of course, knew nothing about us. They weren't one bit helpful either. We were fast approaching the time when we were to meet the country star. I was a bit nervous about meeting Collin, but unusually calm about the situation. I knew Jesus would take care of this. He had set it up. After seeing us lamenting there by the doorway for quite some time, an older man working the door finally decided to search for someone inside who might know something about us. Soon after, he came back and beckoned us inside. There a woman was waiting for us. She checked our names with her list and we were in — finally!

We were led to a table in the theater where our seats would be for the night and then told to go stand in the back where someone would come to usher us backstage. Rita and I stood where we had been directed to stand. Now, no one on the planet knew that I had a desire to tell Collin to keep wearing that pin. No one knew what I was planning to do that night, and that included Rita. It was between me and God. I knew I would be putting myself on the line. I was strictly going by what I had read about Collin in a magazine and what I believe I saw him wearing years ago! I might bring up the pin only to have him say, "What are you talking about?" thinking I was nuts! I was standing first in line with Rita behind me. Four other people arrived and stood behind Rita. They had won tickets to meet Collin through a radio station.

I wondered if I should move to the back of the line; what I had to say to Collin was so personal I didn't want anyone to overhear. I was half-praying and half-asking the question to myself. I felt this calmness come over me saying, "No. Stay right where you are." I stayed put.

A door opened and we were ushered into a darkly lit hallway with neon lights lining the walls and floor. A door opened at the other end. We passed through the doorway and were now backstage. We were lined up along the wall to our left just outside of Collin's open dressing room door. "Collin Raye," printed on a white card with red lettering, was hanging outside of the room and I could hear him talking inside. After just moments, Collin came out and turned right to me. I was immediately struck by how big he was. Rita said that was the first thing she thought too. I had no idea he was as tall as he is, at 6'3". He looked like a pro football player. He could bowl you over with his positive energy too, and he got straight down to business. After all, he did this night after night. The questions came at me: "What's your name?", "Where are you from?", "Do you have a camera?" I did and his band member, Todd, took our picture. After the picture was taken I said to myself, "I'm up!" (for what I *really* had come to say). I knew I had to start talking right then before he went to the others in line.

I said, "Collin, can I ask you a question?" He answered with a positive and resolute, "Yes!"

I plowed ahead, "Did you used to have a pin of the Blessed Sacrament that you would wear?"

He responded immediately, "Yes! But I lost it! It broke, and I lost it!"

I said, "Well, I always told myself that if I ever met you I would tell you to *keep wearing it – it speaks volumes!*" The reaction this got from him I never could have anticipated. The man did a 360° turn right out of business mode. He took a step back with his hand pressed to his chest and uttered, "Uhhh!" from the very depths of his soul and then said, "*Thank you!*" with such sincerity that I was truly touched. We instinctively embraced each other with the pure hug of two souls who recognized Jesus in the Eucharist. Then he looked right into my eyes and repeated to me the exact words I had previously voiced to myself concerning him: he said, "So, you're one of us!"

I had nothing but a resounding "Yes!" to say to that. Then he gave me another big, long hug. By this time I think everyone around us was wondering what was going on.

I then asked a question I felt Our Lady was pressing me to ask, "Have you ever been to Medjugorje?" I was not even sure he would know what Medjugorje was. He answered, "No, but I *want* to go. Time is always a factor." I told him what Our Lady wanted me to tell him, "*Go!*" And then I gave him a medal from Medjugorje, one that had been present during one of her apparitions to the visionaries and that had also been blessed by a priest. (Our Lady stresses the importance of a priestly blessing. She says that whenever a priest blesses something, "My Son blesses it.")

I planned to give him a medal *only* if the question about the pin went well. I had deliberated over which medal to take to him before I left home, as I have many. Finally I dumped my stash of medals into my hand and groaned to Our Lady, "Which one?" At that moment one seemed to spontaneously fall with a thud from between my fingers onto my bureau. I had my fingers tightly together, or so I thought. The medal that fell was a dainty silver silhouette of Our Lady of Medjugorje, very feminine looking. It would *not* have been the medal I would have chosen for him, but I said to the Blessed Mother without a moment's hesitation, "O.K.!" and packed it into my camera case.

I gave him the medal explaining to him how special it was, having been blessed by Our Lady as well as a priest, and Collin thanked me sincerely again. He thanked me profusely, in fact, for the next few moments. I then turned and introduced Collin to Rita and they talked a bit, but when Collin was finished speaking with her he looked straight at me again and said, "Kim . . . *thank you*." with such conviction it blessed my heart. What an exciting night this was, and this was all before the concert even began.

Retreating back into the dimly neon-lit hallway and now inwardly trembling, I said to Rita, "I did what I came to do." She said, "Yeah, what were you two talking about back there? All I could hear was something about Medjugorje. Here you were having this in-depth conversation with him, and all I had to talk to him about was the Red Sox," she said with a laugh. I said, "I'll tell you when we get to our seats."

When we got settled into our seats I explained the whole story to her. I tried to be as discrete as possible as there were other concertgoers seated around our half-table. It was clear to them that we had been backstage, having been gone for a while, and one woman at the far end of the table kept glaring at me. Finally, she could hold back no longer. She boldly and accusingly said to me, "How did *you* get to meet him? I've been a member of his fan club for years and *I've* never been picked to meet him!"

I just shrugged and didn't say too much, chalking it up to fate. I didn't think telling her, "It was Jesus, I had nothing to do with it," would've gone over well with her!

The concert was a blur. I can tell you only a few of the songs that I know he sang for sure because I was so completely awed by his reaction. God was definitely behind this whole thing. When I arrived back home that night after the show I went back to my stash of medals, not knowing for sure why. I dumped them into my hand and stared in astonishment. Some of my silver medals, that were silver before the concert, were now all gold or in the process of turning gold! I picked up one of them and decided to keep it for myself. I chose one that was now split down the middle, being half-gold and half-silver on both front and back.

I wore that one to work the next day. On my lunch break I was looking at it in the mirror and noticed it had turned all gold. *Whoa*, is all I could say. I showed the medals to Paul that night and said, "I think I did something bigger than I know." And Paul, being a man of few words when it comes to these things said, "Yeah." I know he meant it.

Over the course of the next week my newly gold medal began turning blue. Okay, I had heard about and seen medals that had turned from gold to silver and silver to gold, but never solidly to any other color. I wanted to call Wayne Weible up to ask, "Have you ever heard of *this*?"

I didn't know what to think. Had I displeased Our Lady in some way? I began to pray about it. Blue is the color associated with the Blessed Mother. I knew that and I knew she was trying to tell me something. Through prayer I discerned that I was to begin saying the prayers from what we call in our family the "Blue

Book Novena." Also referred to as the "Never Fail Novena," its official book title is *Rosary Novenas to Our Lady* (Benziger Brothers, Inc.). It is a lengthy novena requiring one to say one rosary with other written prayers from the book daily for a total of fifty-four days. It was time consuming, but this sacrifice has always brought answers and graces to all who have said it in our family.

As I began the novena, the mantle of Our Lady on the medal began to turn red on the windswept part of her dress! I knew red meant the Holy Spirit, so I knew I was on the right track with the novena. Approaching completion of my novena, the medal began to turn back to gold. I had done what Our Lady wanted. By the time it was finished, the medal was all gold. Interestingly enough, while Our Lady was gracing the medal with this change of colors, she was also changing a replica of this medal which I kept in my jewelry box in the exact same way! Each change that occurred to the medal I was wearing occurred to the medal in my jewelry box at the same time. I knew this was on purpose.

Our Lady didn't want me to have any doubts. She knew me. She knew that I might be tempted to think that the one I was wearing around my neck might be changing due to skin care products on my neck, or some other false explanation. By turning the other one in the same fashion, this reasoning and questioning would not apply. It was just sitting in my jewelry box, untouched. She wanted me to remember this grace and not dismiss it on account of any doubt later on.

What did I request Our Lady's intercession for in my novena? I prayed through her for a few things, one of which was that my life's purpose would be made manifest. It had been fifteen years, at that point, since I had been to Medjugorje. Fifteen years had passed of me raising my children, working, and going about my daily life. I felt I was supposed to do something that I had not yet done.

Over the years I had been invited to speak about Our Lady of Medjugorje's apparitions in various churches, primarily to CCD students studying the faith. Other than doing this, I really did not have a mission. I was, in addition, growing more and more conscious of being called to write a book, but I hadn't given much thought to starting it. This was not due to laziness. I was busy, ever busy as a wife, mother, homemaker and employee. In fact, though I had always planned on returning to Medjugorje, I had not yet done so due to family responsibilities. Upon completion of this latest novena, however, I knew it was time to return. I actually felt called by the Blessed Mother to return.

A couple of months after the concert I told my friend Theresa my Collin Raye story. She said to me, "Wow, October 7! You got to meet him on October

7! As I was thinking to myself, "*What about it?*" She told me that October 7 was the Feast Day of Our Lady of the Rosary. I was shocked. I had not remembered that. In that moment I had a bit of an awakening. I realized The Blessed Virgin Mary had just as much to do with my meeting Collin that night as her Son. I was also struck with the awareness of something I had not paid much attention to in recent years. I was *consecrated* to the Blessed Virgin Mary. I had consecrated myself to her in 1992 using the St. Louis deMonfort Consecration to Mary (the same format of consecration to Mary used by our late Pope John Paul II). Consecrating oneself to Mary means allowing oneself to be utilized by her in leading souls closer to Christ.

I never forgot I was consecrated to her; I was just again busy and unmindful of her desire to use me on a daily basis. This brought me back to reality. She was reminding me I had given myself to her to do with and use as she pleased, and she wanted to use me. She was knocking at the door of my heart through my conversation with Theresa, reminding me, "Hello, Kim. I have not forgotten you. Do not forget about *me*." As laid out in my consecration, I had given her full credit for any good I was to do in my life — past, present and future. I now had to give credit where credit was due. She had designed the meeting between Collin and me with her Son's blessing.

Consecration to Our Lady is actually consecration to Jesus *through* Mary. Those consecrated to Mary become her ambassadors for Christ by means of her maternal direction, guidance and protection. Jesus respects and honors this loving consecration. He allowed His mother to orchestrate the meeting between Collin and me, and all the subsequent happenings, because through this experience she was calling *me* back to Medjugorje. It was time. She wanted me to wait no longer. There was to be no more postponement of my return. The novena I had begun that October, unbeknownst to me, was also to end on December 8, the Feast Day of Our Lady's Immaculate Conception. This was the icing on the cake for me. I recognized her fingerprints as being involved everywhere, from start to finish. In November the following year I found myself on a plane returning to Medjugorje, this time on my own.

Chapter 5

Divine Connection

I always said that when I went back to Medjugorje I wanted to go with Wayne Weible, the man whose articles brought me to believe in the miracle occurring there in the first place. I had read all of his books. I have religiously received his Medjugorje newsletter for as long as I can remember. I knew I wanted to be on one of his sponsored pilgrimages. He makes several every year, having been there over one hundred times himself. I booked myself on a pilgrimage with a group that he was taking over in November, 2006. I did not know a soul who would be accompanying me, but I soon recognized others who would be with me by their red backpacks in the airports and on the planes — compliments of the agency we had all made our reservations through. There were 110 of us.

For years I had desired to return to Medjugorje for one main reason — to thank Our Lady for changing my life after my first visit there by bringing me closer to her Son. Beyond that, I was also silently hoping she would give me some direction about my future regarding what she wanted me to do. I was trying not to get my hopes up too much, though. I had such a miraculous trip the first time; I didn't want to be disappointed.

I arrived to find a very different Medjugorje than I remembered. Stores, shops, restaurants, housing — even bars and hotels were now there or in the process of being built. This was quite a change from the Medjugorje of sixteen years prior in 1990. At that time there was perhaps one restaurant in town, no hotels, just one public telephone in a small, sparsely appointed post office, lots and lots of poor looking vineyards and tobacco fields, and meager homes all made out of the same concrete materials. It was also communist Yugoslavia when Paul and I arrived in 1990. Back then we were met at the Dubrovnik Airport with armed soldiers carrying machine guns ready to shoot at a moment's notice.

Now, flying in to Sarajevo in present-day Bosnia-Herzegovina, there was no military presence within sight. We even got smiles from some of the workers and the airports, including the one in Dubrovnik (which we visited on our return trip), were larger, cleaner, and much nicer. The after-effects of the horrible ethnic-cleansing war, however, were very apparent. As we traveled by bus three hours from the airport in Sarajevo to Medjugorje, we witnessed apartment complexes, businesses, and homes, with multiple gunshot and mortar holes in them. We saw a considerable number of homes with roofs blown off.

Many refugees were still living in camps as a result of the war, over a decade after its end. They live in poverty and some, close to Medjugorje, rely on infrequent visits from pilgrims who bring supplies of clothing, medicine, toys, and toiletries.

Wayne Weible has for many years made it a point in all of his sponsored pilgrimages to include a trip to one of these camps requesting that pilgrims pack such supplies in their suitcases to bring to the camp from home. It is always one of the most memorable, heartbreaking, but joy-filled parts of a pilgrimage with Wayne. With every visit to the camp people find themselves thinking of ways to bring and do more for these refugees on a return pilgrimage. For some pilgrims, already having been touched by the Medjugorje message, it is their main reason for return. They seek to live out Our Lord's greatest commandment by loving one another in the service of these needy people.

In town even the locals looked more fashion-able in Medjugorje. I attributed it to the fact that they had more money coming in due to tourism, greater thriving businesses and increased trade with other countries. Medjugorje has been the number one tourist attraction in all of the former Yugoslavia for many years. The home I was placed in this time was a beautiful one specifically designed to house pilgrims. We each had our own bathroom, unlike my first trip where several of us shared a bathroom. The building had four or five floors of individual rooms, the dining area where we ate breakfast and dinner was large and beautiful, and the food was absolutely delicious. We arrived in the evening with time to settle into our rooms, have dinner and head to bed after nearly twenty-four hours of travel by car, plane, and bus.

I trusted completely in the Blessed Mother to design my trip. I knew she would orchestrate every-thing: who I would travel with, who I would meet, who I would eat with, talk with, walk with, etc. It was her invitation that we were all responding to in coming, and once there, one could rest assured that she had everything planned.

My first morning there, we had some free time scheduled for lunch after the 10:00 a.m. English language mass got out. As I was walking out of the church among a throng of people, I said to the Blessed Mother silently, "Okay, Mother, who are you going to put me with for lunch?"

No sooner had I said this when Isabelle, a woman I had briefly met on the last leg of our journey, seemed to bolt from across the crowd to me and said, "So! We goin' to Coco's (a local restaurant)?" Not knowing any restaurants around town, but certain this was who Our Lady had picked for me to go to lunch with I said, "O.K.!"

By the time we arrived at Coco's there were six of us: Isabelle and Phyllis, who were two ladies I had met on our last plane; Kathy, who I had met at J.F.K. Airport in New York; and two other girls seated to my right and left that I did not know. To this day, I do not know how the three of us at the end of the table ended up there together other than it being a "divine connection." I began talking to them and soon asked Cassandra, the woman on my right, what kind of work she was in. She said, "I own a publishing company." Instantly, upon hearing her words, I detected the strong scent of roses, the hallmark of the presence of the Blessed Mother — my first on this trip. I knew this woman was to have something to do with my book. This book, only a desire in my heart at that point, was being confirmed to me by the Blessed Mother.

I said nothing, but a conversation ensued between Debbie, to my left, and Cassandra about what kind of books Cassandra published. Cassandra, as it turns out, is a children's publisher, publishing educational materials and I thought to myself, "I don't want to write a children's book." However, that is exactly what Debbie wanted to do. Debbie asked Cassandra what kind of books she was in the market for and Cassandra disclosed the exact type and theme of book she was currently looking to publish. Debbie, in shock, said that she had just written some children's poems with the exact same theme.

The whole time their conversation was going on I continually smelled roses and could finally keep it from them no longer. I blurted out, "I'm smelling roses here!" Cassandra soon followed by saying, "I do too!" I thought to myself, "Maybe I'm just meant to confirm these two in this," thinking my first burst of the smell of roses wasn't meant for my book at all, but Debbie's. I didn't believe that entirely, though. I felt the Blessed Mother was way too clear on that for me. Cassandra, I knew, would have something to do with my book.

Cassandra then asked Debbie if she would write down the poems from memory so that she could take a look at them. She did, and they were excellent. Upon retiring to their rooms, Debbie and Cassandra found that they were both staying at the same hotel, on the same floor, and had rooms directly next to one another. Another coincidence? I think not. Cassandra has begun the process of publishing Debbie's book thanks to this very divine connection.

I never mentioned to the two of them that I felt called by the Blessed Mother to write a book. A day or so later though, during a conversation, Cassandra suddenly stopped, pointed at me and said, "And *you*! *You* need to write a book!" I said, "I know I need to write a book. I've always wanted to write a book. I just don't know what to write it on." Without hesitating she said, "Write about the *journey*." She meant my faith journey. She also believed that she was going to help me in some way. Not only did Cassandra end up being the main catalyst through which the Blessed Mother propelled me to write this book, but she was also a tremendous source of encouragement with her words of praise to me after reading through one of my early rough drafts.

In the days that followed Cassandra and I smelled roses many times whenever she, Debbie, and I were together. The Blessed Mother was constantly confirming our connection to one another. We were not meant to be friendly just during that pilgrimage. We had a future connection together. Once, while exchanging our addresses as we were standing over a stinky garbage can while using its lid as a makeshift table, we smelled roses. Again, a divine sign confirming to us that we were to remain in contact with one another. At the time, we were standing just outside of the Adoration Chapel in Medjugorje where Jesus was present. Several times the three of us visited the chapel together and individually to pray about this connection and what Jesus and Our Lady wanted us to do.

Even though I had received a personal word of prophecy about my life from the priest in the confessional many years before, I was not very familiar with prophecy. Despite the fact that it is one of the gifts given to individuals by the Holy Spirit to build up the church, we don't hear much about it in the Catholic Church. It has not been lost on the Catholic Church; it along with other gifts of the Holy Spirit are just not generally focused upon or largely talked about outside of the charismatic movement and circles within the Church. The Church, in its over two thousand years of wisdom, is very cautious regarding these kinds of matters as there are a lot of false prophets out there.

Needless to say, I was astounded one afternoon when I received a detailed prophetic message about my life from a pilgrim on the trip with us. It came out of the blue, standing on a sidewalk in Medjugorje not far from the church, when I wasn't expecting it. I immediately said, "We need to go to the Blessed Sacrament." I was not going to take any chances. I knew there were prophets from God, but I knew also that Satan can give "knowledge" with evil as his intent. I wanted to test this. We went later that day and I privately prayed, "God, if this is not *of you*, reveal it," trusting that He, in His goodness, would eventually confirm or deny this particular prophetic message.

St. Paul says, "Pursue love and strive for the spiritual gifts, and especially that you may prophesy . . . those who prophesy speak to other people for their building up and encouragement and consolation . . . those who prophesy build up the church . . . prophesy is not for unbelievers but for believers" (1 Corinthians 14:1, 3-4, 22).

We must be very careful when discerning words of personal prophecy. Even if something seems to be plausible, believable, and seemingly for the good, we must always test it. "Beware of false prophets, who come to you in sheep's clothing but inwardly are ravenous wolves. You will know them by their fruits," says Jesus in Matthew 7:15-16. *The Catechism of the*

Catholic Church states that such "Charisms are to be accepted with gratitude by the person who receives them and by all members of the Church as well ... provided they really are genuine gifts of the Holy Spirit and are used in full conformity with authentic promptings of this same Spirit, that is, in keeping with charity, the true measure of all charisms."[7]

"No charism is exempt from being referred and submitted to the Church's shepherds. 'Their office [is] not indeed to extinguish the Spirit, but to test all things and hold fast to what is good'...."[8]

I prayed that afternoon before the Blessed Sacrament about my book as well and I prayed for direction from the Blessed Mother. At a function for our group that evening, the same person came to me directly and said straight away, "Kim, I just came from the Blessed Sacrament and I have a message to you from the Blessed Mother." This was notable because, as I said, I had just been there earlier in the day praying for direction from the Blessed Mother. This person went on to give me the message — a beautiful message that brought tears to my eyes and was so very, very personal. I believed this message to be from God. There were things that were spoken to me in this message that the Blessed Mother had already spoken to my heart during the preceding months — some of them verbatim.

No one would have known these things except God. I had never spoken them to a soul. This message was consoling and encouraging. St. Paul says that one will know a true prophecy because the "secrets" of the heart will be disclosed, and he will bow down and worship God, declaring, "God is really among you" to the one prophesying (1 Corinthians 14:25). That was my reaction to the Blessed Virgin's message that night. I told this person upon hearing the words spoken to me, "I know this is from God because Our Lady has *already spoken this to my heart*." Mind you, at that point I was completely unaware St. Paul had ever said the above words about prophecy in Scripture. I just voiced what came up out of my spirit the moment the words were spoken.

Debbie, Cassandra, and I, along with many other beautiful individuals we shared our trip with, continued having a grace-filled, miraculous pilgrimage. Our Lady was just showering us with graces. I experienced many other miracles on that trip — signs around the moon that I witnessed with other people for three nights in a row, the smell of roses daily — often many times a day, and other experiences that were most assuredly not coincidences. I left Medjugorje elated. God had revealed Himself to me with such force that I no longer felt mislaid, for lack of a better word. I realized all my years of searching for my purpose were not for naught and had culminated in one whopping manifestation of His grace.

During the months leading up to that trip, Our Lady had begun utilizing a new method of instructing me. Having now a very firm and strong foundation in the Catholic faith, she introduced me to the world of some wonderful Protestant preachers. Yes, Protestant preachers. Our Lady was showing me something: We are *all* her children. We are all important to her. We all belong to Christ. Therefore, she is our Mother, collectively. Not that I ever doubted this, she was just showing me that she greatly loved and was calling *all* of us.

Many Protestants I've been exposed to have hit the mark with more spiritual discernment on issues than many Catholics I know, and I respect them greatly. As Catholics, we share great unity with a good number of our Protestant brothers and sisters on important topics such as abortion, the invalidity of same-sex marriage in the eyes of God, the existence of the Devil, Heaven and Hell, the power and gifts of the Holy Spirit, to name a few. Our Lady was filling me with a great love for our separated brethren in Christ — with a great love for *ecumenism,* something our current Pope Benedict XVI has greatly esteemed during his Pontificate. Ecumenism is worldwide tending to and promotion of Christian unity and cooperation. Pope Benedict summons Catholics to the call of ecumenism as an important mission of the Church, particularly in this critical time in history.

Several years prior to my 2006 trip to Medjugorje, I began watching Joyce Meyer's *Enjoying Everyday Life* broadcast. I learned an immense amount from Joyce. This is no understatement. She taught me oodles pertaining to the understanding of and living of God's Word in daily life. She is among the remarkable teachers Our Lady has put me "in class" with, and I consider her a gift. In addition, I have received many holy words of influence from Joel Osteen of Joel Osteen Ministries, James and Betty Robison of *Life Today*, Beth Moore — an international Bible teacher, and Ed Young of Ed Young Ministries. They have helped me in my everyday overall walk with Christ through their powerful preaching awash with wisdom. They live their lives and preach with great devotion to the Bible and Our Lord Jesus. Their collective mission is to bring souls to Christ, and so they are mentors to me. All of the aforementioned have speaking ministries and are authors. These men and women have an anointed gift of teaching. This gift of teaching is another one of the Holy Spirit's gifts given to individuals. They utilize this gift for the good of souls and for building up the Kingdom of God.

This is not to say that I am not likewise influenced by great Catholic teachers as well. As mentioned, Mother Angelica and many of those on EWTN have had an enormous influence upon me. Many of the holy priests on the network have exhibited undying love for Jesus, Our Blessed Mother and the Holy Roman Catholic Church and have taught me exponentially in the faith. EWTN is truly a "light shining forth in the darkness".

I came back from that November 2006 trip to Medjugorje believing that I was to return fairly soon, that I was called to do so. I was hoping to return again in November the following year, but somehow I knew my return might be sooner. Debbie was very devoted to the refugees. That November was her third yearly trip to the area to aid them. Each time Debbie returned bringing more supplies with her. She held fundraisers at home to raise money for the camp and solicited needed items such as toothpaste tubes from her dentist and toiletry items from her pharmacist to bring with her.

One handicapped boy and his family really touched her heart. Each trip Debbie made to the camp included a special visit on her part to see this family. That November Debbie, a few other girls from our group, and I went to this family's hut. These huts were to be temporary shelters for refugee families during the war. Fifteen plus years later, families are still living in them. These aluminum huts are like freezers in the winter and heaters in the summer. They consist of just two rooms, usually with a sheet draped separating the rooms from one another. All those in the camp share common bathrooms and kitchen facilities. Seated in this family's small home I decided I would like to help Debbie as well.

This little handicapped boy's mother carried her five-year-old son around with her wherever they went. He could not sit up for long on his own and could not walk. Debbie and I decided to procure a handicapped stroller for him, one that would last him for years as he grew into adulthood. Debbie came home and solicited funds. She set up a post office box for donations and titled it "Refugee Fund." Paul and I returned that May, six months after my last trip, to deliver this stroller. I am grateful to my husband for deciding to make this return trip with me. We had to disassemble the stroller beforehand and place its parts in our various belongings and suitcases. It, of course, was "gone through" by airport security, something we suspected would happen. Paul also had to reassemble the stroller once we got to Medjugorje. I would not have wanted to attempt this on my own! Paul and I delivered the stroller to this family. It seemed hard for them to accept, which I was prepared for. Not having much of anything, it is hard to accept such a gift from strangers. The boy's mother did not readily put him in the chair, which was understandable. I knew we had to just leave it with them and let them discover it on their own.

Not long after I returned home in May, I began working on this book. It was time. For years I had wanted to keep a private journal titling it *Book of Miracles* to document all of the miraculous stories and experiences I have had through the years. I did not want to forget any of them. I even purchased a journal for this purpose back in the early years of my marriage, but never got around to writing in it because of the busyness of my life raising children and caring for family. I was aware even back then that someday the experiences were meant to be in a book. I knew the book I was embarking upon was to encompass some of these experiences.

I began to write and it came very easily to me. In fact, it was a joy. As said, I love to write and I found that as I sat at the computer words would just flow through me. I always prepped my writing sessions by praying to the Holy Spirit both beforehand and during each session. I prayed for the Holy Spirit to speak through me. I never knew where the book was going. I did not know where it was to end up. I just sat and the words and stories came back to me. Sometimes I would write, re-read what I had written and say, "I wrote that?" in amazement. That proved to me that the Holy Spirit and Our Lady were in charge. Sometimes I would write about something and think, "Well, I didn't think *that* was going to be in there!" And, then there were other things I thought the book might include, but it didn't. I so looked forward to each writing session — it was pure joy for me.

I have learned that wherever God is working, Satan stands ready to thwart His plans. As Joel Osteen says, "The enemy always fights us the hardest when he knows God has something great in store!"[9]

I came home from that May trip to Medjugorje very agitated. Agitation is a sign that the Devil is lurking, and during that trip, the Blessed Mother had spoken loudly and clearly to my whole being repeatedly: "You *must* protect your children through prayer." This resonated with me because, although I prayed daily, I was usually very focused on other concerns. I prayed for things going on in my personal life, friends' lives, and larger world issues just assuming Our Lady and Jesus would take care of my family. While this is true in a sense, and it is important to pray for others, I needed to balance my prayers by additionally focusing on the needs of each family member from my husband and myself to our children. With two teenage boys, a pre-teen daughter and the excessive availability of sin and temptations out there, it was clearly evident to me that Our Lady was offering a pertinent plan of action for the protection of our futures.

How did she want me to specifically "protect them through prayer"? I knew exactly how. Paul and I said the rosary faithfully on a daily basis, but I knew Our Lady wanted us to say it together as a couple and with our children. This would protect our marriage as well as our children and family. I was agitated because I was at a loss as to how to bring this about. Paul is very private when it comes to prayer and the public expression of his faith. I also did not think my two teenage sons would be too keen on getting together for a family rosary time. Any efforts made on my behalf to bring this about were met with resistance, and Satan filled me with hopelessness and despair towards this end. Thus, the praying of the rosary as a family did not come to pass.

The coming months were very difficult for me. Satan was attempting to completely kill my joy and ability to focus to the point that I could not even write. He did not want me to continue with this book. He wanted what I had already begun to be rendered fruitless, and he was using any method of distraction and anguish to accomplish this. I have heard it said that if Satan can't destroy you, he will settle for distraction. This is a great morsel of wisdom for one's life. If you find yourself distracted or in a state of agitation, recognize that he is trying to throw you off course. He will use anything he can to keep you from accomplishing God's will in your life and from having what God wants for you.

The thief comes to steal, kill, and destroy, I've heard Joyce Meyer quip many times (see also John 10:10). Satan wants to steal your joy, she says, because when he steals your joy he steals your *power.* Mother Mary has also said that Satan works "fiercely to take away your joy"[10].

Our Lady further says, "These days Satan wants to frustrate my plans . . . Satan wishes to complicate my plans . . . Satan is so strong and with all his might wants to disturb my plans which I have begun with you. You pray, just pray and don't stop for a minute! I will pray to my Son for the realization of all the plans I have begun. Be patient and constant in your prayers. And don't let Satan discourage you. He is working hard in the world. Be on your guard!"[11] Satan knew of my purpose for writing this book: *To bring people to the belief in Jesus' true presence in the Eucharist and to love of the Blessed Mother.*

I continued to pray. I continued to fast. Our Lady says, "By prayer you can completely disarm him [Satan] and ensure your happiness."[12] The Blessed Virgin sent me many remarkable signs during this season in my life to give me direction, hope, and expectancy. She encouraged me to pray specifically for my husband and for my children. Satan was trying hard to sink me, but I was determined to remain steadfast. When faced with a particularly difficult time in his own life, Joel Osteen said, "The winds that tried to sink me, God turned around, and used them to be the winds to push me into my divine destiny."[13] And, what the enemy means for your harm, God will turn around "and use it to your advantage!"[14]

Six months later, in November of 2007, I again found myself on a plane returning to Medjugorje. This time I went with my mother and a couple of friends. This was now my fourth trip to Medjugorje, three within a year's time. On this trip the Blessed Mother was literally *begging* me to pray the rosary with my husband and family. Not only did she make this overwhelmingly clear to my heart, but she sent three people to actually say it to me. The first was a priest in the confessional who, out of the blue and under the influence of the Holy Spirit, grasped my forearm in emphasis and implored me to pray the rosary with my husband and children. The second was Mirijana, one of the Medjugorje visionaries, who spoke to us from her front yard right in front of me and said we "must pray the rosary with our families!" The third person was Patrick Latta, a Canadian transplant to Medjugorje with a tremendous conversion story, who described how consecrating his children to Mary and praying the rosary transformed him, his children, and renewed his marriage. I returned home resolute. I was going to start the family rosary this time, even if I was to be the only one saying it.

On this trip, one evening after dinner, I approached Wayne Weible to talk for a moment privately. I told him of my desire to continue writing the book I felt Our Lady was calling me to. In a flash, Wayne's hands were atop my head praying with me for discernment. I felt the power of the Holy Spirit emanating through his hands. It was a feeling I have felt a few times before when being prayed over, but only by priests. It is an awesome, yet tender, electrical-*type* feeling I cannot accurately describe in words. This did not surprise me. I had known for years that Wayne was gifted with the Holy Spirit. I knew that he had also received the "gift of healing" years earlier after embarking upon his mission for Our Lady.

Both spiritual and physical healings have been brought about by Jesus working through Wayne's hands. This was not like my experience when being prayed over by the priest in the confessional on my first trip to Medjugorje, but it was power — unearthly power — radiating gently into me. I considered this a heavenly validation for the work I had already begun and confirmation that I should continue.

Paul and I did begin the family rosary together after I returned home from this trip. Our Lady says, "I call you to the renewal of prayer in your homes . . . I am calling you to family prayer . . . I beseech you to start changing your life in the family. Let the family be a harmonious flower that I wish to give to Jesus. Dear children, let every family be active in prayer for I wish that the fruits in the family be seen one day. Only that way shall I give you all, like petals, as a gift to Jesus in fulfillment of God's plans."[15]

Our Lord Jesus says, "Again, truly I tell you, if two of you agree on earth about anything you ask, it will be done for you by my Father in heaven. For where two or three are gathered in my name, I am there among them" (Matthew 18:19-20). There is power in praying together as husband and wife and as a family. Paul and I invited our children to say the rosary with us. We did not force them. Our Lady always "invites" us to pray. She never forces one to do anything. If our children did not want to come, then we would lead by example.

The results in a very short period of time astonished me. My oldest, Conor, came back from a CCD retreat one evening where he and his classmates shared what they were most thankful for. My son publicly thanked God for me, his mother, for teaching him to pray the rosary; something he would never have done before in front of his peers. It was an amazing and surreal retreat night for Conor that came with an added bonus just for him — he was given a note to give to me from one of the retreat speakers, whom I did not even know. It was an invitation to come to hear the Medjugorje visionary, Ivan, speak in a parish about an hour's drive from where we lived. If we attended we would also be present when the Blessed Mother appeared to Ivan. What a gift! The retreat had had nothing to do with Medjugorje. This wonderful man, through the inspiration of the Holy Spirit, was led to Conor not even knowing my connection with Medjugorje. He gave Conor rosary beads that had been blessed by Our Lady during a previous apparition to Ivan. Ivan had said about the beads, "Our Lady chooses who these are to go to." That night blessed Conor to no end.

Next, I received a call one evening from my daughter's third grade teacher. She called me because she had asked each of the children in her class to say what they were thankful for from their parents. The Thanksgiving holiday was approaching and she had given them this assignment. She expected them to say they were thankful for things such as a particular trip, etc. Katerina responded by saying that she was thankful for her parents saying the rosary with her at night. This was amazing. Two of my children were already showing signs of being heavily influenced by the saying of the rosary with us. Paul and I had been unaware of how this was affecting them. I informed her teacher that I didn't even think we'd said it ten times yet. Katerina attends a public school and the teacher said that most of the kids probably didn't even know what the rosary was, but she "just had to call" because she was so impressed by this. She was herself very devoted to the Blessed Mother and found it remarkable that we said the rosary together as a family. This led to a conversation about Medjugorje, which she knew nothing about, that lasted the better part of an hour.

That leaves Anthony, my second oldest. Anthony is a very good student but was having a great amount of difficulty in one of his school subjects. Anthony chose to come with us the night we attended Our Lady's apparition to Ivan. That night was an extensive prayer-filled night. All present went to mass, said three full rosaries in addition to other prayers, and heard two other speakers before Ivan. It was a long evening to say the least, and a bit of a sacrifice, especially for a high school boy. Soon after this miraculous evening, Anthony suddenly came into great favor with his teacher. He improved his grade tremendously and was no longer complaining to us about the class. He even proceeded to take another class with this teacher the following year. This turn of events was nothing short of miraculous, as far as I was concerned, because before this he had been beseeching me for weeks to let him drop the class. Even he was aware of this special grace as events unfolded.

The saying of the rosary together as a family was having another positive effect — we were talking together as a family in a way that was usually hard in our busy lives. Our children were commenting on the fact that they liked how we would talk about other things before and after the rosary just because we were all sitting in the same room together and it just lent itself to that. I also noticed that individual issues we had concerning each one of our children were improving. We were given the grace to know how to deal with each of them the way they needed to be dealt with, and they in turn began exhibiting gifts of increased maturity and peace. God will not be outdone in generosity. When we obey His requests (in this case His mother's request) we will reap the rewards. He responds with incredible grace.

Chapter 6

Miracles of the Eucharist

E ven though I had a strong desire to continue writing this book, Our Lady began directing me to study the Bible as well. I knew the amount of writing and study I wished to undertake would necessitate a sufficient amount of quiet time without interruption at home. With the demands of my job and home life, this was not going to be an easy task. I felt called to give up my job so that I could have the time to both study and write.

I had a great job. I had returned to school several years prior, as mentioned, to obtain an esthetics license. I worked as an esthetician in a world-class spa that ranked among the top 100 spas in the world. I worked in an elegant setting with people I loved, doing a job I enjoyed, and where I had a schedule that allowed me to be home with my children when they came home from school in the afternoons. I was blessed. I made great money for the amount of hours I worked, and it was a much sought-after position in the esthetics field to be where I was.

The first solution to my dilemma of whether or not to give up my job was the decision to relinquish one of my four part-time days of work towards this aim of writing and study. I was bargaining. Didn't I just say I felt called to "give up" my job? I soon found out that one day a week dedicated to my new tasks was not the answer. Too many other things came up: I would get asked to cover for someone else at work on that day and didn't want to say no (especially because I might need that person to cover for me at some point); sometimes there were other work-related functions I needed to be present at on that day such as trainings, meetings, etc., and very soon life just took over, filling up my day. My husband and I had discussed the possibility that if he got a promotion or obtained a new job, I might be able to relinquish my job to devote my time to these new endeavors. Well, Paul did get a promotion. Not only that, but his salary increase was equal to my yearly income and then some! God was providing and making it very clear to me that He wanted me to do this.

This was not something people did everyday — give up their job because they felt God was directing them towards something else. I should caution here that not everyone should relinquish their job if they feel God is "telling them to" without a lot of discernment through prayer amid other considerations. In my case, giving up my job was an option I had at my disposal. If it was not a viable option for my family, financially or otherwise, God would not have called me to it.

I expected the usual reaction from a friend one day when I told her about my dilemma. That common reaction was typically, "Are you *sure* you want to do this?" "Don't you just want to *cut down* a little more on your days?" But after attending mass one weekday afternoon for the sole purpose of praying to God about this issue, I ran into a friend whose godly wisdom I greatly value. I had never seen her at this mass before. Afterwards she asked me if I wanted to go to lunch with her. After talking to her about my quandary, she said, "This will be such a blessing for your family." She blew me away with her words. I felt this encapsulating "presence" surrounding us. I was only vaguely aware of others in the room. The Lord had planned this whole lunch. I went asking for His help that day and He sent someone to meet me and speak His words into me. She said, "Kim, *trust*! You have to let go and trust God!"

That's exactly what I had to do. I had to let go. That's what I was not doing. I was trying to hold onto my job while still holding onto what God was asking me to do. I told my friend that I felt like I was standing at the top of a cliff and the Lord was just waiting for me to jump off. I had to make this leap of faith and trust Him. I attempted it.

When I told my supervisor I was leaving, she, much appreciatively, tried everything to keep me from doing so. She even told me I could just work Sundays. I went home to contemplate again. I made good money on Sundays, especially busy ones. This would give me some spending money for myself and I would keep my foot in the door at work. When I came home from work that day I walked into my bedroom and said, "Lord, what should I do?" It didn't take Him a moment to interiorly respond to me in a soft voice: "You know what you should do . . . keep holy the Sabbath." Yes, I knew what I had to do. I decided once and for all to let the job go — completely.

Once I decided to relinquish my job, Our Lady gave me some time to acclimate to my new life. It was strange at first. I kept waking up thinking I had to go into work each day. Weekends were glorious because for the first time in years I could be home with my family all weekend. It was so freeing. I was able to go to family functions and other events often missed because my time was not spoken for with a work commitment. I did not feel any pressure to continue writing my book just yet. As said, I could tell Our Lady was giving me some time. Then a miraculous story involving the Eucharist was brought to my attention.

Alexandrina Maria deCosta from Balasar, Portugal, north of Fatima, was granted a unique grace in 1942. She began to subsist solely on the Eucharist and Precious Blood of Our Lord, requiring no food or drink to live. Alexandrina had been infirm and bedridden since 1918, long before this grace had begun in her life, following a horrible spinal injury. Jesus told Alexandrina at the commencement of this grace, which lasted for thirteen years until her death, "You will not take food again on earth. Your food will be my flesh; your drink will be my divine blood." He told her, "You are living by the Eucharist alone because I want to prove to the world the power of the Eucharist and the power of my life in souls."[16] Jesus also asked her if she would be willing to suffer for souls (offer up her pain and sufferings) to "spread the message of Fatima and to urge the consecration of the world to the Immaculate Heart" [of Mary]. Alexandrina then began suffering the passion of Jesus every Friday, totaling 180 times before her death.

Alexandrina's doctors were skeptical of this miraculous grace so they kept her confined and under watch for forty days. They testified, "Her abstinence from solids and liquids was absolute during all that time. We testify also that she retained her weight, and her temperature, breathing, blood pressure, pulse and blood were normal while her mental faculties were constant and lucid. The laws of physiology and bio-chemistry cannot account for the survival of this sick woman . . . ."

Jesus said to Alexandrina, "Keep me company in the Blessed Sacrament. I remain in the tabernacle [where the consecrated hosts are kept] night and day, waiting to give my love and grace to all who would visit me. But so few come. I am so abandoned, so lonely, so offended . . . Many . . . do not believe in my existence; they do not believe that I live in the tabernacle. They curse me. Others believe, but do not love me and do not visit me; they live as if I were not there. . . You have chosen to love me in the tabernacles where you can contemplate me, not with the eyes of the body, but those of the soul. I am truly present there as in Heaven, Body, Blood, Soul, and Divinity."

Do not forget that it was Jesus Himself who sol-emnly stated the importance of His Eucharist and

Precious Blood when He said: "Very truly, I tell you, unless you eat the flesh of the Son of Man and drink his blood, you have no life in you. Those who eat my flesh and drink my blood have eternal life, and I will raise them up on the last day; for my flesh is true food and my blood is true drink. Those who eat my flesh and drink my blood abide in me, and I in them. Just as the living Father sent me, and I live because of the Father, so whoever eats me will live because of me. This is the bread that came down from heaven, not like that which your ancestors ate, and they died. But the one who eats this bread will live forever" (John 6:53-58).

There are many documented events recorded throughout history of actual transubstantiation of the bread consecrated by a priest during the mass where the Eucharist has turned to true flesh, as well as many communion hosts that have bled with true human blood. Some of these hosts have been preserved and are on display. Now, these things don't happen on a regular basis (they'd scare everyone too much!), but they have happened here and there throughout the history of the Church to remind us with scientific human proof that this actually occurs.

Wayne Weible, in his February 1996 Medjugorje Newsletter, reports on the "earliest recorded and the most well-known" miracle of the Eucharist — the Miracle at Lanciano. He says:

In about the year 700, a Basilian monk in Lanciano, Italy had continuous doubts about the Real Presence of Christ in the Eucharist. He could not bring himself around to believe that at the words of consecration uttered by him over bread and wine, their substances became the Body and Blood of Christ. But being a devout priest he continued to cele-brate the sacrament according to the teaching of the Church and begged God to remove the doubt from him.

One day, as he was offering the Holy Sacrifice, following the words of consecration, the bread literally changed into Flesh and the wine into Blood. At first he was overwhelmed by what he saw. Then, regaining his composure, he called the faithful present to come to the altar to see what the Lord had caused to happen.

The changed substances were not consumed. The bread-turned-flesh, and the Blood, which coagulated into five irregular globules, were placed in a precious ivory container, where they are preserved even to the present day at the Shrine in Lanciano.[17]

In 1970 the Catholic Church sent a team of medical experts to examine the substances in Lanciano. The chairman was Professor Odoardo Linoli, a skeptic. By the time Odoardo had to send his first message to the Director of the Shrine, his message said simply: "In the beginning was the Word, and the Word was made Flesh."

The complete report of the doctors revealed: "The Flesh is real flesh; the Blood is real blood; The Flesh consists of the muscular tissue of the heart (myocardium); The Flesh and Blood belong to the human species; The Flesh and Blood have the same blood type (AB)"[18]; and the stunning findings continue with information on the proteins, minerals, etc., found within the blood. The World Health Organization has also proclaimed that this tissue, over 1300 years old, is still "living tissue"[19].

In another *Weible Columns Medjugorje Newsletter* article, an additional Eucharistic miracle is cited from the early part of the 13th century in Santarem, Portugal. There, "a poor woman who was made miserable by the activities of her unfaithful husband . . . consulted a sorceress, who promised deliverance from her trials for the price of a consecrated Host." The woman obtained a Host during Holy Communion, took it from her tongue and wrapped it in her veil. Very soon afterwards blood began coming from the Host. "The amount of blood increased so much that it dripped from the cloth and attracted the attention of bystanders." Several people tried to help her thinking she was injured, but she ran home trailing blood behind her all the way, and put the Host in a chest. Later that evening she could no longer hide the Host's presence from her husband because a "mysterious light issued from the trunk, penetrating the wood and illuminating the whole house." Both she and her husband knelt in adoration until dawn when their parish priest was summoned. This church, formerly named St. Stephens, was renamed "The Church of the Holy Miracle" where the Host is still preserved to this day. The Host is "somewhat irregularly shaped, with delicate veins running from top to bottom, where a quantity of blood is collected." According to a New Jersey physician, Dr. Arthur Hoagland, who the article states has observed this Host numerous times, the coagulated blood at the bottom "sometimes has the color of fresh blood, and at other times that of dried blood."[20]

In his March 1995 newsletter, Wayne Weible attested to witnessing, with his own eyes, another preserved Host that had turned to flesh. After meeting with another reported visionary who lived in an area where he had been invited to speak, the visionary took him to a nearby church where a miraculous Host was kept. As Wayne said, "There was no denying it was flesh as small veins could actually be seen in the flesh."[21]

In this same issue, there is also the reported story about Father Robert J. Rooney who was celebrating mass on Mercy Sunday, April 10, 1994 in Yardville, New Jersey. Upon elevating the Host and speaking the words of consecration, "blood flowed out of the Eucharist." The altar servers and readers at the mass "also saw this event and commented on the 'strange' color of the host." Later, the Host bled two more times and "blood could be seen to build up in layers on both the front and back sides of the Eucharist." Two doctors experienced in blood analysis performed a "non-invasive microscopic examination" of the Host. Both stated, "There is no scientific explanation, the red material came from within the Host and it has the microscopic characteristics of human blood; the Church must make the determination as to any miracle."[22]

There are many other documented miracles of the Eucharist, too numerous to mention here, that have been approved by the local bishops of the communities in which these miracles have taken place and by the Holy See in Rome. After acquiring knowledge about these various and fascinating Eucharistic miracles, I felt Our Lady exuberantly propelling me towards the finishing of this book. I smile here as I write this because I knew at that point that my six-month hiatus from writing was at its end. Our Lady turned me back to writing with an enthusiasm and devotion I had not previously had. I longed to write every waking moment. I took advantage of as many hours to write as possible while my children were in school. The hours passed more quickly than I have ever seen time fly. Summer was fast approaching. I knew my occasions of having the computer all to myself, along with corresponding quietness in the house to concentrate, would soon be at an end for awhile.

Chapter 7

The Living Word of God

As mentioned, in addition to writing, I was being called to study the Bible. I had hardly spent any time through the years re-reading the Bible. I would hear Sacred Scripture read at every mass, of course, but after high school and college, where I had been required to read it, I had not made any effort to sit and meditate on God's Word. Father Yozo Zovko, pastor of St. James Church in Medjugorje when the apparitions began, and a very well known priest among Medjugorje followers, always instructs: "The Bible is the *living Word of God*!" He emphatically stresses the importance of reading it daily. I have seen Father several times through the years both in America and in Bosnia and knew this was very important, but I had not invested my time in this area.

The Blessed Mother also stresses the importance of Sacred Scripture. Many times she has called our attention to it in her Medjugorje messages. Here are a few of her exhortations:

♥ *"I call on you to read the Bible every day in your homes and let it be in a visible place so as always to encourage you to read it and to pray."[23]*

♥ *"Every family must pray family prayer and read the Bible!"[24]*

♥ *"Read Sacred Scripture, live it, and pray to understand the signs of the times."[25]*

♥ *"Little children, place the Sacred Scripture in a visible place in your family, and read and live it. Teach your children, because if you are not an example to them, children depart into godlessness."*[26]

♥ *"Put Sacred Scripture in a visible place in your family and read it. In this way, you will come to know prayer with the heart and your thoughts will be on God."*[27]

As you can see, she mentions several times about putting the Bible "in a visible place." Both she and Father Yozo urge us not to put it out as a decoration in our homes, but to have it out in accessibility for the sake of using it.

Pope Benedict XVI also exhorts us to read the Bible. In one of his first messages to the faithful as Pope he stated:

Assiduous reading of Sacred Scripture accompanied by prayer makes that intimate dialogue possible in which, through reading, one hears God speaking, and through prayer, one responds with a confident opening of the heart. If this practice is promoted with efficacy, I am convinced that it will produce a new spiritual springtime in the Church.[28]

Michael Brown from *Spirit Daily* remarks on the Pope's above message by saying, "Reading the Bible on a regular basis allows us to feel the actual move of the Holy Spirit — to reach God through our hearts instead of through our self-important thoughts." He says, "What we need now is familiarity with that remarkable book and the knowing that it is of true supernatural origin."[29]

As I have begun to re-read the Bible, I see it with new eyes as compared to reading it at a younger age. I am truly amazed at how God loved His people and how merciful and forgiving He was towards them when they disobeyed. Once they repented of their sins He renewed His blessing on them. He held steadfast to His covenant with them. I particularly think of Sarah, Rebekah, Jacob, and David. All these sinned greatly; yet they saw their sins, knew they were outside of the will of God, repented before God, were forgiven, and subsequently were blessed in their futures. How people need to know the Word of God. If they know the Word of God, they will not be without hope when they sin. This is not an excuse to sin (knowing that you will be later forgiven), but as humans, we are sure to encounter temptations provoked by the hand of Satan until the day we die. Mother Mary says:

♥ *For now as never before Satan wants to show the world his shameful face by which he wants to seduce as many people as possible onto the way of death and sin. Therefore, dear children, help my Immaculate Heart to triumph in the sinful world. I beseech all of you to offer prayers and sacrifices for my intentions so I can present them to God for what is most necessary.*[30]

♥ *Today again I would like to say to you that I am with you also in these troubled days during which Satan wishes to destroy all that my Son Jesus and I are building. He desires especially to destroy your souls. He wants to take you away as far as possible from the Christian life and from the commandments that the Church calls you to live.*[31]

When you know the Word of God, take its teachings to heart, and live them, you will not as easily succumb to sin. "Whoever obeys a command will meet no harm, and the wise mind will know the time and way" (Ecclesiastes 8:5). Jesus says, "If you love me, you will keep my commandments" (John 14:15). "Whoever does not love me does not keep my words; and the word that you hear is not mine, but is from the Father who sent me" (John 14:24).

Jesus enumerated two great commandments: "You shall love the Lord your God with all your heart, and with all your soul and with all your mind" (Matthew 22:37), and "You shall love your neighbor as yourself" (Matthew 22:39). Some argue that the Ten Commandments are no longer valid because, in their opinion, they are simply "outdated" or because they believe Jesus "replaced" them with the two "great commandments". Jesus in Matthew's gospel deliberately emphasized, "On these two command- ments *hang* all the law and the prophets" (emphasis added; Matthew 22:40).

Jesus told His disciples and the crowds that had come to listen to Him:

"Do not think I have come to *abolish* the law or the prophets; I *have come not to abolish but to fulfil* (sic). For truly I tell you, until heaven and earth pass away, not one letter, not one stroke of a letter, will pass from the law until all is accomplished. Therefore, whoever breaks one of the least of these command- ments, and teaches others to do the same,

will be called least in the kingdom of heaven;
but whoever does them and teaches them will
be called great in the kingdom of heaven"
(emphasis added; Matthew 5:17-20).

The above verses negate the presumption that
the commandments are no longer valid. The following Bible story continues to affirm that the Ten
Commandments are still very much valid. Quoting
from Matthew's gospel, a young man came to ask
Jesus what he must do to attain eternal life. Jesus
responded, "If you wish to enter into life, keep the
commandments" (Matthew 19:16-17). The man then
asked Jesus, "Which ones?" And Jesus said, "You
shall not commit murder; You shall not commit adul-
tery; You shall not steal; You shall not bear false witness; Honor your father and mother; also, You shall
love your neighbor as yourself" (Matthew 19:18-19).

Words of the Virgin Mary reiterating the importance and relevance of the Ten Commandments:

♥ *God gave you the grace to live and to defend all the good that is in you and around you, and to inspire others to be better and holier; but Satan, too, does not sleep and through modernism diverts you and leads you to his way. Therefore, little children, in the love for my Immaculate Heart, love God above every-thing and live His commandments. In this way, your life will have meaning and peace will rule on earth.[32]*

God told Moses that He would show "steadfast love to the thousandth generation of those who love me and keep my commandments" (Exodus 20:6). The very last verse in the book of Ecclesiastes says, "The end of the matter; all has been heard. Fear God, and keep his commandments; for that is the whole duty of everyone" (Ecclesiastes 12:13). Jesus said, "If you keep my commandments, you will abide in my love, just as I have kept my Father's command-ments and abide in his love. I have said these things to you so that my joy may be in you, and that your joy may be complete" (John 15:10-11). To be a friend of Jesus, to love Jesus, and to have His joy complete within us, we are called upon to keep the commandments. How many profess to be Christians today yet do not keep all the commandments?

The similarities of the Israelites in the Old Testament who had fallen away from obeying the commandments compared with present-day society, are striking to me. No story shows this comparison greater than the story of Daniel. Daniel prayed for all of Israel, which had done evil in the sight of the Lord: "I prayed to the Lord my God and made confession, saying, 'Ah, Lord, . . . we have sinned and done wrong, acted wickedly and rebelled, turning aside from your commandments and ordinances. We have not listened to your servants the prophets, who spoke in your name to our kings, our princes, and our ancestors, and to all the people of the land'" (Daniel 9:4-6). " 'All Israel has transgressed your law and turned aside, refusing to obey your voice. So the curse and the oath written in the law of Moses, the servant of God, have been poured out upon us, because we have sinned against you' " (Daniel 9:11).

Daniel pleaded with God to have mercy on His people. He fasted along with his prayers and beseeched God to look at "the city that bears your name" (Daniel 9:18).

Then Gabriel, a man Daniel had seen before in a vision, came and spoke to Daniel. He told Daniel that he was "beloved" by God, and informed him that through God's mercy, the Israelites would be given the opportunity to "put an end to sin, and to atone for iniquity" (Daniel 9:24).

The similarities Daniel describes portraying the Israelites, their sinfulness and "turning aside" from the commandments, reminds me of many in our culture today. And those of us who call ourselves

Christians are those that bear His name! We are largely hypocrites — we cannot "bear His name" and fail to keep the commandments.

Thankfully, we are never without hope when we go astray and sin. If God can be merciful in forgiving a whole nation that has sinned, He can certainly forgive one sinner. We must trust in His love for us, in His mercy, and in His remembrance of our sin no more. As it says in scripture:

For as the heavens are high above the earth, so great is his steadfast love towards those who fear him; as far as the east is from the west, so far he removes our transgressions from us. (Psalm 103:11-12)

But if the wicked turn away from all their sins that they have committed and keep all my statutes and do what is lawful and right, they shall surely live; they shall not die. None of the transgressions that they have committed shall be remembered against them; for the righteousness that they have done they shall live. Have I any pleasure in the death of the wicked, says the Lord God, and not rather that they should turn from their ways and live? (Ezekiel 18:21-23)

I have swept away your transgressions like a cloud, and your sins like mist; return to me, for I have redeemed you. (Isaiah 44:22)

These scripture verses show just how much of a loving and merciful God we have.

Reading the Bible will enlighten one to this merciful God, our loving Father, and our greatest friend and ally. This age of ours is in particular need of re-awakening to the Word of God. Many are in dire need of hope, peace and direction. Following God's Word in the Bible gives this direction for our lives. It is not complicated. It is not burdensome. Following the knowledge set forth in its pages, we are filled with wisdom, Holy Wisdom, and a freedom and peace that "surpass all understanding."

A word of biblical wisdom for those discerning the call to pick up their Bibles more often, meditate on God's word and develop a more magnanimous, rewarding, prayer life is found in the book of Psalms:

Happy are those who do not follow the advice of the wicked, or take the path that sinners tread, or sit in the seat of scoffers; but their delight is in the law of the Lord, and on his law they meditate day and night. They are like trees planted by streams of water, which yield their fruit in its season, and their leaves do not wither. In all that they do, they prosper. (Psalms 1:1-3)

Chapter 8

Spiritual Weapon

I have mentioned the word "fasting" several times in this book already and I would like to address what I mean by it. The Blessed Mother in her apparitions in Medjugorje has asked us to fast on Wednesdays and Fridays on bread and water. She has told us that fasting combined with prayer is extremely powerful. Fasting is not something new. It is mentioned throughout the Bible and has always been practiced in the Catholic Church and honored and practiced in many Protestant churches as well. Fasting is a very high form of prayer. Through fasting you are saying to God, "Lord, I desire (whatever you are praying for) so much that I am willing to 'offer up' in sacrifice all food and drink except bread and water today for this intention."

According to the Medjugorje visionary, Vicka, as I personally heard her state in 1990, the seventh secret, one of the chastisements, was "repealed due to the number of people now praying and fasting." Vicka was telling us that a punishment set for the world was revoked by the hand of God due to His faithful ones' prayers and sacrifices. This reminds me of when the Lord sent Jonah, in the Old Testament, to the large city of Nineveh to announce to all who lived there that He would destroy their city in forty days. When the news reached the King of Nineveh, he made a proclamation: "No human being or animal, no herd or flock, shall taste anything. They shall not feed, nor shall they drink water . . . All shall turn from their evil ways and the violence that is in their hands. Who knows? God may relent and change his mind; he may turn from his fierce anger, so that we do not perish" (Jonah 3:7-9). God did see the people of Nineveh turn from their evil ways, He witnessed their sacrificial actions, forgave them, and the "calamity that he had said he would bring upon them", He cancelled (Jonah 3:10).

These examples, both old and new, exemplify the power of prayer and fasting in mitigating God's rightful anger and invoking His mercy. As you will notice, both the town of Nineveh and the nation of Israel, mentioned in the last chapter, were granted God's mercy through prayer and fasting. Again, the two combined together have great power. Our Lady in her messages also speaks of fasting as a means of expiation for sin:

♥ *Today I call you to prepare your hearts for these days when the Lord particularly desires to purify you from all the sins of your past. You, dear children, are not able by yourselves, therefore I am here to help you. You pray, dear children! Only that way shall you be able to recognize all the evil that is in you and surrender it to the Lord so the Lord may completely purify your hearts. Therefore, dear children, pray without ceasing and prepare your hearts in penance and fasting.*[33]

♥ *Today I call you to renew prayer and fasting with even greater enthusiasm until prayer becomes a joy for you. Little children, the one who prays is not afraid of the future and the one who fasts is not afraid of evil. Once again, I repeat to you: only through prayer and fasting also wars can be stopped — wars of your unbelief and fear for the future.*[34]

Some other biblical examples of fasting are as follows and, if you will bear with me, I enumerate them for good reason:

Yet even now, says the Lord, return to me with all your heart, with fasting, with weeping, and with mourning; rend your hearts and not your clothing. (Joel 2:12-13)

Then I lay prostrate before the Lord as before, for forty days and forty nights; I neither ate bread nor drank water, because of all the sin you had committed, provoking the Lord by doing what was evil in his sight. For I was afraid that the anger that the Lord bore against you was so fierce that he would destroy you. But the Lord listened to me that time also. —Moses (Deuteronomy 9:18-19).

Judas Maccabeus and his brothers saw that their situation in battle was becoming worse and their people were on the verge of being utterly wiped out, so they decided to pray and ask God for His mercy and compassion. *"They fasted that day, put on sackcloth and sprinkled ashes on their heads, and tore their clothes" (1 Maccabees 3:47).* Heaven gave them success in their battle and *"On their return they sang hymns and praises to Heaven — 'For he is good, for his mercy endures for ever'"* (*1 Maccabees4:24*).

While the prophets and teachers of Antioch *"were worshiping the Lord and fasting, the Holy Spirit said, 'Set apart for me Barnabas and Saul for the work to which I have called them.' Then after fasting and praying they laid their hands on them and sent them off"* (*Acts 13:2-3*).

Paul and Barnabas appointed elders for the faithful in each church and *"with prayer and fasting they entrusted them to the Lord in whom they had come to believe"* (*Acts 14:23*).

I recount these biblical examples to illustrate that *whenever* faced with a problem, in need of God's blessing, or when in need of reparation for sin, the biblical figures fasted with their prayers to add power to them and to show commitment to God. Jesus Himself fasted: "Then Jesus was led up by the Spirit into the wilderness to be tempted by the devil. He fasted for forty days and forty nights, and afterwards he was famished" (Matthew 4:1-2). Notice it was the Holy Spirit who led Jesus into the desert and to fast. Heaven knew He needed the power that would come from His fast to be able to endure the suffering and agony He would undergo for our sake.

Our Lady calls us to fast and the Medjugorje visionaries carry this message out by fasting on at least a bi-weekly basis. Many others touched by Our Lady's request have also incorporated fasting into their lives. I began fasting upon my return from Medjugorje in 1990. I'll admit I did it sporadically for sixteen years, sometimes being diligent every Wednesday and Friday for several weeks at a time, and sometimes not being so diligent and only fasting occasionally. Since my 2006 return trip, however,

I have tried to remain very committed to fasting. I won't say that all my fasting days are absolutely perfect bread and water days or that there is never a Wednesday or Friday when I am not fasting, but, by and large, I try to honor what she requests from us as closely as possible. I believe she asks this of us because it is of utmost importance. If she, such a loving mother, is calling us to fast this often and to this degree, we are in a serious situation here on earth needing reparation for sin, obedience (submission) to God, and hope for our future.

We need the hope that springs forth from fasting, acknowledging it as a powerful weapon to effect positive change for our future. As a mother, Our Lady's aim is to protect her children. She is trying to protect us from unnecessary and worse suffering, expiation, and punishment for sin to come, by requesting that we make this milder loving sacrifice of fasting now for ourselves, for our brothers and sisters, and for the world in which we live. By coming under God's authority now, and honoring Him by these selfless acts including fasting, we will gain honor's reward.

Fasting is not so hard. Fasting is not so easy. Our Lady says to do it out of love and then it will become easy for you. This is true. Pick something you wish to do it for — a family member, a situation, a crisis in the world, or our Blessed Mother's intentions — and then it does become easier. Throughout the day be steadfast when you are tempted to give in to eating something other than bread, or when tempted to give up fasting entirely, by remembering your petition. This will strengthen you to say, "No!" because what you desire is so important. Fasting strengthens you to resist temptation in general. If you can control your natural inclination to eat, you can control other passions as well. This is a grace you receive from fasting. Fasting strengthens body and soul.

After twenty years, I do have some tips on fasting. I would like to share them in the hopes of aiding those who wish to utilize this powerful spiritual weapon. The most important thing is to eat good quality bread of substance. Breads containing some whole grains and fiber are best. These keep you satisfied and give you your needed energy for the day. Drink lots of water. This helps you to stay satiated as well and you need hydration, especially if you are taking in more fiber. I find I need to vary the bread I eat. Sometimes I make my own bread in a bread maker; sometimes I buy it in a store or bakery. Variety helps me to continue fasting on a bi-weekly basis.

I am not one to keep eating the same bread over and over again for weeks at a time. Some people are okay with this and with eating very little bread as well. I once met a man whose father fasts three times a week as fasting is not a hardship for him! While I see this more as a rarity, everyone is different. The visionary Vicka often fasts strictly on water (not even any bread) as an extra sacrifice for Our Lady's intentions.

People ask many questions about fasting such as, how much bread can you eat? Can I have coffee? Can I have butter on my bread? The only answer I can give you is that Our Lady has said that the best way to fast is on bread and water. That is what the visionaries tell us. That is what she says. Our Lady is a loving mother and does not want us to make ourselves sick. She says that if one cannot fast due to medical reasons, etc., then one can fast from something else one likes very much — may it be another food item, or fasting from things such as television, etc. When asked this question concerning fasting from other things, I heard the visionary Vicka respond, "Our Lady would like it if we would give up sin in our lives." This should be a lifelong fast.

When I fast, I treat the day as normal. I still exercise and I go on about my daily duties — cooking for my family, shopping and cleaning. I don't let it have any negative effect on my life and I try not to let it have any negative effects on my mood. Jesus says, "And whenever you fast, do not look dismal, like the hypocrites, for they disfigure their faces so as to show others that they are fasting. Truly I tell you, they have received their reward. But when you fast, put oil on your head and wash your face, so that your fasting may be seen not by others but by your Father who is in secret; and your Father who sees in secret will reward you" (Matthew 6:16-18).

Mother Mary says the same thing in one of her messages, that when we fast we are not to let others know we are fasting. That means not to complain about it, not to lament about it and not to be in a bad mood because of it. Just peaceably go on with your life. When I fast, I sit with my family at the dinner table as normal. While they are eating, I eat bread instead. Most of the time, they don't even notice that I'm fasting. If we have an important function to go to on either Wednesday or Friday, I will fast on a different day of the week in place of either day or, oftentimes, I will fast right up until the time of the particular function. These are just ways I have found that work for me and keep me faithfully responding to Our Lady's request for fasting.

I know a priest who lost thirty pounds when he began to fast for Our Lady a few years ago. He continues to work out on fast days and says that on fast days he actually has more energy. He has also kept the excess weight off. Not everyone will lose weight, however. That will depend on your metabolism, what kind of bread you are eating, how much bread you are eating, and your regular intake of food. Now that I have been fasting regularly for quite a while, I realize the importance of healthy eating on the other five days of the week. I have learned it is important to concentrate on eating proteins, vegetables and fruit on the other days. Eating only bread two days of the week makes me less desirable of bread and many other starchy carbohydrates during the remainder of the week.

This way of eating has produced healthier eating on my part, overall. Although certainly not a diet plan, and not the motive Our Lady desires from us for fasting, I do believe better eating habits can come about by grace through this act of self-denial. Late in the evenings on fast days I do lose energy and long to retire to bed, but, occasionally, I even stay up until midnight when my fast has ended, to eat. Many of us who fast have done this — including the visionaries. Generally, though, I just go to bed at my regular time and look forward to the morning. Thursday and Saturday mornings are glorious! The feeling when I wake up is one of accomplishment and gratitude that I was able to fast the day before, and thankfulness for being able to now eat. When you fast, you become aware of how much less food you can live on, and you become increasingly grateful for the food you do have. Food tastes exceptionally more flavorful and delicious. These are beautiful revelations that show us how much we take our sustenance for granted.

The most important thing to remember about fasting says Our Lady, is to "fast and pray with the heart." She says, "There are many people who are fasting, but only because everyone else is fasting. It has become a custom which no one wants to stop."[35] She asks us to fast out of gratitude for God allowing her to continue to appear in Medjugorje. "Especially live the fast, because by fasting you will achieve and cause me the joy of the whole plan, which God is planning here in Medjugorje, being fulfilled."[36]

Our God is a loving God and He will gladly accept anything we wish to give Him in sacrifice. On Wednesdays or Fridays when I do not have the dedication for a bread and water fast, I make the commitment to at least fast from something else such as hot tea, which I usually drink several cups of a day. Offering up something that we desire in any given moment for God is extremely powerful — even if it's a small piece of gum or candy or our favorite TV show!

We can also make a habit of offering things up during each day as sacrifices for offences made to God, for the reparation of sin or for those who do not yet know the love of God. I have learned to make a habit out of offering up little inconveniences to God for the salvation of a soul or for many souls. For example, whenever I stub my toe, or bump myself accidentally or get hurt, or sick, I offer up my sufferings for the conversion of sinners. I like this and feel particularly called to pray for those whom Our Lady says "do not yet know the love of God." In that moment of pain I like to stick it to the devil by saying, "I offer this up for the conversion of a hardened sinner, Lord." It helps to lessen the pain. It can set you in a better mood knowing it has value. The pain and the suffering are *worth* something.

Another thing one can do, something that I have even taught my children, is whenever you see someone on the side of the road in a broken down vehicle, or pulled over by a police officer, or in some other kind of distress — pray for them. Sure you can be the one to lend assistance if they need it, but also pray for them. I began doing this many years ago and had an experience that fills me with teary emotion whenever I think of it. I was driving my van on the Massachusetts Turnpike one rainy dark evening, and my whole family was in the van with me. All of a sudden something went terribly wrong with the van while I was driving it, and I knew we would need assistance. No sooner had I thought this, when I saw the headlights and flashing yellow lights in my rear view mirror of a turnpike assistance vehicle practically riding my bumper!

Without a moment's hesitation, I knew the Lord had sent this vehicle before I'd even had a chance to ask because of all the prayers I had said for others on the side of the road. Our van ended up being towed and we were given transportation to a service station. I am moved just thinking again of this incident.

God's presence and message to me were so strong and clear in that moment.

Our Lady calls us to offer up sacrifices and to fast. The Bible is full of examples of those who did so. These are worthwhile gifts we should all try to incorporate into our lives. They show our commitment to God, plead our case before Him for His mercy, and add strength and influence to our prayers resulting in divine graces of discipline, fortitude, favor, mercy, and peace.

Chapter 9

Medjugorje: The Fruit

Exposure to Medjugorje changes a person. The sheer fact of knowing about it can change your life, let alone traveling there and allowing oneself to become immersed in the environment and Our Lady's messages. Friends of mine who have been touched by Medjugorje have seen their lives transformed as well.

My brother, Fred, for one, thought I was a little bit nutty when he heard of my wanting to go to Medjugorje. He grew more curious after my return and after witnessing the transformation and greater devotion in me to Jesus and Our Lady. He decided to take a trip of his own. He went during the Bosnian War. He, too, came home changed. Slowly, he was allowing what he had witnessed and learned to transform him. It took a while for things to settle in him as well.

Change sometimes takes time and, like me, he really had to contemplate things in his heart and mind concerning what he had been exposed to. It's not always easy to change in our walk with the Lord. You have to change the way you live and conduct yourself once you become aware of certain truths. My brother began praying more and going to Adoration. He became a teacher in our church's RCIA (Rite of Christian Initiation for Adults) program; he attended religious talks, and watched and listened to EWTN on both television and shortwave radio. My family, I, and others in our community saw great devotion in him to the faith. He didn't think I was nutty anymore! And don't let me forget to tell you that he stayed in the home of the visionary Ivanka and her family while he was in Medjugorje!

My friend, Teresa, was also transformed through Medjugorje. As of this writing, Teresa has not yet made a physical trip to Medjugorje, however, her belief in Our Lady's presence there has changed her thinking and the way she is living her life. Teresa was a lot like I was in that she was also pro-choice and against some Church teachings on such topics as birth-control. She had a family situation that was different than mine in that two of her siblings and their families were estranged from her parents.

After I returned from Medjugorje and shared with her what I had learned, she said it really clicked with her. As she said in her own words, "These were things that my old Irish grandmother used to say: 'Say three rosaries a day' and 'you have to believe in miracles.' "[37] She also realized she needed to attend mass on a weekly basis and frequent the Sacrament of Reconciliation as well. She began praying the rosary. She witnessed her rosary bead links change color and she, too, has many times experienced the scent of roses from the Blessed Mother. And Teresa witnessed something even more miraculous from her prayers than the changing colors of rosary links: her estranged family members made peace with her parents again after thirteen years. That was the biggest miracle she had ever witnessed from personal prayer.

Something in Teresa's soul troubled her, though. She said, "I was praying the rosary and thought — *something's* wrong with me." She asked God, "What's wrong with me?" and suddenly she had a huge revelation: "There is something wrong with being pro-choice." She was told, "You cannot *be* pro-choice. There *is no* choice!" That was a major revelation in both her thinking and her life.

Another one of my friends, also named Theresa was, likewise, transformed through Medjugorje. Theresa and I have been friends since becoming roommates together in the Boston area after college. We both married in the same year, within two months of each another. Theresa was another soul like mine in that she, too, was pro-choice and also didn't believe in the same church teachings as mentioned above. Theresa had never heard of any apparitions before I took my first trip to Medjugorje and, after I returned, she said she was "unconsciously or subconsciously not ready to hear about it!"[38] "I distinctly remember being at a family picnic with my mom," she recalled to me, "and she kept asking me about your trip. She wanted to know everything about it." Theresa's mom was very devout. She strongly believed in Catholic school, Our Lady's apparitions in Fatima, praying the rosary daily and confession. Her mom proceeded to read *Medjugorje: The Message*, Wayne's book. After finishing it, Theresa began reading it and thought, "Wow. What an eye-opener for me. You definitely believe after you read it." Theresa was changing and allowing Our Lady's messages to penetrate her heart, mind and soul.

Theresa began to get interested in other apparitions of Our Lady as well and took a trip to Betania, Venezuela (another apparition site) before taking a trip to Medjugorje. An interesting thing to note here is that Theresa and her husband had been trying to have a baby together for a couple of years with no success. Before Theresa left for Medjugorje she was prayed over, and six days upon her return she found out that she was pregnant. She wholeheartedly believes she became pregnant due to the graces that began to flood her life once she decided to go to Medjugorje. She and her husband, Ken, are now the parents of five blessed children! Theresa has also been graced with the beautiful scent of Our Lady's roses on several occasions during mass and other religious events.

While in Medjugorje, Theresa received the gift of being able to be present in the apparition room during Our Lady's apparition to Ivan. She said, "There was a young priest who was present on our trip who was very skeptical." While they were in the apparition

room, this young priest later told how during the apparition he "saw the Blessed Mother come to life in a
picture on the wall. He was changed after that for the
rest of the trip!"

Theresa said, "Before I went to Medjugorje I realized I needed to change my life." One of the things she
knew she had to do was start going back to church.
She had stopped attending after college. Theresa said
that once you go to Medjugorje, "There's no going
back. You're on this path even if you don't want to be.
You are forever changed."

Theresa was saying what all who have been
touched by Medjugorje know: once you know the
truth, you cannot return to your former ways. It will
dog you if you continue to resist the loving touch of
God, the simplicity of His ways and the beauty, peace,
and freedom that flow from following His laws and
commandments.

One of the most moving testimonies I have personally heard from someone regarding how Our Lady's presence in Medjugorje and her messages there have transformed them is from my friend, Chris. I have known Chris for years, long before we became close friends, as she is my brother-in-law's sister. I'll never forget the first time I heard her story and, feeling it would greatly benefit others, I asked her if she would mind sharing it with the readers of this book. I repeat Chris' story now, largely in her own words, and I thank her for being so honest, forthright, and willing to share it so that others might be forever changed.

Chris describes her Medjugorje conversion experience as "kind of like my turning point in life between my Old Testament and my New Testament," and she says that Medjugorje was another integral part of what is hopefully for all of us, a lifelong, continuing conversion experience.

Chris is a happily married wife and mother of three grown children. Over the years, as her married life progressed, her family was blessed materially and monetarily. She said everything in her life was about "the jobs, the money, the social life, and wanting my kids to keep-up with other kids with what they owned. That's the path we were walking down. We were going to church. My kids were in Catholic schools, but I was losing focus, or I didn't have focus of what was truly important in life — that all things come from God and those other things have no meaning or importance."[39]

All was going well in their lives until she said the "rug was ripped out from underneath us." Her husband lost his job. "Our means of having all that stuff" she says, was gone. Once the job was gone, "the prestige was gone. We lost the friends that we thought were so dear to us, you know, the social life and everything else — all I had left was God. That's all I had left. It brought me to my knees." Chris saw how God was using the unfortunate situation of her husband's unemployment to bring them closer to Him. She said, "We were humbled."

Chris and her husband had previously booked a family vacation that had already been paid for before her husband lost his job. It was a vacation they could not get out of, so they went, not knowing how they were to sustain themselves once they returned. While on vacation, Chris said to the Blessed Mother, "If you find my husband a job, I will go to Medjugorje." She says, "I was bargaining with her." What prompted Chris to make this promise was a book she read while traveling. Before leaving home, Chris grabbed a book on her dining room table. She didn't even know where she got the book or who gave it to her.

She said, "It was just laying there. We were running late and I grabbed the book. Usually I read some mindless romance novel, some nothing-book, on vacation, and I didn't have a book, so I whisked it up and took it with me." The book happened to be *The*

Visions of the Children by Janice T. Connell about Medjugorje.

Not long after their return home, she and her husband were able to purchase a franchise and start their own business. Chris was clearly aware that the Blessed Mother had come through on her end of the bargain, but she had not fulfilled her own end. She said, "Our Lady started on me — 'You have to come to Medjugorje. You have to come to Medjugorje.' "

She continued, "I kept putting it off saying, 'Well, we really don't have much money, and I really can't do that, and my husband needs me.' " After all, "It was a new business starting up, and we were just trying to get on our feet. I was making all kinds of excuses. This went on for three years. Finally one day I threw my hands up in the air and said, Fine! You win! I'll go home and tell my husband I need to go to Medjugorje, but he's going to look at me and say, 'What are you, crazy? You can't go to Medjugorje!' And if he says that, then I can't go because he is my husband. There I was, having this conversation with the Blessed Mother!"

"So," she said, "I went home and I told Greg, 'I need to go to Medjugorje.' His response was a simple, 'Fine. You go to Medjugorje, and I will take care of everything at home.' My jaw dropped, because I didn't expect that. And I said to the Blessed Mother, 'Well, you have won. I am going to Medjugorje.'"

Chris left and traveled to Medjugorje along with two of her brothers. It was during the Bosnian War. Amazingly, they were placed in the home of the visionary Ivanka as well. "I hadn't asked to be placed there. It just fell into place," she recalled. Chris saw God's providence in this because, "There was a lot I needed to learn as a mother and a wife. I was able to see how I should be living my life because we had just come from that spot where it was all about climbing the corporate ladder, making more money, socializing with work colleagues and all of that. I believe the Blessed Mother put me there so that I could see how my family really needed to be. In that spot, in that place, Ivanka was the example she put in front of me."

Chris took in everything going on around her in the home of this visionary in a way only a mother could. My brother, although having stayed with Ivanka as well, was young and single when he made his trip. He was not at all aware of the dynamics of family life, as he would be later on as a married father. He was more understandably impacted by the war refugees he saw living in train boxcars than he was by seeing Ivanka simply taking care of her family and home. But Chris, a wife and mother of three, was getting a front row seat into the life of a visionary of the Mother of God, who also happened to be a wife and mother of three!

Chris said Ivanka is very loving and very peaceful. However, she was quick to add that Ivanka is "no different than we are in any way. She's very human. She has the same troubles and anxieties and everything in her life that any mother or wife would have. None of that has been removed from her. I found the miracle was that I looked at Ivanka and I thought of myself. She had three children, like I had three children, and a husband, and a home, and she had all of the work that I have at home — the cleaning, the cooking, the grocery shopping and the care of the children. Yet, she takes in approximately twelve pilgrims into her home at a time, cooks two meals a day for them — *two meals a day*, makes up all the rooms, washes all the linens and just has total faith that God will provide because she's part of His plan to save us — to save *all* of us! I don't know if I could do that," Chris said with her voice and lip quivering, "*That's* a miracle!"

"When I looked at her," Chris continued, "she's not fancy, she doesn't wear make-up — I saw how shallow I was in comparison. She has a friend, (and I thought of the friends that I was choosing based on what their husbands did, or the money they had, or the clothes they wore, or how great they spoke or whatever), and there was Ivanka's friend who, despite missing teeth, radiated such immense spiritual beauty and was so filled with the joy of the Holy Spirit, standing by Ivanka's side helping her wait on all of us — I saw that there was so much more to life than where I was at."

Chris was grateful to God that through the financial/social/emotional setback in their lives, "I saw just how out of focus I had become and was grateful for a chance to *refocus*." Chris and Greg — like so many others who look back over the difficult situations in their lives — were able to see the scripture verse, "We know that all things work together for good for those who love God, who are called according to his purpose" (Romans 8:28), in action in their lives as they were being led to reexamine their thinking, acknowledge God's grace and mercy, and redirect their lives.

Chris continued about Ivanka, "Her kids were no different. They were climbing all over the place and she had to keep them in line just like any other mother would. But she wasn't screaming and yelling at them. She simply went over, took them in her arms and hugged and kissed them when they were acting up. I was thinking about how often I fly off the handle, lose my temper and yell. She was setting an example for me."

Chris related to me how Ivanka's children would sit in the living room watching television with the volume off so that the noise wouldn't disrupt the pilgrims and their conversations. Her children just accepted this and didn't buck or complain about this. Chris also washed dishes with Ivanka side by side after meals at her kitchen sink. Ivanka refused to sit and let Chris take over. She would even hold dinner for all of the pilgrims until they came in at night, refusing to eat any earlier herself. Chris said Ivanka "just has complete faith. She's so humble and so pure."

One day when Ivanka was asked to give a talk to their group by their pilgrimage director, Chris said Ivanka became "very humble and shy and embarrassed. She probably would have rather not come. She probably would rather just be left to her example." Here she was bringing people into her home, feeding them and doing what Our Lady was asking of her, but, no, she still came. Chris said, "Here's this woman that sees the Blessed Mother. She could be arrogant and filled with pride. She could have the attitude, 'I'm better than you,' but no, she was so humble."

"The minute before she came in to talk with the pilgrims," said Chris, "Ivanka's car was hit in an accident. It was smashed. Ivanka had saved pennies forever to have a car to drive her kids to school. But she came in to talk to us in total peace. She gave her talk like nothing had even happened, just completely knowing that you don't need to worry about those kinds of things. They are so unimportant and God will take care of it all if you do what He wants and needs. If you are obedient to Him, He will take care of the rest. Do you know, everybody passed a hat during our stay and came up with enough money, to the penny, for the repairs she needed on her car!"

From this example, and many others Chris witnessed on the parts of Ivanka, her husband, and her family, it was very evident they lived "in the moment." She said, "That's another lesson I learned while there. They're not working for ten years from now. As soon as what they need for that day is earned, they come home and enjoy the love of their family. Ivanka's husband goes to work. The people in Medjugorje go to work. They work for the bread they need to provide for their family that day. They had so much more than us. My own husband wouldn't be home until 7:00 at night, we had more than enough for years to come, and we were wasting it on material things. And here God gave us this beautiful family, the *soul*, as well as the ability to love and enjoy each other, and we were missing it because we wanted more and more and more! And I learned," said Chris in tears, "that they only work for what they need for the day — the *daily bread* from the Our Father. And then they come home and enjoy what is really important in life — one another!"

Having spoken with one of my former pilgrimage directors specifically about how our two countries differ in our priorities, he related to me some interesting examples. This director has been to America many times and says that in Medjugorje, for example, during the Christmas season they don't go overboard like we do in America. In Medjugorje, as well as in the surrounding areas, the focus of the holiday is more on the holy beauty of Christ's birth and being together with family than it is about presents and decorations. Yes, they do exchange presents and have decorations, but not anywhere near to the extent that we have them, nor do they allow themselves to stress and/or obsess about either the way that we do. Likewise, weddings, holy days and funerals are much more sacred, holy, family events as well. And the whole community comes together to help defray the costs of these events, thus taking the financial pressure off of families during these times.

Everyone spends their time when their workday is through at home with their families. They do not do all the running around that we do here. Those in Medjugorje say three public rosaries together and attend mass every evening with their families before dinner. I mean everyone — teenagers, toddlers, husbands and wives, etc. I have been among them many times during their Croatian rosary and mass. My mother and I often commented to one another about how good their little children were through hours of the rosary and mass each night. I find it so beautiful that this is an unquestionable, uncompromised routine in their lives. Their way of life is so much simpler, purer, and holier.

After being exposed to everything in Medjugorje, Chris experienced a heaviness that many of us who've been there can relate to on her trip home. That heaviness is the burden of knowing that you have to change. Chris said, "When I left Medjugorje, I remember sitting on the plane and realizing that this was so big. For God to be sending His Mother to earth everyday — since 1981— it must be of monumental importance — *monumental importance* — that we all need to pay attention. Never in the history of mankind has He provided a grace of this magnitude. We are living in a time of great difficulty. There is war. There is hatred in families — divorces. There is abortion, AIDS, drugs, and violence. There is prostitution, criminals, children shooting children . . . He is trying to save us. It's a great grace."

"So," said Chris with her lip quivering again, "while on the plane I was thinking, 'Wow. I almost wish I hadn't come.' The responsibility is of such magnitude, and once you have been a part of it, you can't pretend you haven't learned what you just learned. Now you are a part of it. You're in it! So, I cried tears on the plane thinking, 'can I even *do* this? Can I even *do* this because I have to change my entire life?' I have to *change my entire life!* The only way that people will believe that Our Lady's presence in Medjugorje is real, is if they can see a huge conversion and change in me — that I've bought into it!"

"So, I came home and I gave it my all. I had to try to avoid temptation. There was a lot of my life that I had to cut out. And it was painful. People don't understand, but you have to move forward. I wasn't always at peace because it hurts when you come home and you have friends that make fun of you. They can't understand. They think you're a spiritual nutcase! There is no peace in that. I had to go to God for my peace in that. It was a struggle for years. In the end you end up with the friends that are on the same course you are on, and you continue in your example of love for everybody, hoping that through your love they will come to understand."

Chris said this new way of living blessed her home. "It blessed my children. It blessed my family." The way she was now choosing to live her life (including praying the rosary with her family), was bearing fruit and gracing them all. Chris struggled at first with how to get her whole family praying the rosary together as well. She and Greg wisely decided to invite their children to prayer, as Our Lady does with all of us, and remarkably they began joining them on their own. Chris has also been the recipient of many extraordinary personal graces from Our Lady along her journey of faith since her Medjugorje conversion.

In addition to all the newfound blessings in the lives of this family, there was a financial blessing as well. Her husband got offered a job by the corporate office of the franchise he'd been working for. And not only did they offer him the job, they so wanted him in the position, that they were willing to allow him to work from his home instead of moving his family across the country to work at their corporate office!

The Blessed Mother comes to Medjugorje under the title of "Queen of Peace," and peace is one of the most important things she calls us to. Chris said that "peace is probably the greatest gift" from God and she reminded me that the last thing Jesus gave us before He ascended into heaven was peace. She said, "He could have given us anything, but He chose to give us peace." In the Gospel of John, Jesus is heard saying, "Peace I leave with you; my peace I give to you" (John 14:27). Chris went on eagerly: "Out of a single heart you create peace in the world, but that peace starts in one heart. All *I* have to be concerned about is what's in *my* heart. It will trickle out to other hearts through the example of love." Chris mirrored what Our Lady of Medjugorje is always telling us: that we must first have peace in our own individual hearts, and then that peace will spread to our families, to our communities and to our world at large.

"If you walk around with anxiety, stress and all of those other things that are absolutely everywhere today, who's going to be attracted to your lifestyle? Nobody wants that. But if you walk around and you're filled with joy and love and peace, people want it. They are going to ask you, 'How come you're so happy?' Or, 'How come you just have this way about you?' It's from the Eucharist. It's from daily mass. It's from living in the moment. It's from not getting caught up in the things of this world. It's by keeping your sights on God always. Because, when you focus on Him, He gives you everything you need — *everything* — sometimes before you even ask for it it's dropped at your feet. All you need to do is put God first. He gives you the graces and the gift of free will. We have free will so that we have the choice to love Him. He never forces His way on anyone. There is no merit in any behavior that is forced. It is when you choose to avoid temptation that you receive merit for your behavior."

Chris summed up what she learned in Medjugorje this way: "I learned I had to have patience. I had to have more tolerance with my kids. I had to have more love. I had to have more generosity. I had to have forgiveness. It taught me to try to live in the present moment. It's not rocket science, but it's not easy, either. I'm human. When I lose my patience, I try to catch myself. If I'm in a situation that I can't control, I try to stop and go to God. If you live your life without Jesus, it is such a miserable struggle and hard work. It's so easy to invite Him into your heart, to give Him your day and your life. He created the universe. He will give you anything that's good for you."

All those touched by Medjugorje, including those who have traveled there, are affected by Our Blessed Mother's messages. We come home carrying these messages and examples in our hearts and we come home knowing we have to pass them on. These are the "fruits" of Medjugorje. Many of us come home from Medjugorje convicted about our own lives. We know we need to make changes. We come home knowing our examples are imperative. Out of them, others can be brought to faith and light or plunged into darkness. It is a huge responsibility but it really is not hard, ultimately. Living God's way is the most peaceful way to live. We realize, even if we resist acknowledging it at first, or even if it's merely on a subconscious level, that our only true peace will be found when we align ourselves with His will and live according to the commandments and His Church.

We are all Our Lady's children. She desires that we come closer to her Son, Jesus, and that we come to recognize Him in the Eucharist through His Church. She is praying for us, interceding for us before the Most High, and granting us her help, protection and very great graces. We are all called to play a part in this mission through the living of these messages of prayer, conversion, fasting, penance and peace. By doing so, our lives become examples for others to learn from and imitate. Our Blessed Mother says it is more by our example than by our words that others will be converted. Utilizing the gifts, talents and resources that the Lord has given to each one of us, we are to be "our brother's keeper" in leading others to salvation.

♥ *You are the ones responsible for the messages. The source of grace is **here**, but you, dear children, are the vessels which transport the gifts. Therefore, dear children, I am calling you to do your job with responsibility. Each one shall be responsible according to his own ability. Dear children, I am calling you to give the gifts to others with love and not to keep them for yourselves.*[40] ***You shall be answerable to "me" and to my Son, Jesus.***[41] *Pray to the Holy Spirit for enlightenment. If you only knew how great are the graces God is granting you, you would be praying without ceasing.*[42] *— Our Mother*

She continues to commission us for this task as she said on June 25, 2007, the 25th Anniversary of the Medjugorje apparitions:

♥ *Dear children! Also today, with great joy in my heart, I call you to conversion. Little children, do not forget that you are all important in this great plan which God leads through Medjugorje. God desires to convert the entire world and to call it to salvation and to the way towards Himself, who is the beginning and the end of every being. In a special way, little children, from the depth of my heart, I call you all to open yourselves to this great grace that God gives you through my presence here. I desire to thank each of you for the sacrifices and prayers. I am with you and I bless you all. Thank you for responding to my call.*[43]

Conclusion

A Final Word of Encouragement

My hope, dear readers, is that I have conveyed to you the reality of Jesus' presence in the Holy Eucharist, the great blessing available to us in our loving Mother's intercession, and the truth of God speaking to us through His Word. I hope I have enlightened you to the value of fasting, the "offering up" of sacrifices and the importance of confessing our sins. I hope to have reminded you that we have a forgiving all-powerful God as Father, His loving Son Jesus, our Redeemer and example, and the help of the Holy Spirit guiding us in our daily lives.

I'm sure I have conveyed to you how much the Roman Catholic Church means to me, personally, and how it provides me with our Living God through the Eucharist, Sacred Scripture, Sacred Tradition — as passed to us through the apostles — and through the wisdom of the Magisterium. And I hope through my example, and the examples of others mentioned in this book, that the "fruits" of souls being led more deeply to Christ through Medjugorje have been made manifest.

I am truly grateful to the Blessed Virgin Mary for taking me under her wing and guiding me as a mother leads a child to what is best and most important for them. She is a mother continuously coaxing all her children to come to the right truths and to do the right things. She points us only to her Son for our salvation and for our direction. Her last recorded words in scripture are, "Do whatever he tells you" (John 2: 5). She has come down from Heaven to Medjugorje to repeat those words, to redirect us on our often-misguided paths, and to strengthen the faithful in their walk with our Lord by reminding us unceasingly to "Look at the **SON!**"

Endnotes

1. See: Weible, Wayne. "Sister Lucia, Last Fatima Visionary Dies." Weible Columns Medjugorje Newsletter 14.32 (2005): 1, 3.
2. A Friend of Medjugorje, Entering A New Time, Caritas of Birmingham, AL, USA; Saint James Publishing, 2001, p.13.
3. Klins, June. The Best of "The Spirit of Medjugorje" Volume II. 2007 Bloomington, IN, USA; AuthorHouse, 150.
4. McFadden, Joe and Eleanor. Messages of the Queen of Peace, 2007 Ed., Ireland: Dublin Medjugorje South East, 155.
5. A Friend of Medjugorje, In Front of the Crucifix With Our Lady, Caritas of Birmingham, AL, USA; Saint James Publishing, 1999, p. 16.
6. McFadden, Joe and Eleanor. Messages of the Queen of Peace, 2007 Ed., Ireland: Dublin Medjugorje South East, 24.
7. Libreria Editrice Vaticana, Catechism of the Catholic Church (Missouri: Liguori Publications, 1994) 212.

8. Libreria Editrice Vaticana, Catechism of the Catholic Church (Missouri: Liguori Publications, 1994) 212.

9. Osteen, Joel. Be Glad Continually. 19 April 2009. Joel Osteen Audio Podcast, #421.<http://rss.streamos.com/streamos/rss./genfeed.php?feedid=111&groupname=lakewood>

10. McFadden, Joe and Eleanor. Messages of the Queen of Peace. 2007 Ed., Ireland: Dublin Medjugorje South East, 36.

11. McFadden, Joe and Eleanor. Messages of the Queen of Peace. 2007 Ed., Ireland: Dublin Medjugorje South East, 28-29, 35.

12. McFadden, Joe and Eleanor. Messages of the Queen of Peace. 2007 Ed., Ireland: Dublin Medjugorje South East, 36.

13. Osteen, Joel. Seizing Your God-Given Opportunities. 27 Sept. 2007. Joel Osteen Audio Podcast, #361.<http://rss.streamos.com/streamos/rss./genfeed.php?feedid=111&groupname=lakewood>; (See also Genesis 50:20)

14. "Stay Open for Something New"- #409, Joel Osteen, Joel Osteen Ministries. 11 January 2009.

15. McFadden, Joe and Eleanor. Messages of the Queen of Peace. 2007 Ed., Ireland: Dublin Medjugorje South East, 32-33, 54.

16. Fr. Tommy Lane.com <http://frtommylane.com/homilies/year_b/18.htm>

17. Weible, Wayne. "Miracles Of The Eucharist." Weible Columns Medjugorje Newsletter 7.9 (1996): 6.

18. Weible, Wayne. "Miracles Of The Eucharist." Weible Columns Medjugorje Newsletter 7.9 (1996): 6.

19. EWTN Live (Encore), Fr. Thomas Milota, Eternal Word Television Network. 8 January 2009.

20. Cruz, Joan Carroll. "The Eucharist Miracle Of Santarem, Portugal." Weible Columns Medjugorje Newsletter, July (1996): 6.

21. Weible, Wayne "The Great Miracle: The Eucharist." Weible Columns Medjugorje Newsletter, 6.11 (1995): 1-2.

22. Pladek, Robert. "1994 Eucharist Occurrence In New Jersey." Weible Columns Medjugorje Newsletter 6.11 (1995): 1, 8.

23. McFadden, Joe and Eleanor, Messages of the Queen of Peace. 2007 Ed. Ireland: Dublin Medjugorje South East, 31.

24. McFadden, Joe and Eleanor. Messages of the Queen of Peace. 2007 Ed. Ireland: Dublin Medjugorje South East, 36-37.

25. McFadden, Joe and Eleanor. Messages of the Queen of Peace. 2007 Ed. Ireland: Dublin Medjugorje South East, 102.

26. McFadden, Joe and Eleanor. Messages of the Queen of Peace. 2007 Ed., Ireland: Dublin Medjugorje South East, 116.

27. McFadden, Joe and Eleanor. Messages of the Queen of Peace. 2007 Ed., Ireland: Dublin Medjugorje South East, 160.

28. Brown, Michael. "Pope Benedict XVI Hits the Mark." Weible Columns Medjugorje Newsletter.14.38 (2005): 1.

29. Brown, Michael. "Pope Benedict XVI Hits the Mark." Weible Columns Medjugorje Newsletter.14.38 (2005): 1.
30. McFadden, Joe and Eleanor. Messages of the Queen of Peace. 2007 Ed., Ireland: Dublin Medjugorje South East, 91-92.
31. McFadden, Joe and Eleanor. Messages of the Queen of Peace. 2007 Ed., Ireland: Dublin Medjugorje South East, 97.
32. Medjugorje.org, 2010, The Medjugorje Web, 25 May 2010 htttp://www.medjugorje.org.
33. McFadden, Joe and Eleanor. Messages of the Queen of Peace. 2007 Ed., Ireland: Dublin Medjugorje South East, 65.
34. McFadden, Joe and Eleanor. Messages of the Queen of Peace. 2007 Ed., Ireland: Dublin Medjugorje South East, 136.
35. McFadden, Joe and Eleanor. Messages of the Queen of Peace. 2007 Ed., Ireland: Dublin Medjugorje South East, 30.
36. McFadden, Joe and Eleanor. Messages of the Queen of Peace. 2007 Ed., Ireland: Dublin Medjugorje South East, 45-46.
37. Friend - Teresa. Telephone interview. June 2008.
38. Friend - Theresa. Telephone interview. May 2008.
39. Friend - Christine. Personal Interview. July 2008.
40. A Friend of Medjugorje, Understanding Our Lady's Messages, Caritas of Birmingham, AL, USA; Saint James Publishing, 1997, 26.

41. A Friend of Medjugorje, Understanding Our Lady's Messages, Caritas of Birmingham, AL, USA; Saint James Publishing, 1997, 24.
42. A Friend of Medjugorje, Understanding Our Lady's Messages, Caritas of Birmingham, AL, USA; Saint James Publishing, 1997, 12.
43. Medjugorje.org. 2007. The Medjugorje Web. 25 June 2007 htttp://www.medjugorje.org.

CPSIA information can be obtained at www.ICGtesting.com
Printed in the USA
BVOW070922160112

280523BV00001B/4/P

THE RIGHT MADNESS

Also by James Crumley
in Large Print:

The Final Country

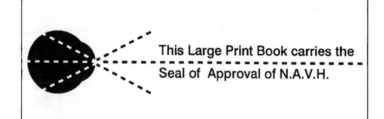

This Large Print Book carries the
Seal of Approval of N.A.V.H.

THE RIGHT MADNESS

MADNESS

James Crumley

Thorndike Press • Waterville, Maine

Published in 2005 by arrangement with Viking Penguin, a member of Penguin Group (USA) Inc.

Thorndike Press® Large Print Americana.

The tree indicium is a trademark of Thorndike Press.

The text of this Large Print edition is unabridged. Other aspects of the book may vary from the original edition.

Set in 16 pt. Plantin by Minnie B. Raven.

Printed in the United States on permanent paper.

Library of Congress Cataloging-in-Publication Data

Crumley, James, 1939–
    The right madness / by James Crumley.
        p. cm. — (Thorndike Press large print Americana)
    ISBN 0-7862-7876-5 (lg. print : hc : alk. paper)
    1. Sughrue, C. W. (Fictitious character) — Fiction.
  2. Private investigators — Montana — Fiction.
  3. Psychotherapist and patient — Fiction. 4. Montana —
Fiction. 5. Large type books. 6. Psychological fiction.
  I. Title. II. Thorndike
Press large print Americana series.
  PS3553.R78R54 2005b
   813'.54—dc22   2005013450

THE RIGHT
MADNESS

As the Founder/CEO of NAVH, the only national health agency solely devoted to those who, although not totally blind, have an eye disease which could lead to serious visual impairment, I am pleased to recognize Thorndike Press* as one of the leading publishers in the large print field.

Founded in 1954 in San Francisco to prepare large print textbooks for partially seeing children, NAVH became the pioneer and standard setting agency in the preparation of large type.

Today, those publishers who meet our standards carry the prestigious "Seal of Approval" indicating high quality large print. We are delighted that Thorndike Press is one of the publishers whose titles meet these standards. We are also pleased to recognize the significant contribution Thorndike Press is making in this important and growing field.

Lorraine H. Marchi, L.H.D.
Founder/CEO
NAVH

* Thorndike Press encompasses the following imprints: Thorndike, Wheeler, Walker and Large Print Press.

This novel is dedicated to my hometown, Missoula, Montana, to the readers, writers, book lovers, and friends — the people who stepped up to the mark when things went badly for me. Neil MacMahon, Michael Koepf, and John Keegan organized a benefit that kept us up and running during the time I couldn't even write my name. Charles Umhey, M.D., and his wife, Tavy provided food, bandages, and sympathy. Ed Wells and Mike Muncie of the Depot Bar deserve thanks, as do all the good kids who worked on the benefit. The nurses at the ICU at Community Hospital saved my life as kindly as they could, although I wasn't always the best of patients. I apologize for my moments of foolishness and thank them for their understanding.

I also have to express our thanks to the estate of John Chesley and Grace Lundin, of Richmond, Virginia. Without its generous help, we would never have made it.

I can only say thank you to my friends

who stood with me, and promise to do the same in return.

And, of course, the novel is dedicated to Martha Elizabeth, perhaps most of all. She stood next to my bed and never gave up. Even when I made a drugged pass at her, when I didn't know who she was, she forgave me. Ain't the world grand? My love and thanks to everybody.

One

It was a lovely, calm Montana summer evening, a Saturday night after a long weekend of softball. The full moon rose blazing over Mount Sentinel, outlining the maw of the Hellgate Canyon with silver fire. A streak of summer haze like a line of blood lay across the moon's idiot face. The motel's pool lights were reduced to dim glows. The hot tub shimmered around us like a pot of silver. The early August afternoon had been as hot as a fiddler's bitch, and a molten slice of sunset still glowed with a hot golden flame along the jagged edge of the western horizon, but the early evening air had cooled quickly enough to draw vaporous swirls of steam from the heated water. The rising moon seemed to muffle the night for a moment. The only sounds were faint — the hiss of traffic over the Clark Fork bridge, the soft paddles from a gaggle of children in the pool, the romantic whispers of two young blond girls in oversized softball shirts leaning into each other, and the brazen chuckles squirting out of a coven of young men brewing drunken plots of disorder and early sorrow at a poolside table.

Then Mac ratcheted up the hot tub's timer and broke the spell. The Jacuzzi jets thrashed the water, scouring away the moon's blush. A whisper of fabric brushed my thigh and a flash of something black and shining caught my eye. I grabbed it automatically. When I realized what it was, I quickly stuffed the scrap of sparkling cloth into the pocket of my trunks.

"Random madness in the ER tonight, Sughrue," Mac murmured from the other side of the hot tub. I assumed he would know. After a quick Vietnam tour and a stint in ERs up and down the West Coast, he had gone back to school, taken his boards, and become a psychiatrist, a position from where he could at least help, sometimes, and where he didn't have to deal with blood and guts anymore.

Once, when I asked him why he had changed medical careers in midstream, he answered thoughtfully that he had enjoyed the battle against bloody injury and sudden death too much. Winning made him hysterical with victory, and losing nearly killed him. The ER was no place for a budding manic-depressive, he maintained. "A dangerous night, Sughrue," he added, grinning. "What's your pleasure? Shall we confront the danger?"

"The most dangerous thing I'm going to do tonight," I said as I cracked my last beer, "is put my pants on and go downtown."

"It's downtown Missoula on a Saturday night," Mac said, then dropped his cigar into the remains of his watery vodka. "You could be eaten by vegetarian hippies falling off the wagon, raped by closet Republicans," he said, then added, nodding toward the table full of bulky and besotted young men laughing, "or beaten to death by deranged and defeated softball players." State softball tournament weekend.

"I'll take my chances," I said. "You want to come along?"

"Is Whitney coming?"

"I don't think so," I said. "I can almost hear her pounding her laptop keys from here. Being married to a lady lawyer ain't all it's cracked up to be, Doc. Hell, she probably won't even notice when I stop by the room to put on my pants."

"How's the separation going?" Mac said as he climbed out of the Jacuzzi.

"It's not a separation," I insisted. "She just took a new job."

"A thousand miles away?" he said. "But

it's my personal and professional opinion that you're handling it the right way."

"How's that?"

"You're not taking it personally." Then he added, smiling, "I'll get dressed, tell Lorna we're going, and meet you at the Depot. I need to talk to you about something anyway. It's important."

"Sounds like a deal," I said. As do all people who keep secrets professionally, Mac knew too many, and had a way of making anything he said sound like a deal.

Although he was several years past fifty and had played two softball games in one day, Mac still carried his stubby body with an athlete's strut, a sense of easy strength in his oddly shaped frame. Like Babe Ruth, he didn't look like he could hit the ball, but he could; and he had a winner's confidence in his carriage as he walked the twenty feet from the hot tub to his room. He'd earned that strut. In spite of a torn ACL in high school, he had been a small-college all-American linebacker in his youth, a ranked amateur squash player in his middle years, and now was probably the best softball player over fifty in Montana. Even with a twisted knee, his play at short-stop — two doubles and a seventh-inning home run — earlier that evening had won us the state title in the O.F.S. League. Over Fifty League, they called it. Old Farts Softball, we said.

Our wives had endured the semifinal game earlier that hot afternoon, thinking as everyone did that the Old Goats had come as far as they could, farther than they had ever dreamed. We were bound to lose to a team of very athletic peace officers from Billings, fundamental Christians to a man, their eyes untroubled by doubt, drugs, or even rumors of strong drink. Our defeat seemed so certain that we had made dinner reservations at the Redbird for that night.

But Satan kept the score book that day. Their starting pitcher walked four men in a row before giving up as many dink singles. Then the shortstop, short fielder, and center fielder, mad with frustration, crashed together chasing a high, lazy pop-up. The result was a separated shoulder, a serious concussion, two lost teeth, and four more runs for our team. For them, everything went to hell after that. The next inning, their catcher and the umpire collided face to face, then rushed off to St. Patrick's ER to have their noses removed from their cheeks and recentered in their faces. In the fourth inning, they were forced to recruit two drunks from the stands to save themselves from a forfeit. When the ten-run mercy rule was applied after the fifth inning, they were truly thankful to leave the arena. Christians, 0; Old Goats, 21. So much for dinner reservations. Our wives elected to skip the night game final in favor of a soak in the hot tub and room service dinners in their rooms. We were so stunned by our win that we didn't argue with them.

Mac paused at the sliding glass door of the bridal suite. "Actually, give me an hour," he said, his broad grin shining in the shadows. Mac and Lorna weren't newlyweds, but new enough to still have fun with the notion.

I answered with a wave and a smile of my own. My friend's grin was as happy and excited as a puppy's when he turned to go in to his young wife. Unfortunately, my smile felt as if it had been gouged into my face with a rusty nail. The scrap of fabric I had snatched from the water was the top of Lorna's swimsuit.

As the sliding glass door rumbled shut, the laughter from the young men's table took on a sharp snicker that I didn't much like. I finished my beer, tossed the empty can into the cooler, then climbed out of the hot tub. As I walked past the chuckling table, I clipped one kid's knee with the cooler, hard, then stumbled into the table, spilling drinks all over the other two. Apologizing profusely and promising to call room service to send them a round of drinks, I trotted over to the motel's side entrance, trying not to limp.

A small revenge, I realized, but I knew the indignities facing an older man married to a younger woman. I was fifteen years older than Whitney, but I still had most of my hair, and it was blond and didn't show the gray like the blue-black curls that draped Mac's head and his rakish goatee. He was twenty years older than Lorna, but she looked so young, the age difference seemed greater. She had wide-set wild green eyes, a cap of deep red hair, and the clear skin of an Irish child.

My wife, on the other hand, carried herself like a woman wise beyond her years. A finely etched set of crow's-feet, shadows left from our time hiding in the hard sunlight of the slickrock desert and later in the Davis Mountains of West Texas, flanked the fierce and determined intelligence shining from her deep blue eyes. And I suspected, like many beautiful women, Whitney had never looked like a child. Just as I suspected that Lorna wouldn't stop looking like a child until she was suddenly very old.

A trash can sat just inside the side entrance. I started to stuff the top of Lorna's swimsuit deep into the refuse, then changed my mind, and walked down to our room. The hallway was filled with the wails of the losers and the cheers of the winners. A room service tray with a half-eaten club sandwich and an empty coffee pot sat outside our door. Whit must have heard my key in the door because she was standing just inside, waiting for me, the deep laugh lines flickering around her wide mouth.

"Are you guys ever going to stop acting like kids?" she said, smiling and shaking her head. Then she gave me a long kiss and a hug hard enough to make me flinch. In our league, base runners weren't supposed to try to run over the catcher. But sometimes they forgot. "Aren't you guys ever going to grow up?"

"We'll start working on it tomorrow," I said, when we disengaged.

"I'll believe it when I see it, CW," she said. "Tomorrow?"

"Tonight we're going downtown."

"And here we are with a room all to ourselves," she said, grinning. Our son, Les, had gone to basketball camp back in Minnesota. At twelve he thought softball nearly as boring as baseball and football. He was a basketball fanatic. Pro basketball. "You mind if I keep working?" Whit asked, and she really meant it. She sat back down at the desk. That was one of the many things I loved about her: she always meant what she said. "If I get through this brief tonight, we'll have all day tomorrow to ourselves."

"A brief hurrah, huh?" I said. Her flight wasn't until eight the next evening. "All too brief."

"I wish you wouldn't take it that way," she said, looking into the gray screen. "I'm getting a late start at this lawyer thing, and this job is a chance to skip a few grinding years." Then she added, "Anyway, we've survived worse times than this." Her new job in Minneapolis was a good one, right, and her mother needed help with her aged father, true enough, and sure as hell we had survived worse times. "It'll be fine," she said.

"I'll get a dog," I said, "and wear out an airline seat."

"Thank you," she said, wrapping a slim, manicured hand around my wet knee, but her eyes were already back at the screen.

"I'll be back before closing time," I said.

"I've heard that before," she said. "Is Lorna going?"

"I don't think so," I said. "Too many vodka tonics and too much sun this afternoon."

"Did you see the size of that blister on her thigh where she missed with the sun block? Jesus."

"I try not to look at Lorna's legs," I said. Even though they were long and lovely, often she seemed a bit too proud of them, too ready to show them off.

"Liar," Whit said as she gently slapped the back of my knee. "I used to envy her that beautiful white skin. Until I found out that she doesn't tan. Hell, she doesn't even bother to burn; she's so pure, she blisters." Then she patted me on the ribs again, laughing. "Are you sore? That asshole ran into you pretty hard. I thought that was against the rules."

"I held on to the ball, honey," I said, "and that's all that counts."

"You'll never grow up."

"I'll be as sore as a boil tomorrow, but we've got at least an hour before the pain starts."

"*You've* got an hour, cowboy," she said.

"*I've* got to get back to work."

"All work and no play makes Jack —" I started to say.

"My name ain't Jack, dude," she interrupted, laughing again, "and if you think I'm dull, I can fix that in a heartbeat."

"No, thanks," I said.

She went back to her laptop, and I stepped over to the telephone to order a round of drinks for the boys at the pool.

"What the hell was that about?" Whit said without looking up.

"I stumbled into a table coming back from the hot tub."

"Time to take up golf?"

"I was thinking of chess," I said, but she was already deep into the brief. I showered and changed, trying not to think about why the top of Lorna's swimsuit was floating around the hot tub, and trying not to worry about what Mac wanted to talk to me about.

"Eat something," she said by way of good-bye as I left. Since the day I'd been gutshot down on the border, eating had lost a lot of its charm.

Actually, Whitney had brought Dr. William MacKinderick into our lives. She had been trying to run a pro bono diminished capacity defense for a fourteen-year-old Benewah teenager who had hitchhiked off the reservation down to Meriwether, where he'd stuck six inches of sharpened screwdriver into the neck of the first bartender who wouldn't serve him a drink. The kid was lucky the bartender hadn't died. Whit was sure that the kid suffered from fetal alcohol syndrome and had no more control over his emotions or actions than a rabid coyote. Of course, in this new world, the state wanted to try the kid as an adult for attempted murder. Mac was the only psychiatrist in Meriwether who volunteered his time as an expert witness. The case dragged on forever, but they finally got the kid remanded to Warm Springs for treatment instead of Deer Lodge Prison, where he would have become just another piece of red meat.

Mac could afford the time. Before he'd left a successful practice in Seattle after the scandal surrounding his divorce and quick marriage to Lorna, who had been one of his patients, Mac had written four best-selling, down-to-earth self-help books: *Other People's Troubles*; *Your Demon Family*; *I'd Be Okay if You Weren't Such a Mess*; and *They Need You as a Witness*. They were funny, practical, without cant or pretension, and full of absolutely practical advice about changing behavior. Mac believed that whatever method helped, in each individual case, was the right method and that most people's problems were caused by listening to friends and family. The psychiatric world was suspicious of him because he refused to belong to any school and had the gall to suggest that most people needed therapy, not because of their personal demons but because they allowed the other people in their lives to be demonic. Enough readers, though, loved Mac's advice so much that he never had to worry about money again.

Lorna had grown up in Bigfork, Montana, the late child of a retired runway model and a mediocre professional golfer, so her move back to Montana had satisfied her family. And Mac's practice in the small city of Meriwether had seemed to suit him perfectly. Until the malpractice suit.

The suit had gone on for a year when it became clear that an eyewitness was needed. Mac's lawyer, Ron Musselwhite, recommended me. Captain Fucking Bloodhound to the rescue. It cost Mac thousands of dollars and me six months of my life, but I finally came up with a witness, and the malpractice suit was settled last winter. During the breaks through that long, hard time, Mac and I became confidants, then drinking buddies, then close friends.

When I got to the Depot that night, it was full of men and women still in their sweaty softball uniforms and plastic spikes. Because of our winters, it often seemed that summer softball was a religion in Montana, the only religion to which I had ever belonged. Some of the guys I saw from the Old Farts League had changed clothes, but their faces glowed with the same inner light as the kids'. We were past middle age, perhaps almost old, but we were still swinging the bat. And thanks to the miracle of modern technology, occasionally hitting one out of the park.

Mac was sitting on a tall stool at the corner of the bar beneath the chalkboard that displayed the beer and wine list. He wore olive khakis and a dark cashmere sport coat over a white knit shirt. I felt like a bindle stiff in my jeans, Slumgullion's T-shirt, and Old Goat's windbreaker. As I worked the rest of the way through the crowd, Mac tapped the kid beside him on the shoulder. The kid gave up his stool happily and moved back into a clot of standing players. I knew that Mac had bought the kid and his friends a round of drinks to save me a stool. The two pudgy young blond girls from the pool were billing and cooing on the stools beside me.

"I saved you a place, darling," Mac said as he slapped my cheek when I sat down. The kids nearby gave us a look, then shook their heads and laughed. "You want a drink?" He had an almost untouched martini in front of him, a drink I usually avoided like sin, but it looked clean and cold and perfect for the moment.

"I'll have one of those," I said.

"Todd," Mac said in a normal voice. But the bartender heard him and looked up alertly. I was fairly good company in bars, but Mac made himself a neighborhood within minutes after climbing on a bar stool. "A Bombay Sapphire martini for my friend, please."

While the bartender made the drink, I looked around the bar. As had happened too often recently, all the women looked very young, impossibly pretty and sharper than the popper on a blacksnake whip. But I was with Mac, a member of the neighborhood, so my openly admiring stares were met with smiles instead of frowns.

When my martini came, I raised it to

Mac. We clicked glasses. "Victory," I said.

"Unless it's victory over death, my friend," he said, "it's as empty as an old man's condom." He stared at the clear drink, his face deadly serious.

"Excuse me," I said, trying not to think about the piece of Lorna's swimsuit in the inner pocket of my windbreaker. Or her bare breasts. Or her legs. "Jesus, I thought this was supposed to be a celebration."

"I need you to go to work for me again," he said abruptly, his voice almost inaudible beneath the crowd noise.

"No," I answered without hesitation. "I don't think so."

"You won't even think about it?"

"The last gig almost killed me, partner," I said. "I didn't shit right or sleep through the night for months after all that time on the road. And you know how I feel about working for friends."

"You'd be working for Ron Musselwhite," he said as he pulled out a cigar and snipped off the tip.

"Can't smoke that in here, dude," said a passing blond waitress with massive energy and a dangerous edge to her laughter, who quickly lost the edge, then slipped into a happy voice that defined her personality. We were the entertainment in her world.

"Can I at least chew on it?" Mac suggested.

"Anytime, dude. Anytime," she said, then swept on past with a tray full of drinks.

"Look," he said, leaning toward me. "You won't have to leave town, and I promise it will be an easy job. I'll pay twice your usual rate."

"What the hell?" I said. "We live in the same town, man. We even live in the same neighborhood. We have drinks at the Scapegoat at least twice a week, right? So why did we have to drive all the way to Missoula, play two softball games in the same goddamned day and come down to this madhouse so you can offer me a job?"

"You always had a great perspective on the obvious," he said. "The timing seemed right. Whitney's on her way back to the Twin Cities —"

"Thanks for reminding me."

"Sughrue, I need your help. A professional and personal favor."

"Jesus fucking wept," I said, then sighed, and gunned my martini, then waved my glass at the bartender. Of course, he ignored me. Mac raised his finger and Todd was there in a microsecond.

"Another?"

25

"For him, please," Mac said, then turned to me again. "Look, this is worse than the malpractice suit. Far worse."

"It's always about you, isn't it?" I said as I picked up my second martini. Gin had always made me silly. "It's never about me," I said, probably louder than I meant. Now the kids shifted gently away. We were almost alone in the crowd.

"If I worked for you," Mac said, perfectly calm, "it'd all be about you. But when you work for me, by definition, it is about me, my friend."

I didn't say anything, just looked at my empty martini glass and wondered how it had gotten empty. "Goddamn," I said to no one in particular, "I fucking miss drugs."

"Don't we all," Mac said. "How did you get here?"

"My dad was pretty fucking crazy when he came back from WWII," I said, "and my mom was an Avon Lady who loved gossip."

"The Depot, man," Mac said. "How did you get to the bar?"

"I walked," I said. "I knew you'd stay sober and give me a ride back to the motel."

"I'm glad I'm dependable, CW," he said.

"I'm dependable, too," I said, "in my own way." I pushed the third martini aside, ordered a rack of ribs and a glass of water, then bummed a cigarette and a light from the young woman on the stool beside me. She didn't seem to mind so I assumed that she belonged to the clot of kids drinking on Mac's tab. She gave me an almost empty pack of Dunhills and a box of Swan matches. "Just keep them."

"Thanks," I said.

"Just one more I don't have to smoke," she said. The young woman had a thin, pleasant face and fair, almost creamy skin. And the same accent as an old friend of mine, a Chicano dog trainer whose mixture of Mexican and Southern accents gave him one of the best storytelling voices I'd ever heard.

"Thanks," I said again. "Where are you from?"

"Billings," she said. That's what her jacket said.

"You didn't get that accent in Billings," I laughed, but she turned away. Old guys get used to it. So I turned to Mac. "So what the hell's up?"

Then he told me. Unfortunately.

Most of Mac's patients dealt with their problems with drugs or group therapy, but he still had seven patients in old-fashioned long-term analysis. Like all his records, the notes and tapes of these sessions were tightly controlled. But shortly after the conversion from tapes to minidisks, his secretary had discovered that somebody had broken into either the office or the files and copied the stack of minidisks. There was no evidence of a break-in, and the secretary only caught on to the fact that the minidisks had been copied when she was checking the computer logs for something else entirely.

For reasons that weren't quite clear to me but seemed obvious to Mac, he was convinced that the theft had been accomplished or engineered by one of his seven patients in analysis. He claimed he couldn't expand on his reasoning without violating his doctor-patient confidentiality.

"These patients are the only ones who have ever been in the back office where the computer is," he said as Todd set the plate of baby back ribs in front of me. "Patients in analysis are always curious about each other," he added as he set an envelope beside my drink. "That's why I have two waiting rooms and a secluded exit from the back office."

"Blackmail, you think?"

He paused, then said, "Lord knows I've been fooled before, but I am almost certain, my friend, that none of these patients are being blackmailed. Yet."

"Almost?" I said, then stubbed out the cigarette, had a sip of my last martini, and a slug of water. I picked up a rib but left the envelope where it set. "How 'almost'?"

Mac leaned closer as if we were under a cone of silence. And perhaps we were in our quiet island in the confusing froth of late-night bar conversations, a tangle of voices as opaque as the smoke floating above our heads. "My patients are your average band of unhappy neurotics whose lives would probably improve if they could just get out of their personal situations," he said. "Look over there." Mac pointed across the barroom toward the fake fireplace in the corner.

Our first baseman, Charlie Marshall, a lanky accountant with a narrow, long-suffering acne-scarred face, leaned on the couch next to his tiny wife, Ellen, who was talking to him as if she were lecturing a child. I knew she was seeing one of the other shrinks in town, a lady doctor known for her quick moves with a prescription pad, so Ellen lived on a half-dozen psychotropic drugs. Behind his glasses, Charlie's eyes were deeply unfocused, and his grin was so painful his feet might have been on fire. Another couple — our third baseman, George Paul, and his bony wife, whose name I couldn't remember — sat on the opposite couch. I didn't know what George had to be unhappy about; he owned a successful Internet company that provided business advice, information, and accounting services to small hospitals and clinics all over the country. The catcher, Ken Forbes, an ex-college baseball player, now a business lawyer with a wife who never left the house, sat alone on the hearth.

"Charlie and George and Ken are patients?" I said. When Mac didn't answer, I suggested, "Their wives?"

"Not a psychotic among the group, and they all have plenty of money," he said, ignoring my questions. "Sometimes I think that the people around them are the fucking crazy ones," he added. "If you'll excuse my French."

"I'll excuse your French, my friend," I said, "if you'll excuse my reluctance to do this personal favor for you."

Mac nodded slowly. We sat silently as I finished the ribs, then thanked the young woman with the cigarettes again. "Let's get the hell out of here," I said as I slipped the envelope into the inner pocket of the windbreaker, next to the scrap of cloth, then picked up my martini.

"It's on me, buddy," Mac said.

"No shit," I said.

Mac settled the check while I finished a cigarette and half of my drink. Then I followed him out the back door and into the soft luxury of his new Range Rover, both of us still silent. We drove back to the motel without a word. Mac parked in his space beside the bridal suite, turned off the engine, then lit his cigar.

"You picked up the envelope, CW," he said.

"I was drunk," I said. "What the hell did I pick up?"

"A twenty-thousand-dollar retainer from Ron Musselwhite," he said. "And the names and address of the seven patients. Some you'll know, others you won't. And for pity's sake, don't lose it. It's the only copy. I'm on very shaky ground here, friend."

"I suspect you're not alone," I said.

"Just follow them around randomly now and again; watch them from a distance," he said. "But not to or from my office, okay? You've got a blank check for expenses.

Rent or buy whatever you need. But don't hire any other PIs, and don't listen to any private conversations. Whatever you overhear in public, that's okay. You can report that, along with movements and impressions. But just to me. And nothing on paper or tape, audio or video. You can't tell anybody what you're doing. Not even Whit."

"How long do you want me to work on this?"

"Until I know which one has the copies," he said.

"How the hell are you going to know?"

"I just will," he said.

"You know this job is even crazier than the last one?"

"I told you. I'll double your hourly rates."

"I'd have to be out of my mind to get involved in something like this, Mac," I said. But I had to admit that the notion of being paid like a lawyer without bothering about law school had its attractions. "This is not my kind of job, man," I said. "I find people who want to be lost — skip traces and bounty hunts, runaways and lost spouses — that's what I do. I don't do surveillance. It's too fucking boring," I added. I could hear the acceptance slipping into my voice.

"But you'll do it, right?" he said, holding out his hand. "Thank you, Sughrue. I truly thank you."

"You're less than welcome," I said.

We shook hands warmly, smiling ruefully at each other.

Making friends had always been hard for me after we moved to Vado, Texas, at the end of WWII when I was a kid. I was always the new kid in town, the one who wore feed-sack shirts and no shoes. The one with the crazy and often missing father. Nothing like being an outsider in a small Texas town to make an old boy cranky and adept with his fists. As far as I knew, the first group of men I'd really cared about were the guys in my squad in Vietnam. So in late middle age making friends was problematic at best.

Women usually make friends talking, by exchanging confidences, and men, traditionally, by working together. But the only work Mac and I had ever shared was the occasional firewood foray on nice fall weekend afternoons. Unless playing softball together was work.

Sports often revealed the cracks in a man's character, the frayed edges of his personality. Maybe friendship between men was as inexplicable as love. Whatever,

Mac and I were friends. Good friends, who depended on that friendship more than either of us admitted. We both dealt in the secrets of damaged lives, but we could never talk about them. Our bonds were silent but stronger, perhaps, for the silence.

"When we stop holding hands," Mac said, "I've got a bottle of twenty-one-year-old Springbank single malt. Let's have a nightcap?"

"Sounds good to me," I said. I had hoped he would ask me in for a drink when we came back from downtown.

I followed him into the inner entrance of the bridal suite, which opened into a short hall between a toilet and a closet, then into the sitting room. Except for the glow from the master bath, the bedroom was dark beyond the partially closed door, but Mac went to the wet bar without even looking in on Lorna. Once he had told me that she slept like a cat: deeply, quickly, often, and anywhere. He put ice cubes in a couple of glasses and drenched them with four fingers of peaty Scotch, then we settled with our drinks into armchairs across the coffee table from each other. Mac offered me a cigar, but I declined. I wanted another cigarette. So badly I couldn't remember why I had quit. We sipped our Scotch and chatted aimlessly in low voices until we had almost finished our drinks.

"I thought I smelled your cigar, honey," Lorna said from the darkened doorway, a depleted ice bag dangling from one hand, a tattered, barely recognizable stuffed elephant from the other. She held two condoms in green silver foil against the stuffed animal's chest. Whitney had suggested that Lorna was so afraid of getting pregnant that she was on the pill, still used a diaphragm, and probably made Mac wear two rubbers. But until I saw them in her hand I thought Whitney had been joking.

"Oh hi, CW," she added. She seemed to have gone to bed wearing full makeup, but standing in the shadows her face was half dark. Unlike some women's green eyes, Lorna's never glittered metallically. They were always softly smudged, sleepy dissipated like the smoke drifting from a green flare. Except for the blister on her thigh — fingerwide and perhaps four inches long — Lorna's elegant legs were very white and very long beneath the short jade silk nightgown she wore. "You boys havin' fun?" she said. Although she had never been any closer to the South than South Dakota, she had an almost unaffected Southern accent.

"We always have fun," Mac said. "That's

why they call us boys." Then he rose and walked over to his wife to kiss her on the corner of the mouth. Even barefoot, she stood a few inches taller than Mac. And she almost always wore heels. "Let me fill this up," he said as he took the ice bag from her.

Lorna lifted a slim hand in a languid farewell, then floated into the darkness behind her. Mac stepped over to the bar, dumped the water, and began to load ice cubes into the bag. I excused myself and went into the toilet off the sitting room. I took the swimsuit top out and dropped it on the floor, only partially hidden behind the toilet.

As far as I knew, Lorna had never fooled around, but she had that air of availability about her, and she had always been a bit casual about exposing her body in ways that made me uncomfortable. One of her large and lovely breasts seemed always about to slip its mooring into public view. And she seemed unable to cross her legs without offering a glimpse of her dark red and neatly trimmed muff through transparent thongs.

Unfortunately, I knew what I was talking about. Once when the four of us were on a float trip down the Smith River, camped at Sunset Cliffs, after an evening of wine and whiskey, elk steaks, and *mota* shared with the guides, Whit and I had curled into our bags to sleep as calmly as rounded stones under the soft murmur of the river. But sometime during the middle of the night, I'd woken with an aching bladder. When I climbed out of our tent, but before I could trek up to the outdoor toilet, I noticed Lorna standing naked in the moonlight on the sandbar at the edge of the river.

We had camped at the mouth of the canyon where the cliff's shadow covered the campsite like a widow's shawl, but down by the river the moonlight glistened off Lorna's body as if she were a pillar of rock salt. She stood so still, I walked down the slope to see if she was all right. When she heard me, she turned, a joint in one hand, a wine bottle in the other, and looked at me. She raised the bottle as if to offer me a drink but quickly lowered it to her side. The look in her eyes and the slight smile on her face signaled neither invitation nor anticipation but acceptance. Of what, though, I didn't know. Whatever it was, it unnerved me. I retreated, pissed on a tree, then crawled back into my sleeping bag for a night of red-wine marijuana dreams.

★ ★ ★

The visible portion of the swimsuit-top microfabric sparkled vividly against the pale tiles of the floor beside the toilet. I'd done what I could. I flushed, then washed my hands and face. When I looked in the mirror over the sink, I was, as usual, shocked. I'd never regained the weight I'd lost after I'd been shot. The dark blond ponytail, which I couldn't seem to give up, was shorter, but the beard had fallen by the wayside. The mustache fit into the decently earned wrinkles, and somewhere behind that blue-eyed dusky face, I hoped, a younger version of myself might still live, maybe an aging surfer or a retired dot-com millionaire. Then I laughed at my foolishness. Just another piece of footloose border trash staring back at me, a redneck with a *corazón mejicano,* a Mexican heart.

When I went back into the sitting room, I could hear the rattle of ice cubes as Mac rubbed the ice bag against Lorna's blistered thigh. I finished my drink, whispered "Later" at the bedroom doorway, then let myself out.

I just made last call at the motel bar, grabbed a bottle of Rainier, bummed two Camel straights from the bartender, then went out to the empty poolside. The full

38

moon had lodged at the zenith, smaller but still white-hot, as intense as a halogen flood. The night seemed full of scraps of party sound — pointless laughter, the bass-line thrum of overamped car stereos, and loud voices, hoarse with senseless anger. South of the Clark Fork River a siren whooped for a long moment, then stopped. I didn't really want the beer, just the cigarettes, the ephemeral clarity of nicotine. I smoked slowly even though I knew my throat and sinus cavities would hurt in the morning, a throbbing ache as if I'd spent the night snorting ground glass.

Beyond the pool I could see that the light in our room was still on. Whitney, I assumed, burning the midnight keystrokes on her notebook. Damn. Goddamn love. But I did owe her my life. When they got me to the hospital in El Paso after I'd been gutshot, the only number in my wallet was hers. When they'd called, she quit her job and flew down from Montana, although we'd only been out once. She sat by my bed until she persuaded me to live. She smuggled tacos and beer into my hospital room, and for reasons neither of us exactly understood, she married me. We'd never slept together, we'd had a single date, and there we were doing the vows in a hospital room.

And she ran with me during the crazy times, hiding from the *contrabandistas* who had tried to kill me, hiding first in Utah, then later in the Davis Mountains of West Texas. I owed this woman my life and what little sanity I possessed.

When I finished the second cigarette, I left the rest of the beer, then went back to our room.

Whit was sprawled across the bed, asleep among a scattering of legal documents, her long, lean, lovely body stretched across the bed. When I leaned over to kiss her, her eyes opened slowly, eyes the clear blue of the desert sky reflected in a slickrock pool after a passing shower.

"You've been smoking," she said quietly.

"Just a couple," I said. "Four actually."

"Well, just because I'm gone, don't be smoking in my house," she said, smiling widely. "I'll be back." I took that as a good sign. She rolled into my arms, whispering, "Get in the shower, cowboy. I'll wash the stink right off you."

Later, in the predawn half darkness of the room, she asked, "What did Mac want? Does he have another wild goose chase for you?" Then she kissed me on the shoulder.

"I caught the goose last time," I said. Sometimes her mind startled me. "How the hell did you know?"

"He's been making calf eyes at you all weekend," she said. "Like a virgin in heat. What did he want?"

"Just an odd chore for a few weeks. He asked me not to tell you, hon," I said without any hope that Whit would settle for my answer.

"His last odd chore took you out of law school, love," she said. She was never going to let me forget that. Or forgive the way I lived my life.

"It paid off your loans," I said. "And set up your office."

"True," she said cautiously. "Watch your ass," she said. "Remember, he deals with crazy people." Then she rolled away. She was asleep before I knew what to think. Maybe this case wouldn't be as hard as it seemed.

The hard part was saying good-bye to Whitney as she climbed on the flight from Missoula to Minneapolis. Really hard. When I got home, I found myself sitting in my office glancing seriously through the classified ads looking for a dog I didn't actually want.

As it turned out, moving to the white-shoe, latte-sipping heart of the frozen Midwest would have been easier all around.

Two

People have a lot of theories about life — what it means, how to survive it, and other unadulterated bullshit. The only thing I've ever heard that made any sense came many years ago and in a country far away, not on some windswept mountaintop but among the crumbling sandbags of a night defensive position, and my guru wasn't some bearded, balding wise man but a giant Hawaiian-Black-Mexican M60 gunner in the middle of his second tour in Vietnam.

Because my job as a private investigator lent itself more toward the mundane and realistic, I didn't have much use for theory, but it was a fine late-summer morning in the Winding Woods neighborhood of Meriwether, Montana, and I was lulled into aimless illusions of theory as I carried a clipboard and wore a fake name tag on my short-sleeved white shirt that identified me as JOE DON LOONY, REAL ESTATE AGENT, ostensibly checking for somebody who wanted to sell his house in the old neighborhood, but actually working a job I didn't much care for, the crazy chore for my old buddy Dr. William Mac-Kinderick, when Nacho's dark face suddenly rose before me, not like a flashback — I knew about those — or a nightmare, just a sudden solid vision out of my past, a moment of unexpected laughter.

The past hit me in the face like a bloody hand. Back during the Vietnam War, Nacho and I had survived a hard day in the bush. My first one, really. We had nearly lost a reinforced platoon patrol through the usual stupidity and lack of leadership. All of our officers were new guys getting their tickets punched in the combat zone, and most of the experienced NCOs were back at the base camp club or drunk in Bangkok. The company commander, a young first lieutenant, was an ROTC jerk from Georgia. An NVA company was cleaning our plows — 30 percent casualties in ten minutes — and we would have gone the way of that idiot Custer if a passing flight of Cobra gunships that had been fogged out of their mission hadn't been close enough to save our badly charred bacon. Their rockets and miniguns cleaned the NVA off the ridge top, flattened the hidden encampment, and showed me what hell really looked like.

When it was over, it was too late to extract anybody but the dead and wounded, so we set up a night defensive position on the ridge line. Just before good dark, Nacho calmly stirred coffee over a burning scrap of C4. My hands were still shaking so badly that I had trouble holding my cup still when he asked me how I liked my baptism of fire.

"Jesus, we were lucky," I said breathlessly.

He laughed, then reached over to poke his finger through a hole in the pocket of my fatigues. "Hey, man, look at it this way," he said, still chuckling, "fistfights, firefights, and fucking love affairs — nothing counts but luck and geography, man." Then he tugged on the bullet hole, laughing even harder as I shit my pants. Again. "Luck and geography."

For me it was laugh or cry, or some of both.

I didn't have much to laugh about, exactly, now or then. I already missed my wife. But it was my fault. I had refused to even consider moving with her a thousand miles away to Minneapolis, where she had taken a job at a high-powered firm in the Twin Cities. She was still miffed that I refused to go back to law school, and if that wasn't bad enough, she had also taken my son with her. Insult to injury as they say. And I'd been having endless nightmares since the day they left.

So I turned my face into the late-summer Montana sun and collapsed against a little table in a small park, smoked a quick doobie, laughed for no reason until I almost cried, ignoring the curious neighbors, the lazy yardmen, the remodeling teams, laughing until I stretched out and went to sleep.

Surveillance is never as easy as it looks in the movies, and working a one-man job in a small city like Meriwether made it that much harder. Plus Mac's restrictions made it much harder than it needed to be. Television or telephone repair trucks always seemed to call forth angry neighbors who wondered why you hadn't come to fix their sets or phones. Delivery trucks were only good until one of the real drivers drove by your fake van. You couldn't park a plumbing truck anywhere there weren't a dozen clogged drains in the neighborhood. It took a couple of days to work it out and get equipped. I finally settled on a ruse I'd used before: scouting for the real estate broker. Mac had talked one of his broker friends into vouching for me, so I put on a short-sleeved shirt, a tie, and the Joe Don Loony fake name tag. I rented an anonymous Taurus sedan, equipped it with my handheld police scanner and cell phone, added a small pair of binoculars and the Leica 35-mm camera with the 150-mm telephoto lens, a bouquet of gimme caps, a selection of windbreakers, and a couple of pairs of sunglasses, and I was ready: your average, run-of-the-mill, hardworking private investigator perfectly equipped to track a bunch of Dr. MacKinderick's neurotics around town.

Except for a weapon. They were all hanging in the gun safe in my office in the converted garage. They had been in the safe since the day I discovered that my son, Les, was as agile as a raccoon and smarter than your average PI. I hadn't had much occasion to carry a gun since my partner and I had taken our revenge on a bunch of *contrabandistas* some years before, and, after almost thirty years of carrying a weapon, I had gotten out of the habit.

Mac's patient list was organized by appointment times instead of the alphabet, with one name on each page. I assumed that meant something so I didn't bother looking beyond the first name on the list.

And it was one I knew, as Mac said might happen. When he had given me the prohibitions on this case, he hadn't said anything about background checks, which make my job easier. So I took it on myself. The background on this guy was easy. I just hung around the college bars for a couple of nights posing as a retired English professor on vacation, logging a half-a-dozen expensive hours and picking up gossip.

Professor Garfield Ritter saw Mac at 8:00 a.m. Monday, Wednesday, and Friday. Ritter had been the chairman of the English Department at Mountain States since gasoline was eighty-nine cents a gallon. Ritter had come west with his Yale Ph.D., shoulder-length curly hair that went with his politics, and a bellyful of academic ambition. Twenty-five years later, the hair, like the politics, had disappeared; none of his scholarly papers had ever been published; and now he had the belly of a Republican banker with the only fire inside his spastic colitis, caused, perhaps, by his fat, rich Main Line Philadelphia wife, Charity, who by all accounts had none and was reputed, when drunk, to be meaner than a tow sack full of drowning cats.

The Ritters lived in a large restored Victorian in the Winding Woods neighborhood south of the Meriwether River, a collection of winding streets that often fooled even the natives. By nine o'clock that Wednesday morning I was parked and ready. Except for a pair of house painters struggling down the street with their scaffolding toward the Ritters' neighborhood, the streets were empty. I started out going through the motions: carrying my clipboard around and asking dumb questions, waiting for Ritter to come home after his appointment with Mac and before he went to the college for his eleven o'clock office hours. I thought I would see what the professor did with his free time between nine and eleven. Mac had told me that he didn't want me to follow his clients to or from his office. I didn't think it would be a problem. But after moving the Taurus several times, filling a dozen sheets with useless real estate information, wandering around, and drifting into some very vivid and very bad dreams, I began to wonder if this was the job for me.

Winding Woods was beautifully calm. It had been built after the First World War; the trees were mature, the houses richly maintained. West of the divide, the mountains cut into the horizon, so it wasn't Big

Sky Country exactly, but on a clear late-summer morning there seemed to be more blue than the eye could absorb. The Norwegian maples and elms glowed with fringes of gold as the sun topped the foothills of the Diablos, and the morning chill retreated into the pools of shade.

Around a quarter to ten, I was suddenly awakened by the slap of a nightstick against my boot soles and the rasp of smoky laughter. Then I looked up into the bloodshot eyes of Sergeant Fergie Ferguson, just about the last of the old guys on the Meriwether police force.

"What the hell's going on, Sughrue?" he growled.

"Just a little snooze, officer," I said. "You know about a little snooze." Fergie was famous for cooping on the night shift, but equally famous for hearing his radio calls through a dead sleep.

"No," he said. "What's with your boots?"

I looked down to find that some smart ass had painted the soles of my boots white.

"I don't know, man," I said.

"Well, clean them up," he said, laughing again, "or I'll run you in for defacing public property." He tossed me a dirty rag, and when I finished, he tossed it in the park's trash can. "I don't know what you're doing, man, but try to stay awake." Then he walked to his unit, where his new partner, a kid who had the makings of a good street cop, grinned as he watched his partner carry his laughing face and bouncing beer gut in front of him.

As far as I could tell, Ritter still hadn't shown up. I walked up to the door of his house, picked up the rolled paper on the steps, and rang the bell. It seemed that I could hear distant chimes through the thick oak door, but I wasn't sure. After a bit, I rang again, waited, then knocked. The heavy doors unlocked, swung open slowly. Nobody answered my "Anybody home?" shout, either.

I glanced at the alarm keypad and the security company sticker below it. I suddenly felt very exposed. I dropped the newspaper, trotted to the rent car, and moved it to a wandering cross street where I could see the front door. All the way I told myself that nothing was wrong, that I was just unsettled, perhaps even slightly nervous because this case had seemed so ambiguous from the beginning. I'd always been better at finding people than following them. I also knew better than to work for friends.

It seldom worked out as well as the malpractice suit I worked for Mac had done. But we weren't friends then. I watched and worried. The longer I looked at the open door, the more it bothered me.

I called the Ritter residence several times on the cell phone, without an answer. The professor didn't answer his office telephone, either. So I called Mac on the hour.

"What's going on?"

"Did Ritter show up for his appointment this morning?"

"Of course, why?"

"How did he seem?"

"Fine, why?"

"The front door of his house is open," I said.

"Oh, hell," Mac said. "I know his wife's at home. He told me they had words this morning. But they have words almost every morning with their bran flakes."

"And you can't tell me what they were, right?"

"I can tell you that they were just the usual, nothing out of the ordinary," he said.

"Look, buddy, I've got a bad feeling about this," I said. "We've got three choices. I can go in and out like a cat burglar, and if nothing is wrong, we're cool.

Or I can place an anonymous call to the alarm company. Or the police."

"What do you think?"

"He forgot to lock the door on his way out," I said, "and she's sleeping one off. Except . . ."

"Except what?"

"They've got a three-car garage, so he probably went out that way," I said. "And rumor has it that she has her first vodka of the day with the morning paper."

"And the paper is still on the front steps?"

"You got it," I said.

"You better check it out," he said without further explanation.

"Be prepared, Mac," I said.

But no one could have been prepared for this.

The double front doors opened directly into the bright light of a large atrium formed by a skylight cut through the attic and the roof above, with living and dining rooms and library set off to the sides, the kitchen at the end, and a wide stairway on the right leading to a balcony. But I didn't know that then. That information all came later. As I stepped across the threshold, I heard a strangled scream from above.

Through the flood of sunlight pouring into the atrium, I glimpsed a giant pale shape teetering on the balcony rail, a flash of light behind her — Mrs. Ritter in a white nightgown and robe, I later learned — then the figure screamed and swooped down toward me.

The cotton clothesline around her neck had been tied to an open roof beam just below the skylight. Time congealed. I had a moment to think that, like many people, Mrs. Ritter probably hadn't the vaguest idea how to hang herself. Too much slack in the rope for her weight. But when she hit the end of the slack, her head popped off with a sound that can't be described, one which I'll spend the rest of my life forgetting, and her body plowed into me, a fountain of blood drenching me and the room. The head flew toward the other end of the room, tumbling into the shadows, and the body's momentum blew me backward out the front door, in a cloud of blood. As I rolled down the front steps, I vomited through a dark burst of laughter that I couldn't stop no matter how hard I tried.

Three

Given the way the police treated me that afternoon in front of Ritter's house — except Fergie, who grabbed his chest and collapsed, stroked out by the headless gore, and his partner, the kid, who stood like a stone statue — the other cops would have been pleased to see me stroke out, too. They didn't want to touch me, drenched in Charity's blood and my vomit, but they really wanted me to stop laughing hysterically. So they did what any good cop would do: took me down, jerked my arms behind me hard enough to dislocate my shoulders, cuffed me, and started to throw me into the back of a cruiser. Until they considered the chore of cleaning out the backseat. So I was led around like a country idiot until the new chief of detectives, Johnny Raymond, showed up. Johnny and I had a long, unhappy history and he was more than happy to stuff me into his backseat because he planned to make me clean up the mess with my tongue.

My life and sanity were saved only because I had managed the energy and sense to call Mac just after I called 911. I must have sounded insane, stuttering and stammering and shouting as I sat on the front steps covered with blood and vomit as I waited for the law. Who came in droves. By the time Mac and Musselwhite arrived, I had talked to any number of cops who were as disturbed as I was but didn't know it, including Johnny Raymond. I was shaking so badly in the back of his unit that I thought I was going to break my wrists before help arrived.

Johnny Raymond was a native son of Meriwether, a longtime hardworking police officer, a Vietnam vet, a highly decorated ex-SEAL, too, and an all-around good guy. As far as I knew, his only personal flaw was that he hated me worse than crotch rot. He wasn't too fond of Mac or Ron Musselwhite, either. When working, I was always more interested in justice than the law, so I had skated along the icy edges and deep water cracks of the law while I was on a case. Although Raymond had busted me several times, he was never able to make anything stick. And although he had tried, he had never managed to inter- fere with my license. But he was sure he had me now. A B&E, perhaps, an illegal entry at the very least. He thought he'd find something to stick this time. It was clear on his large, blond farm boy's face and in his aggressive questions.

I was so shaken that I might have answered him if I could have spoken, if he hadn't drowned me out with a barrage of questions. But I couldn't tell the truth about why I was at the Ritter house. Not without Mac to explain it for me. It was never a good idea to lie to cops. And I had learned a long time ago not to answer any of their questions without a lawyer sitting in my lap. With a lawyer, not even the innocent had to answer questions. Raymond gave up and told his driver to transport me. But Mac arrived at exactly the right moment and pulled medical rank on Johnny, making him open the back door of the unit. Mac leaned in, checked my eyes with a penlight, my pulse with his fingers, then stepped back and turned to the red-faced officer.

"This man's going into shock, officer," he said to Raymond. "Get him out of there, get the cuffs off him, and call for medical transport."

"I want him in the jail wing," Raymond said.

"What's the charge?" Musselwhite said.

Raymond looked at Musselwhite, a Kiowa-Comanche breed from Oklahoma who affected braids and beaded leather jackets, which didn't quite conceal his bear-trap mind and his dangerous warrior's grin. Or his Boalt law degree hanging like a scalp on his office wall. Raymond sighed, then reached in to help me out. "Sughrue," he whispered, "I'll nail you with something. You can count on that. Fergie's dead, you bastard." Then because he was a good cop, Raymond eased me as gently as a mother out of the backseat.

I nodded, smiling an idiot's smile, as if I agreed with him completely, as if I wanted him to put me in a cell. But before he could get the cuffs off me, Mac hit me in the arm with a hypodermic. I hiccupped a couple of dry heaves, my eyes rolled up, and I went down as the ambulance. Arrived. Thankfully.

When I awoke in the private room in St. Vincent's that night just before midnight, I remembered everything. Unfortunately. Until I had fainted. Perhaps I had been going into shock. Or perhaps I had seen too much bloody death over the years. The last few had been relatively quiet, though. Almost civilized. Maybe I was out of practice. Whatever, I wanted to go home. But my butt was sticking out of a hospital gown, a saline drip was sticking into the back of my left hand, and I had to pee before I did anything.

The call button for the nurse was easy to find, clipped to the pillow next to my head, but nobody showed for a long time after I punched the button. I only did it once — some years before, St. Vincent's had become a for-profit-managed hospital, an economic machine run by MBAs for money instead of mercy, so the nurses were treated like serfs — then I pulled off the tape, jerked the drip out of my hand, and rolled off the bed. Whatever drug Mac had injected into me to cause that long dreamless sleep seemed to have worn off. I did my business, switched off the drip, and climbed back into bed to wait for the nurse.

"I'm sorry, Sughrue," the nurse said as she swept quickly into the dim room. She was a bright, sunny woman I'd known around the bars for years, but I couldn't remember her name.

"No problem," I said. "I took the drip out myself, then pissed about a quart if anybody's interested." Her smile glowed in the scant light. "Now I'm hungry," I added.

"You slept through dinner," she said, chuckling. "Hell, a decent human being would have slept until breakfast," she said, then paused. "But the doctor knew better. He left you a change of clothes and a sandwich and a Coke when he was here earlier."

"What?" I said.

"You want a sandwich?"

"You're a darling," I said, and she didn't argue with that.

"I'll just put this back in," she said as she stabbed me with the drip and retaped it quickly, efficiently and almost painlessly. "And I'll call Dr. MacKinderick," she added as she left. "He left orders to call him no matter what time you woke up."

I had the drip out again before she got back. She put down the sandwich and the Coke, then hooked me up again. "Leave it alone, or I'll tape you to the bed, you silly shit," she said, grinning, then left me to my own devices.

Which mainly consisted of chewing and dreading. I dreaded Mac's visit all the way through the sandwich. And I was right to dread it. But the sandwich and the dread had cleared my mind wonderfully.

"CW," he said as he stepped through the door, shutting it quietly behind him and picking up my chart. "Have you ever fainted before?"

"All the time," I said. "Every fucking day."

"Just as I thought," he said. "We're going to keep you here for a couple of days, run some tests."

"As my daddy used to say, you're going to shit and fall back in it, too," I said. "I'm out of here in the morning."

"As long as you're in here," he said, "they can't question you. Ron says if we stall Raymond for a couple of days, he'll lose interest in finding out what you were doing at the Ritter front door."

"You know better than that," I said. "He's never going to give up. I'll just dummy up until they come back with a suicide ruling, then there's no crime to investigate."

"Are you sure it was a suicide?"

"I'd guess her blood's going to be full of vodka and drugs," I said. "And she thought I was her husband, so she jumped when the door opened. But you'd know more about that than I would. And surely you know how many people try to kill themselves and fuck it up. Put a piece to their temple and miss. Don't take enough pills. Or take too many and throw them up . . ."

"I know something about suicides," he said sadly, so I shut up. "Okay, I'll get you out tomorrow."

"In the morning," I said. "And get this thing out of my hand."

"Stop complaining," he said. "Ritter is down the hall. Unlike you, he actually went into shock — collapsed in his office when I told him. And it looks as if he had a small cardiac event."

"Then he really should be glad he wasn't there," I said, meaning it.

"When do you think you can go back to the job?"

"Oh, I forgot to tell you that, my friend," I said. "I fucking quit."

"You can't," he said quietly. Then he left before I could argue with him, an argument I knew I wouldn't win anyway.

At least the smiling nurse came back a few minutes later to relieve me of the drip.

"Thanks, Sunny," I said, suddenly remembering her name. "Thanks."

She just smiled as she patted me on the head as if I were a child. A good nurse is a great treasure.

They released me before noon the next day. I stopped by Ritter's room on the way out of the hospital. I wondered where he had been between nine and eleven that morning, but he wasn't exactly able to answer questions. A gray stubble frosted his jowls, drool puddled on his pillow, and he snored like a passing freight. He must have gotten better drugs than mine.

I ran a few errands, did a few chores, had a burger at the Goat, then went home. The house was too empty, so I sat on the front porch until almost sundown, then retreated to my office, a converted garage. When Whit passed the bar exam, we split the two lots the house and garage sat on and moved my office out of the house so that my bad habits wouldn't affect her legal standing. I was watching some more secrets of Nazi Germany on the History Channel when Mac called, asking, "Can I buy you a drink?"

"I thought you recommended rest," I said.

"Now I recommend a cocktail."

"I don't know, man," I said. "I thought I'd catch the ten o'clock news."

"You'll just be disappointed," he said.

"Whit's supposed to call in a few minutes."

"Take your cell with you."

"Hey, man, between two hundred pounds

of Christian Highway Patrolman and three hundred pounds of Charity, I'm sore as a boil."

"Don't make me beg."

"Give me one reason why I shouldn't," I said.

"Because I'm your friend."

I didn't have a smart-ass answer for that. "Okay, I'll walk down to the Goat and meet you for one," I said.

"Just step out the door, my friend," he said. "I'm parked in the alley."

Goddamned cell phones.

I used mine to call Whitney but I got her voice mail again, so I assumed that she was asleep. I left word for her to call in the morning, then left my cell at home.

The Scapegoat Bar and Grill nestled comfortably in the basement of an old bank building in downtown Meriwether. The food was western standard but good, and the drinks were generous and Montana cheap, but its major attraction was a complete lack of gambling machines or loud music. Too many Montana bars had been ruined when the state legalized poker and keno machines, which were a constant burping and beeping presence. And at least as addictive as crack cocaine.

I'm not against gambling, but a quiet bar is worth its weight in gold. But what Mac liked about the Goat was that he could have his single cigar for the day in the cigar bar nestled in the old vault.

Mac ordered a cognac, but I opted for a bottle of Negra Modelo. Except for "Hi," we hadn't spoken on the short drive from the Northgate neighborhood to the bar. Mac did his business with his cigar — a Havana smuggled from Canada, I suspected — while I dug out a pack of American Spirits that I had bought when I got out of the hospital that morning.

"So you're smoking again," he said before I could get one lit.

"Hey, man," I said. "I saw some ugly shit in the Central Highlands, and I've seen some ugly shit since then, but I've never . . . Oh, well, fuck it."

"Sorry," he said.

"You had all those years in emergency rooms," I said. "I'm only used to ordinary violence — you know, fistfights, gunshot wounds, exploding bodies, that sort of shit. So I'm smoking cigarettes to keep from slamming heroin into my arm."

"I am sorry," he said, carefully not looking at me.

"Not sorry enough," I said. "I can't go

on with this chore unless you tell me what's going on."

"Even if I knew, my friend, I couldn't."

"Beautiful, man. Just fucking beautiful."

We sat, mostly silent, for a long time. Desultory hellos and good-byes directed to friends and acquaintances, aimless exchanges with the young bartender. I had two beers and four cigarettes while Mac sipped cognac and contemplated his cigar.

"You're not going to quit on me?" he finally asked, knocking an inch of ash off the cigar.

"If nobody's being blackmailed," I said, "what the hell does it matter who has the disks?"

"I'll be happy to pay a generous bonus when it's wrapped up," he said, ignoring my questions again.

"You're already paying me too much," I said. "Enough to make me nervous."

"I'm sorry," he said sarcastically.

"If you're not going to come clean with me, man, I'm going to do it my way now," I said. "No more pussyfooting around. I'm going to work these people my way, work them hard until I know who copied the disks. You stay out of it. Otherwise, I quit. For real this time."

"I guess I don't have any choice now," he

said. "Just don't burn me."

"I've never burned anybody," I said. "But I've got to tell Whit."

"Please don't," he said. "Please."

"Have you told Lorna?" I said.

Mac stared at me for a moment, wild-eyed, then he smiled oddly. "Not a word, my friend. Not a word."

"You know Whit won't say a word to anybody," I said. "And nobody can make her, legally, so what the hell are you worried about?"

Mac studied his cigar again, ordered a second cognac, which was unusual, then insisted that I have another beer. When he stopped stalling, he set his cigar down and finally turned to me, talking but not answering me. "You know my mother still lives over in Dakota. Outside Bismarck on the old home place. In her youth she was a tall, white-blond Swede. Even at almost ninety, CW, she's a handsome woman, still got fine clear skin and those steely blue eyes, the kind of eyes you only see on the plains. She looks as if she can see over the horizon, see the wind, see winter . . ." He paused, watching his cigar consume itself. "My father was a knotty little Scot," he continued. "A tough little fucker. A coach . . ." Once again he paused. But he had been talking to himself. Perhaps even his silence was for himself.

"And this has what to do with me not telling Whit?" I said, interrupting his silence.

"I'd be professionally embarrassed," he said with some finality, a lopsided grin on his face.

"You weren't embarrassed to tell me," I pointed out.

Suddenly Mac laughed, lifted his snifter, and slapped me on the back. I realized that this wasn't his second cognac. More like his sixth. "I didn't think you'd judge me," he said.

"Hell, Whit doesn't judge anybody," I said. "Least of all you."

"I know," he said, "I know. Forgive me; it's my weakness, not her nature. But that face, those blue eyes . . ."

"You mind if I tell her why I can't tell her?"

Mac's silence was answer enough. He looked away, picked up the cigar. "I hear you stopped by Ritter's room on your way out of the hospital. How did he look?"

"Like a dead man," I said.

"I just hope he isn't," Mac said. "Even through their long years of anger, they really depended on each other. Desperately."

I didn't want to think about it. I don't know, sometimes it seemed that most sorts of madness were simply a convenient way to avoid life. But then I didn't know. When I'd gone mad, I had had good reason: people *were* trying to kill me back then.

I told Mac that I'd walk home to clear my head so I could decide how to tell Whit that I couldn't even tell her why I couldn't tell her.

"Call me," he said as I was leaving.

"In a week or so," I answered, "unless I clear it up before then. And get me the alarm code for Ritter's place."

Mac started to protest but stopped himself, nodded curtly, then I was gone.

I had missed Whitney's calls by the time I got home. All three of them. Somehow she'd gotten word of the incident at the Ritters'. I missed the calls because I'd taken the long way home, I had stopped at the Slumgullion, the Low Rent Rendezvous, and Mickey's on the walk. Slow beers and conversations about nothing. I didn't let the job cross my mind. Mike, the bartender at Mickey's, fronted me a couple of doobies, one of which I smoked on the pedestrian walkway over the railroad to the Northgate neighborhood.

I took one tour around the house, then retreated to my office. The little refrigerator was stuffed with cans of Pabst beer along with a chunk of rat cheese and several rings of homemade smoked deer sausage. My office wasn't exactly plush, but it was comfortable — a La-Z-Boy in the corner, a great desk chair in front of the computer, a small television, a compact stereo, and snuggled into one corner a bathroom that would have fit into a small fishing boat. The back was filled with free weights, two bags, speed and heavy, and the gun safe built into the wall.

I put a Lucinda Williams CD in the player, booted up the computer, cracked a beer, then opened the safe buried in the concrete pad under the floor. As Lucinda sang mournfully about lost places and times and loves, I opened the next envelope on Mac's patient list. The name on the sheet was Carrie Fraizer. Monday, Wednesday and Friday at nine. When I ran a search, the computer told me that she lived in a funky old hotel that had been converted to apartments, near the abandoned railroad station at the north end of Dottle Avenue. The Pacific Northwest. It had been an important railroad hostel in the old days, but now it served as a home for unrepentant hippies, local starving artists, and musicians who could afford the rent. In the city directory her occupation was listed as "artist." I wondered how Carrie Fraizer could afford analysis with Mac. Hell, I wondered how she could afford a telephone.

But I didn't wonder very long. I went out into the alley and smoked the other doobie; then before settling into the La-Z-Boy, I sliced up a chunk of cheese and deer sausage, cracked another beer, and found one of those goofy Falcon movies from the forties with an impeccably arrogant George Sanders. I had been on this case three days and was already near collapse and dreaming of a simpler, more amusing, life.

Whit's morning voice mail had been a bit terse, and I was still tired, guilty, and suffering from a mild hangover when I decided not to call her back. I started to back the rent car out of my driveway. A black Ford Explorer laced with mud pulled in behind me. As I got out, Johnny Raymond, in civilian clothes, jeans, and a T-shirt, waved me over to his rig.

"Get in," he said. "We're going for a ride." It didn't seem worth arguing about, since he was wearing his Colt Commander .45 man killer holstered high on his hip, so I climbed in. "Scooch down," he ordered. "I don't want to be seen with you."

Raymond didn't say another word as he drove a few miles out of town, then turned up Bear Creek, one of the few drainages around town that hadn't been covered with new developments or expensive houses. After a bit, he pulled off the gravel road onto a dirt track, then parked behind a screen of piss firs and cut the engine. As the road dust settled around us, he rolled down the windows and sighed deeply.

"Get out," he said sharply.

"Are we going to have a fistfight?" I asked, my hand on the door handle. "Or are you just planning to drop the hammer on me without ceremony?"

"Just shut up and get out of the rig."

"Aren't you going to say 'please'?" I said. Some sort of massive struggle was going on behind his large, open face, so I added, "Okay."

We climbed out. Raymond looked relieved that I hadn't forced the "please" out of him. But when we met at the front of the rig, he crossed his massive arms as if he were holding himself away from me, protecting himself from me. We were about the same height, but he outweighed me by thirty pounds, so if I had to put him down, I'd have to hurt him.

"Sughrue," he said softly, "you know I don't approve of you."

"Actually the word on the street, Raymond, is that you despise me," I said. "Simple disapproval seems somewhat of an improvement."

"This is hard enough for me without you running your smart mouth," he said. "I hate your attitude, hate the way you only obey those laws that suit you, and hate the fact that you're a dope-smoking bum. But you've got a wonderful wife, even if she is a defense lawyer, and you two are raising a great kid, so maybe you aren't as bad as I think —"

He had some more things to say, but I interrupted him, "When I give a shit what you think of me, Johnny-boy, you'll be the first to know. So just ask me what the fuck you want to ask me —"

"You've got a foul mouth, mister."

"They're just words, man."

"But the attitude behind those words — don't push it," he said. "You cost me a good man."

"Fergie wasn't your favorite officer, man."

"Not Fergie, the kid," he said. "He's still nutty as hell, and he put in his papers. He would have made a good cop."

"Are you nuts?" I said.

He waited a moment, shook his head dubiously, suddenly confused, then answered seriously, "I don't know. Maybe I am crazy, but I need your help on this one." Then just as quickly he turned again, red faced and steaming. "Goddamn it, I need your help."

"You know I can't work an open case, plus anything I know from the Doc is confidential." I wouldn't have been any more shocked if he'd asked me for a date.

He started to say something angry and insane again, then paused. "Look, I know you'll go to jail before you tell me what you were doing in front of Ritter's place, but I need —"

"You don't have any room in jail."

"Believe me, I'd be happy to make some," he said, then unwrapped his arms from his chest. He threw them in the air in disgust, slammed them on the hood of the Explorer, then turned his back on me.

"Don't hit this piece of shit too hard," I said, "the tires will explode."

He turned back quickly as if the insult to his ride had been the final straw, then grabbed a deep breath and said, "What the hell happened? You were a good soldier, mister, what happened?"

"Drugs," I said.

"Drugs?" He was confused.

"Hey, I'd already been involved in losing one senseless war," I said. "You guys got the drug war all fucked up. I couldn't tell the good guys from the bad, man, the budget suckers from the real cops."

"That's what laws are for," he said.

"In your dreams," I said. "What the hell do you want, Raymond?"

"I need your help, mister," he said again.

"What?" I said. I couldn't have been more amazed if he had asked me for a blow job.

"Listen, I'm the only person in the department who wanted me to have this job," he said, an admission so difficult I had to believe it. "When I got promoted, they wanted to put me in charge of patrol, but I badgered them until I got this job. And the troops who work for me have made it clear that they think I'm either a dumb farmer or a little tin soldier, a marionette —"

"That's martinet," I interrupted.

"Whatever," he said, waving me off. "Listen, I don't know what you were doing at the Ritters', CW, but after going over the scene, I have to believe that you had just walked into the house," he said. "And there's no way in the world that fat woman got that rope over that beam," he added, "and no way she tied a perfectly knotted bowline around her neck and climbed up on that railing —"

"Maybe she just wanted to hang out with her husband when he came home," I joked, then regretted it.

"To hell with that," he said, then actually blushed. Curse words seemed to have that effect on him. His two tours in Vietnam must have been more kinds of torture than just the usual nightmares of guerrilla warfare.

"What was it you wanted?" I said.

He grabbed another breath, then said, "I've seen a lot of crime scenes in my life, mister, and even though the lab reports aren't back, I know this one is going to be clean. Too clean."

"Crime scene?"

"Listen to me," he said, "it is."

"Well, hell, man, I believe you believe it, but I don't have any way of knowing," I said. "What do you want from me?"

"An open and honest exchange of information," he said, then added sternly, "within the limits of the law, of course.

Our investigation, such as it is, will be over shortly. Case closed — suicide. I don't have any idea what you were doing there, but I know you were on the job, so if you come up with anything that makes you think that it wasn't a suicide . . ." He paused, the word sticking like a fork in his throat, "*Please* let me know. If only for Fergie." The please came out in a croak, as if he had dislodged a piece of lung tissue just to get it out.

"I'm going to have to think about this," I said, without even knowing what to think, "and I have to consult with my client."

"That's fair," he said, digging a business card out of his jeans. "But don't call me at the office, okay? That's my personal cell phone number on the back."

"Hell, Raymond, I won't even tell anybody that I talked to you," I said. "My reputation would be just as screwed as yours."

"Thanks," he said and seemed to mean it. "Listen, just because I respect the law doesn't mean that I can't have a hunch," he said, embarrassed now.

"I've got to go to work, okay?" I said, glancing at my watch. "You probably do, too."

"It's my day off," he said. "I'm taking my little brother fishing up at Dog Lake." I must have raised an eyebrow. Raymond blushed, then said, "Little Brother-Big Brother program, you know."

Even though we weren't at the hand-shaking part yet, I nodded in approval, then shook my head. Nothing is more tire-some than a good guy who really is a good guy.

Four

By the time I got back on the job, Carrie Fraizer was walking swiftly through the low hedges just out the back door of Mac's office. She was a tall, buxom young woman bearing a tangle of earrings in both ears, dressed in what looked like rumpled second-hand clothes — a peasant blouse, a flowing skirt, and sandals full of dirty toes — only her hair looked clean and cared for, a sleek black bundle pulled back into a ponytail. Once again I wondered how she afforded Mac's sessions. She climbed into an ancient but beautifully preserved VW van. She looked familiar, but I couldn't place her. I pulled in behind her and followed her to the parking lot behind the Pacific Northwest Hotel. I stashed my rented ride down the alley where I had a clear view of the rear of the building and the parking lot.

The old maze of wooden balconies and fire escapes that once had hung from the rear of the brick building had been replaced with steel painted to look like wood. The balconies were cluttered with potted

plants, wind socks and chimes, cloth butterflies, music posters, and coarse, unfinished art work. Twenty minutes later
Carrie Fraizer came out on a balcony on
the top floor. She had changed into waitress gear — a white blouse, black skirt,
black panty hose, and flats. She leaned
against the rail on the south end of the balcony and smoked. She was talking to
somebody I couldn't see at the other end
of the balcony, a hulking shadow behind a
hanging screen of bamboo strips. After two
cigarettes, she went into the apartment. A
few minutes later she came out of the hotel's
rear door, climbed into the van, and took
off.

I followed her out to the Eastgate Mall,
then through the mall into a faux Asian
restaurant, the Ginger Snap Dragon,
where it seemed she worked as a waitress.
The restaurant was so modern it squeaked
like a new shoe: bundles of exposed pipe
and wiring snaked among raw chunks of
abstract art. I pulled up at the bar and ordered coffee.

"Too early for a drink, Sughrue?" the
bartender said. When I didn't respond, he
added, "Dave Moore."

"Little Davy Moore," I said as I shook
his small, strong hand. "Long time no see,

man. How the hell are you?"

"Good," he said. "Really good."

"I wouldn't have recognized you," I admitted. The scraggly beard, butt-length hair, and biker tattoos had disappeared as if they never had existed. I had met Davy years ago when he helped me snatch a runaway girl from the clutches of a motorcycle gang. "Not for a second."

"Did a little jolt over in Monroe," he said. "State of Washington cleaned me up." He handed me my coffee, then glanced at his arms, which except for a few faded blue dots were unmarked. "Decided the outlaw life wasn't for me, man," he said, "and it's wonderful what lasers can do." He leaned over the bar to add, "My mother's aunt owns a piece of the place. I'm moving up to bar manager next month. White-collar job."

"You've already got a white collar on," I said.

He laughed, then walked away when Carrie Fraizer called him in a husky voice.

I nursed a couple of cups of coffee and a bottle of Tsing Tsao before ordering lunch. I wanted a cigarette, but the only place you could smoke inside the Dragon was in the gaming room, a small cubicle stuffed with gambling machines, so I ate my addiction. Peace seemed more important now than nicotine. I didn't know what to think about Raymond's appeal for my help. Help with what? He might have a hunch, but all I had was nightmares waiting. I hadn't had any yet. Of course, I hadn't gone to sleep clean yet, either. But the bad dreams always were waiting in the shadows, flirting around the fringes of sleep. They didn't mean anything, I knew, but that was sometimes hard to tell myself when they blundered like drunken bears into my unconscious.

Over an odd lunch — mediocre sushi, decent pot stickers, and slices of Chinese barbecue that, even with hot mustard, had the taste and texture of roasted shoe tongues — I watched Carrie Fraizer work and pumped Little Davy a tad, just enough so I could learn something without him knowing it. He had an ex-con's desire to please and accommodate, plus a native Montanan's love of stories, so the lunch wasn't wasted.

Carrie was an excellent and hardworking waitress. She had grown up on a ranch in eastern Wyoming, then fled when her father tried to marry her to the neighbor's son. Something about water rights on the Powder River, maybe. She'd run to the college in Meriwether, on her own, worked her way to a B.F.A. in art education, hopping tables during the school year and working the slime line in Alaskan canneries in the summers. She taught high school for two years in Alaska, then came back to Meriwether to paint and hop tables again. Carrie painted enamel miniature western scenes on pieces of weathered barn wood.

Hell, no wonder she looked familiar. Whit owned a couple of her pieces that she had bought at a gallery opening she had made me attend, one of those cold-cheese, warm-wine affairs. That night Carrie had worn makeup; her hair had been loose, a black flood across her wide shoulders, and her tall, strong body had been draped in a red sheath. She was a striking woman. No wonder I hadn't recognized her as either a starving artist or a waitress.

I ordered another beer after the lunch rush had subsided and carried it into the gaming room, where I leaned in a corner and finally had a couple of cigarettes. The retired couples working the machines on a wasted afternoon looked at me as if I were either a crazy preacher or a cop because I hadn't bellied up to lady luck's bad little sister. Maybe they should have felt guilty. Maybe we all should. What sort of mistake had been made in their lives that led them to believe the only fun left was stuffing twenty-dollar bills into an empty hole controlled by a computer chip? Perhaps I only felt sorry for them because they had fallen prey to a vice I had managed to avoid. Sort of the same way I felt sorry for golfers.

When I had had enough beeping and burping, sounds that sounded too much like the electronic chortle of the house's edge, I went back to the bar to settle my bill. Davy stopped in front of me just as a tall, beefy young guy with muddy, clotted dreadlocks, dressed in a mixture of combat camouflage and Salvation Army chic, strode in from the mall, followed by his pals, two giggling bookends.

"Oh, shit," Davy said, something almost biblical in his voice. "The beast returneth."

The guy, who wasn't nearly as young as I'd first thought, walked up behind Carrie, slapped her on the butt, then squeezed. She batted his arm away, but her heart wasn't in it. Not as much as I would have liked, anyway. After a quick kiss, the tall, bulky guy led his merry pals to the far end of the bar. Perhaps because Whitney had complained so much, during these past few years I had only smoked dope in the dark alley behind my office or other shadowed lanes, and I'd forgotten how much fun it was to be stoned on a summer's afternoon.

"You want another beer, Sughrue?" Davy asked.

"Sure," I said. "Then bring me the tab." I wanted to watch this visit for a bit.

Davy brought me a beer, then waited on the boys down the bar. They all had complex concoctions in shot glasses that I didn't recognize. Expensive concoctions, I guessed from the amounts Davy rang up. He handed me my bill and started to walk away.

"Awfully nice-looking lady to be hooked up with trash like that," I said. "If this was my place, I wouldn't let people dressed like that in the door."

He nodded with energetic agreement. Nothing like a reformed biker to drum up disapproval of the badly dressed.

"Fucking trust-a-farians," Davy said.

"East Coast money?"

"Lots of it," Davy said. "Arno owns the Pacific Northwest Hotel. Or his dad does. Somebody paid for the remodel with cash. He and Carrie have the whole top floor."

"Arno?"

"Arno Biddle," Davy said. "He's kind of a barfly, Sughrue. I'm surprised that you don't know him."

"I guess I fly in different circles these days," I said.

"Don't we all," he offered. "I'm married and have two little girls now."

"Congratulations," I said. "Not many people beat the odds, man."

"Tell me," he said.

But I didn't know what to tell him. I didn't have to wonder now how Carrie could afford Mac's professional hours, though I almost asked Davy why she worked. I assumed I already knew the answer: the work ethic of a ranch kid. And who knew? Maybe she loved the creep. Stranger things have happened. But then I wondered what sort of unhappiness had forced her into Mac's office.

I paid my bill, then went home for a nap. To hell with these people.

When Charlie Marshall, the next name on the list, walked out of his accounting firm that afternoon about six, I was in the Taurus parked in the firm's lot, a Broncos cap pulled down over my dark glasses. Summer sunset was hours away, full dark hours beyond that. So I needed a bit of camouflage.

I'd known Charlie for years but still

didn't really know anything about him, except for a few random things. His wife, Ellen, was completely batshit. She had been hospitalized a dozen times, twice for suicide attempts, and they had been separated as much as they had lived together. Charlie looked unhappy, not just his long hangdog face, but also his infrequent smiles that looked more like grimaces of pain than grins, as if he were sitting on a toilet passing a small animal with sharp claws. His watery gray eyes hovered on the edge of tears behind round glasses, and his shoulders slumped under an invisible but terrible burden. Even his lank gray-brown hair looked sad. And he couldn't sit still. I'd seldom seen him sit down in a bar. He always stood up, his feet shifting constantly, as if he were trying to balance the dismal weight on his shoulders. Once in a dim study at a party in a mansion up Gold Creek, I'd seen Charlie rubbing an antique French inlaid escritoire with both hands, his fingers touching the intricate woodwork as if it were a woman. His eyes were closed and he was smiling sweetly. But when he realized that he had drawn an audience, he stood up quickly, grabbed his glass of bourbon, and hurried away as if ashamed.

That afternoon I waited until Charlie climbed into a Lincoln Navigator, then headed downtown. Just where I'd expected. Friday night at the Scapegoat. Charlie stopped between George Paul and Ken Cole to lean on the long curved bar. Almost immediately they were engaged in a serious, animated conversation. I'd dumped my disguise in the car, found an empty stool at the other end of the bar, and settled down. The barroom was filled with end-of-the-week drinkers, people waiting for a table in the dining room upstairs on the main floor of the old bank, and a crowd of young women with loud, high voices. A bachelorette party I assumed, since the table was covered with dildos, blown-up rubbers, and scraps of lingerie. In Montana, women were allowed, perhaps even encouraged — if not required — to go see the elephant, too, as if they were cowhands just off the trail. The crowd of young women would have shamed even a bunch of Texas cowboys. But they were having fun.

Just after Ken left, George and Charlie noticed me, lifted a hand, but didn't wave me over. Charlie had been standoffish since the night I'd seen him stroking the furniture. Perhaps because I'd made the mistake of mentioning it to him during a party at his house. I had drifted downstairs, looking for the smokers, but had found Charlie standing alone in a workshop worthy of a professional cabinetmaker. But I could tell that Charlie didn't want to talk about wood or his shop.

On the other hand, George and I had sort of been drinking buddies once. We'd grown up in small southwestern towns — Vado, Texas, for me; Hobbs, New Mexico, for him. So we usually had plenty to talk about. Until one drunken night when we had followed the bartender into the basement of the Low Rent and snorted half a dozen fat lines of cocaine and gunned half a dozen shots of Patrón tequila with it. Later George had gotten on a crying jag, complaining about his early childhood. His father had either died or run away — it wasn't clear — when George had been in the third grade, and he was convinced that his classmates had always felt sorry for him. "Poor little Georgie Paul," he had blubbered endlessly until I finally got him home, *"pobrecito Jorge,* he ain't got no daddy." George had a pugnacious forehead and a brutal jaw, but his face was softened by jug ears, a short gray beard, and close-cut curly, gray hair that fit his head like a knit cap. He almost looked benign. But I had seen a sneaky meanness on the ball field — stepping on the first baseman's foot, catching the second baseman with a flying elbow, banging the catcher on the knee as he warmed up at the plate, or making a tag like a punch. Also, to George women were bitches, cunts, or dykes.

An hour or so later, the stool next to George opened up, so I drifted over, sat down, and ordered a round of drinks from my favorite bartender, Steve, a former political science professor. "For the State Champion Old Farts," I said as I raised my glass. Charlie and George didn't look all that happy to drink with me, but they raised their bourbons on the rocks and nodded thanks.

"Well, I guess it's better to go out champions than on a stretcher," George said.

"Like those other poor bastards," Charlie added shyly.

"Sounds like you guys are giving it up," I said. They both nodded in agreement. "Yeah," I said, "when we were driving back last Sunday I felt like I'd either fallen down the stairs or had the shit beaten out of me."

"It's just not fun anymore," Charlie said quietly, as if nothing were.

"Hell, I spend more time in the hot tub than on the field," George said. "And frankly I'm sick of that fucking Mac-Kinderick acting like he's the manager. It's our team. I mean who the hell died and elected him Casey Stengel and Babe Ruth?"

"Hey, we'll miss you guys," I lied. George's comment about Mac sounded strange to me, since I thought I had noticed his name when I dropped Mac's pages. Then I remembered that his wife's name was Georgia. GG for short.

"How about you, Sughrue? You gonna hang in there?"

"Like a hair in a biscuit," I said. "They'll probably have to carry me off like one of those poor Christians — tote me straight to the graveyard across the street."

"They did sort of wander into the wrong arena, didn't they?" George said, something cruel in his laugh.

"What are you boys doing out tonight?" I said.

"The wives are in Seattle," Charlie said, a sick but hopeful grin twisting his features.

"The ladies are competitive shopping," George said bitterly, low-tar smoke drifting out of his mouth. Hell, his wife could afford to buy a floor at Nordstrom's. "Or getting shitfaced in the Four Seasons," he added, "offering free blow jobs to Asian software millionaires."

"A good woman would keep her blow jobs at home," Charlie said, then giggled, his grin almost becoming a true smile. He was more than a bit tipsy.

"That's for shitsure," George said, his grin full of large, crooked yellow teeth, his blue eyes glittering. I wondered why he didn't spend some of his fortune on his teeth.

We made inane small talk for a while until it became clear that they weren't going to resume their former conversation, so I paid my tab, said good night, and went out to wait for Charlie in my rent car. I didn't have to wait very long. He came out thirty minutes later, followed by George, and they climbed into separate vehicles without saying good night. I followed them up Dottle, then down to the corner of Railroad and Vender, where the Low Rent Rendezvous occupied the ground floor of another old railroad hotel that had been converted into an office building. They parked in the back lot and walked into the bar together. I knew that Eric Ray was playing to a Friday night crowd, and I wouldn't have a chance to listen to their conversation, so I backed the Taurus into a space in the overflow lot across Railroad Street, beside the tracks.

From my position, I could see their rides, but I could also see the back of the Pacific Northwest Hotel, the tallest building between Vender and Dottle. The setting sun poured down Railroad Street, the old bricks of the hotel shining as if newly fired. The light on the balconies behind the hotel was as bright as noon. The gaily colored wind socks and cloth butterflies hung unmoved in the sundown air. Several of the balconies were filled with scruffy young people chattering through clouds of dope smoke, competing stereos blasting.

I opened all the windows to let the soft evening air in and the new car smell of the Taurus out. I had a cooler full of beer, a Thermos of chicory coffee, two chicken salad sandwiches from the Frog Pond Deli, and a capped plastic bottle for piss. So I was ready. I switched on the radio. *All Things Considered* was over, and having grown up among displaced hillbillies, I didn't care much for blue grass. The only other things I could find on the radio were hard- and soft-rock stations, creamed corn country, mystical stock tips, and Ronald

Reagan's boy whining, so I cut it off, stuffed *The Last Coyote* into the tape deck, and settled back to wait. Recorded books had made surveillance jobs almost bearable.

Down the street, up on the top-floor balcony, the screen door slammed open with a bang and the bamboo awning rolled up with a snap. Nosy by nature, I grabbed the Leica with the telephoto lens and quickly focused on the balcony. Arno and Carrie were standing on the balcony arguing in loud voices that I couldn't quite make out and waving their arms at each other. Arno threw a green can of Heineken's straight out into the sunset, where it twirled, spewing foam in loops until it landed on the roof of Peale's secondhand store across the alley. Carrie lit a cigarette, shoved Arno out of the way, then stormed over to the north side of the balcony, where she propped her right elbow into her left hand and puffed furiously, staring into the sun as it set behind Sheba Peak in the northern Hardrocks. Arno disappeared into the house, then came back out with another Heineken's, cracked it, then chugged beer for a long time. Carrie ignored him until he shouted at her. Watching his mouth, I guessed that he had screamed, "Fucking cunt!" but I could only guess. Arno raged back toward the screen door. Carrie threw her cigarette at his retreating back, then quickly lit another, sighed deeply, and leaned back against the rail.

Even though they had been shouting, I couldn't hear their words exactly, but I didn't have any trouble hearing the screech as the balcony rail pulled away from the bricks; I heard that very distinctly. More out of reflex than purpose, I hit the shutter release. I heard Carrie's gasp of horror, then the descending scream. But I was out of the car and running before the body hit the bricks of the alley, so I missed that sound. At least I hoped I had missed it.

Carrie lay on her side, her right arm smashed into a maze of blood and white bone shards beneath her, the side of her face flattened in a spreading bright red pool against the alley bricks. She still had a faint thread of a pulse when I squatted to place two fingers on her carotid artery; then the beat paused. Another longer tremble slipped wetly beneath my finger-tips, followed by a longer pause, then a single tick, followed by a soft moan that escaped her bleeding mouth from among the clatter and grind of her broken jaw and teeth. Then nothing. I looked up into

Arno's white face, a shocked, bloodless moon staring down at me. I shook my head sadly, but he didn't acknowledge it.

A siren whooped from the police department two blocks away, answered by another from the fire station only four blocks in the other direction. If any life remained in the crushed body, I wasn't going to be able to draw it out. Professional saviors would be here in moments. I heard the pounding of running feet on wooden floorboards as they echoed out of the hotel's rear entrance. I pushed my sunglasses tighter to my nose, tugged the bill of my Broncos cap down around my face, then walked away.

It was only about fifty feet down the alley to the Iron Butterfly, a crowded yuppie bar, but I kept my gorge down long enough to get past it, then across the street to Mickey's. I gunned two shots of cheap tequila and half a can of beer, then went into the john to throw it up, came back to the bar, had a shot of peppermint schnapps and the rest of the can of beer. When it felt as if that might stay down, I had another, then left.

I was on the sidewalk heading for my car when I heard my name shouted behind me. It was the bartender, Mike.

"Hey, man," he huffed when he caught up with me. "You okay?"

"Sure. Why?"

"Well, you're white as a sheet, tears are pouring down your face," he said, then cocked his grizzled head, "and you didn't pay for your drinks."

"Oh, hell, sorry," was all I could say. I handed him a twenty, then walked on toward the burning sunset. "Catch you around."

"Don't you want your change?" he asked somewhere way behind me.

It should have been dark, as black as winter midnight, but the sun was so bright it hurt my eyes.

When Mac moved to Meriwether, he bought up an entire block that nestled against the base of Grasshopper Hill on the east end of the Northgate neighborhood and north of the abandoned railroad tracks; then he had all the small houses either demolished or moved. He built a spacious but not huge Craftsman house and filled it with a fairly good collection of local art, a variety of seascapes, and three great Winslow forgeries. The house nestled into the south face of the hill and a tall brick wall bordered by a line of poplars on the street side. A small stone-banked ditch carried irrigation water across the yard. The ground was sodded with thick grass and landscaped into small hills and dales. It was a perfect place. In town, but almost a country estate in its solitude. He could walk to his office just across the river in thirty minutes, or to the Scapegoat in fifteen. Cemetery Park, where we played ball, was six blocks to the west. My house was only another two blocks farther.

Northgate was a nice neighborhood, a nice mix of all incomes and all classes, a neighborhood with no room to expand, no bars, and almost no businesses. Grasshopper Creek, spouting small irrigation ditches for large gardens, wound past the cemetery, through the park, then around the community. There had been a spurt of gentrification in the seventies, but it hadn't lasted. It was an easy neighborhood where you could, if you tried, forget the present and dream of a kinder past, one of those brief periods of peace between wars.

Lorna answered the door when I rang, blocking the doorway. She was dressed to the nines: a little black dress, patterned stockings, spike heels, and an emerald as big as a small cracker hanging on a gold chain around her neck. The stone was surrounded by tiny diamonds, as were her matching earrings and dinner ring.

"CW," she said. "We're just on our way out. Dr. MacKinderick is getting dressed now. Can I do something for you?"

"I need to talk to him," I said. "Now, please."

"Just for a second, though, hon," she said. "We're already late now. You can wait in the den."

"It won't take a second," I promised. Lorna led me down the hallway toward the den and ushered me inside.

"May I get you something?" she said, poised in the doorway, glowing in horizontal bands of red-gold light, her hair shining like fresh blood.

"I know where everything is," I said. "Don't bother. By the way, you're looking sharp tonight."

"Why thank you, kind sir," she said, smiling. She flipped on the lights and the exhaust system that filtered Mac's cigar smoke out of the room. "Mac says you're smoking again," she said, then spun on a delicate heel and headed back down the hallway, the tapping of her heels as light as the blows of a fairy's wand.

I had a smoking cigarette and a handful

of sixteen-year-old Scotch before the sound of her heels disappeared. Then I leaned on the back of a huge black leather couch. Mac's den was more like a library or an art museum than a den. No animal heads, gun racks, or pictures of bird dogs on the dark oak walls. One wall was nothing but books, floor to ceiling. The other walls displayed three Chatham winter landscapes, a subdued western scene, and three small seascapes Mac had painted and brought back from a long honeymoon with Lorna in the Hebrides. Two ceramic rat pots flanked the fireplace. And on the wall between the French doors that led to the veranda, strips of faded barnwood climbed the oak like a rough ladder, gleaming landscapes and ranchwork scenes that reminded me of Japanese miniatures. I walked over to look at the work more closely. Perhaps I had been wrong about Arno paying for Carrie's analysis. Perhaps she had paid in art. Mac probably wouldn't tell me, but I knew how to find out.

Mac stepped into the den as he finished the Windsor of his rich silk tie. As he slipped into his linen suit coat, he said, "Sughrue, what's up?"

"You guys are a little overdressed for this

poor ol' country town," I said, trying to ease the mood and avoid the news.

"Since when are you the fashion police?"

"Actually I'm no kind of police at all," I said. "I'm really bad news. You better get a drink."

"Sunset champagne at the Mansion," he said. "Life donors of the art museum."

"You get the alarm code from Ritter?" I said suddenly, finding a new way to avoid the bad news as hard and fast as I could.

"It's in your mailbox," he said, "with the key, too. By the way, don't bother breaking into his house. I told him that somebody would stop by to feed the cats and water the plants. There's plenty of food in the pantry and a list of directions inside the door."

"Do I have to clean the cat box?" I asked.

"Also sit down with the cats, watch a little television, too — nothing too violent, though — and pet Chloe and her sister, Charmaine."

"How am I supposed to know which one is which?" I asked.

"Chloe's got one blue eye," Mac said calmly, "and a bad attitude."

"Jesus, you don't ask much, do you?" I said.

"CW," he said, a boyish grin flittering

around his face. "You're one of those loyal romantics. You'd do anything for a friend. And probably have, right?"

"Maybe," I said. "You have any samples of a sleeping pill that will put me to sleep without making me crazy?"

"Sure," he said, then rummaged in the top drawer of his desk, dug up a small box, and pitched it to me. "Ambien. It will put you down, but it won't interfere with REM sleep. Safe as mother's milk."

"What if I don't want to dream?"

"Oh, shit. What's happened?" he asked, suddenly serious. "What are you so carefully not telling me, my friend?"

I couldn't evade it any longer. "About half an hour ago, Carrie Fraizer fell off the top-floor balcony behind her apartment at the Pacific Northwest."

"Dead?"

"You're talking to the lucky son of a bitch who felt the last tick of her blood," I said.

"Oh, hell," he said. "I'm so sorry." He staggered back as if I'd just hit him in the face, his hand to his eyes. He grabbed the Lagavulin off the bar and had a quick shot from the bottle. Two deep breaths and he was professional again. "The bastard finally did it?"

"She fell, man," I said. "I saw it. Hell, I may even have a picture of it."

"It's Friday," Mac said, "her best night for tips. She worked a split shift. Always." He couldn't take it in, either. He was perplexed, his forehead wrinkled, his black eyebrows reaching for each other. "She should have been at work. Jesus, I'm so sorry. And you were there? Were you following her?"

"Earlier in the day," I admitted, sounding guilty even to myself. "But I was hooked up on Charlie, sitting in the overflow lot across from the Low Rent. I had a clear view of the balcony. They were shouting. I wanted to look closer, so I picked up the Leica."

"My god, what am I going to do?"

"Go get drunk with the bigwigs," I said. "Act like nothing happened. Use a glass, and you'll be all right."

Moving like the living dead, Mac picked up a champagne flute off the bar, poured four fingers of Scotch into it, then drank it like a man who wasn't going to stop, even to breathe. The flute was almost empty when Lorna came to the door of the den.

She leaned into the room, stomping her long narrow foot, saying, "What the live-long hell are you boys doin' in here?" Then she noticed the dark Scotch in Mac's hand. "Mac, honey what are you doing? We're runnin' late already, dammit."

"I'll just be a moment, darling," Mac said softly as he poured more Scotch into the flute. "Just a moment. CW just gave me some bad news."

"Not too bad, I hope," Lorna crooned and started in his direction.

"I'll meet you in the car," he said, and she looked mildly hurt. I noticed, but he didn't. "Just give me a second."

"Well, sir, if you're gonna be a-drinkin' like some ol' fish, I guess we'd better take my car. Nobody's gonna care if my hair's blown all to hell and gone," she prattled, then walked toward the rear of the house and the garage. "I'll meet you in front, darlin'," she added, casting a coy smile over her shoulder.

Lorna's thick red hair was as heavy as a helmet, and it looked as if it would take a war ax to muss it, but I didn't tell her that. Mac stared into the flute as if it held the secret to everlasting life.

"I must be losing my mind," he said. "I'm drinking Scotch out of a champagne flute."

"Actually, that's an improvement from sucking it straight from the bottle."

"Jesus," he said. "Surely there's no connection between Carrie and the Ritters."

"Probably just a coincidence," I said. "But any time I see two dead bodies in three days, it makes me nervous. So I'll make damn sure there's no connection."

"Would you, please?" he said, then gunned the whiskey. "Guess I should let Lorna drive. 'Cept every time I do, she scares me sober." Lorna drove her little BMW Z car too fast and too aimlessly for comfort. Faster than a speeding bullet with no more sense of direction than a ricochet. Mac set the flute in the sink. "Finish your drink, Sughrue. Take your time. Lock up and set the alarm, will you? And stop by tomorrow afternoon, okay?"

"Not tomorrow," I said. "Sunday. You pick me up about two at the Missoula airport, okay? In Lorna's ride. I want to drive that little car, okay? And fast. I need to work it out, boss. Perks of the job."

Mac laughed for a second as if he had forgotten what had brought me here, then the sadness fell across his face. He turned, shook my hand with both of his. "Thank you," he said. "I'm in your debt, my friend. Forever."

"Don't sweat it," I said as he trotted out of the den, wobbling a bit, on his way to sobriety courtesy of a windy adrenaline rush. I wished him luck.

After pouring another stiff drink, I slipped a Kelly Willis disk into the CD player, adjusted the volume, then stepped through the French doors onto the wide veranda and sat down in a wonderfully comfortable wicker chair. I assumed that Sunday would be soon enough to pass along Johnny Raymond's hunch. The sun had finally eased behind the Hardrocks, casting long shadows across the greensward. A brace of magpies strutted along the small ditch as if waiting for their daily carrion delivery. Three does — an old fat one, a yearling, and a late fawn with a few spots still left — clattered down the slope of Grasshopper Hill, leaped the five-foot fence as gracefully as if they were swimming in air, and settled down to their jobs, nibbling the short grass of the lawn peacefully, pausing occasionally for a quick flower snack or a brief munch of pale willow leaves. When I struck a match for another cigarette, they looked up with brown eyes as wise as children's.

What are you doing here? they seemed to say. *This is our place.*

"I ate your grandmother and your grandfather, and half of your fuckin'

105

cousins!" I shouted. The deer didn't seem all that interested in the seasons of mortality. The fawn hunched slightly, deer pellets raining like hail on the smooth surface of the lawn. "Well, fuck you," I said. "I've got rows to hoe for Massa MacKinderick. Again."

Five

The malpractice suit had been the longest row I had hoed in my life. At least that time I didn't have to deal with any dead bodies in person.

A San Francisco brokerage partner, one Turner Landry, who had been forced out of his firm for cocaine abuse, drunkenness, and several counts of sexual harassment, had retreated to the languid climes of Meriwether, Montana, after a messy divorce and an unsuccessful trip into the spin dry. Unfortunately, shortly after he moved to town a few years back, he wandered into the Low Rent Rendezvous one summer evening and bumped into an off-shift lady bartender, a pretty woman except for her pockmarked face, who introduced him to the joys of crystal meth. For the first time in his life, Landry could drink to his heart's content and command a blow job when the occasion arose. The sexual part of the affair only lasted a few months, but his love for crystal lasted into the next summer. It lasted through three car wrecks, several ugly incidents in local bars — one of which I witnessed, a fistfight with a wino about who was pitching when Kirk Gibson hit one out against the A's in the '88 series — and two arrests for shooting at his neighbor's cows with a .44-magnum Ruger Redhawk.

Only his money and his promise to stay in detox this time kept him out of jail. Much to everybody's surprise, Landry was loosely paroled into the caring arms of Dr. MacKinderick. After six months of five sessions a week with the doc, Landry seemed dry and clean enough for a weekend pass to see his son in Denver.

Coming back that Sunday, Landry picked up a fourteen-year-old runaway named Doug Foley in Casper, Wyoming. A spring blizzard trapped them in a cheap trailer-house motel outside Hardin, Montana. The next day in the gray, frozen morning their motel room was engulfed by fire, then the whole motel was leveled by an explosion. As far as the authorities could tell from the remains, the .44 magnum had been used to beat the kid to death, then Landry had turned the piece on himself and scattered bits of skull across the room.

But when he pulled the trigger he didn't

know about the leak in the heating system or the large puddle of propane collected in the crawl space beneath the trailer. The explosion broke windows all over the west side of Hardin and killed two other guests, the owner, and his wife, who was filling in for the maid who had been too stoned to come to work that day. The trailer-house motel looked as if it had been hit by a firestorm, a tornado, or an Arkansas divorce. Not much was left but piles of charred fiberglass, smoldering particle board, and melted aluminum. And the remains of six bodies, of course. A mess but a fairly straightforward mess. Until the overworked and understaffed Montana crime lab, an outfit that usually did forensic work worthy of a much larger and well-endowed state, lost all the blood and tissue work. There was plenty of evidence of drug and drink paraphernalia in the room, but without the blood and tissue work, no evidence of actual abuse, or who had fired the pistol.

Once word of the "misplacement" leaked to the press, Landry's son from his first marriage, a thirty-year-old bum who had been disowned by his father after endless problems with drugs and other people's checks, showed up in Meriwether with a copy of an e-mail that could be considered a suicide note, an ambitious Denver lawyer, and a five-million-dollar medical malpractice suit against Mac, claiming he should have anticipated Landry's suicide.

Mac, who had freely admitted to me that he cared too much for his patients, offered to settle for a million. But the lawyer wars had already escalated so quickly that no wiggle room was left. Ron Musselwhite was convinced that Landry had fallen off the wagon, back into crystal and drink again, the instrument of his own destruction. But with the loss of the blood and tissue work, he needed a witness.

That's where I entered the picture. I didn't want the job, but because Mac had testified for Whit at the trial of the Benewah kid, I owed him a favor. Six months had passed, all the motel records had been destroyed in the explosion, and I had no place to start. No place but the bars of Hardin, a hard-drinking town just off the Crow Reservation, where I spent three weeks of suicidal drinking. All I learned during that cloudy and confused time was the name of the stoned maid who hadn't come to work that day, Shirley Looks at the Ground. Her mother thought that she had moved to Sacramento. Maybe. Turned out it was Rancho Cordova, just outside Sacramento.

For five hundred dollars, which she needed to bail her Sioux boyfriend out of jail, Shirley told me that the only person she remembered, aside from Landry and the kid, was a long-haired guy who drove an old white Ford pickup with one red front fender. Maybe it had a lawn mower or something in the back. Maybe he had been a marine, a Vietnam vet, she suggested, based on a glimpse of a blurred tattoo on his butt. But she refused to tell me how or why she'd seen his butt.

Five months later, most of it spent on the road, after spending a ton of Mac's money, with a little luck and thanks to an old friend of mine, a retired alternative newspaper owner living in Boston, I found the kid's drunken uncle sitting in a recliner in a rundown clapboard house in the middle of an untended orchard outside Delta, Colorado. His guesses led me to Lonnie Howell as he cleared a driveway outside Denver, up in a fancy neighborhood above Evergreen, Colorado, one afternoon just after a heavy, wet October snowstorm.

The woman of the house watched

Lonnie as he ran his snowblower up and down the driveway. I might have watched Lonnie, too. He was a completely unreconstructed bush-vet hippie straight out of the seventies. Lonnie's beard was gray and wispy, his jacket was the color of dried blood, except where it was black with grease or white with leaked feathers, his snow pacs came from two different pairs, and his knit cap had a large hole in the very top. Only his snowblower and pickup, which now also sported a blue rear fender, showed any signs of normal maintenance.

The woman had straight black hair streaked with gray, but lively amused dark eyes in a sharp face. She wore a mink hat that matched her coat, and she held a muzzled rottweiler bitch on a rolling leash. When I climbed out of my car onto the freshly blown sidewalk, the dog trotted toward me, unreeling the leash.

"Don't worry," the woman said in a musical voice. "She's a teddy bear. She wears a muzzle to keep her from eating rocks." I must have looked confused. "Bitch eats rocks for fun. Last time it cost twelve hundred forty-three dollars and fifteen cents to have them cut out of her."

I took this as good news, since the dog had her muzzle buried in my crotch.

"Can I help you?" she said.

"I'll bet he's a-lookin' for me," Lonnie said over the roar of the snowblower. Then to me, he added, "I heard you were lookin' for me, man. I'll be done in a bit."

And he was. I followed his pickup down to south Denver, where he parked it and picked up his few belongings. When we stopped for meals or motel rooms, he was oddly silent, as if bearing some unnamed guilt, but I attributed it to the war, although he never said a word about it. His silence seemed very important to him.

After that, the lawsuit was over. Lonnie hadn't had a drug or a drink in years. The single blot on his record was that he had a general discharge rather than an honorable, which could mean anything from misbehavior to madness. He lived under the middle-class radar because he still hated the government that had squandered his youth and innocence in a useless war. He cleaned up nicely and his deposition was intelligent and to the point. He had been in Landry's motel several times during the blizzard, trying to help the kid kick drugs. In country, he had seen hundred of kids hooked on CIA heroin. Lonnie knew the destructive horror of addiction. He had witnessed Landry and the kid slamming crystal, smoking dope, and guzzling everything from butterscotch schnapps to green Chartreuse.

So they settled happily. Mac's insurance company was happy, Mac was relieved, and Landry's son had replaced a bit of his lost inheritance. Lonnie spent his days standing on the frozen bank of the Meriwether River and his nights drinking Cokes at the motel bar. As soon as he was finished, he grabbed his piece of change and left town on the first plane, headed for a winter in Mexico. I went back to my family; Whit's college debts, office expenses, and salary were paid for a year. Of course I had lost any interest in continuing law school. I was too close to the criminal mind to give a shit about the law.

And the lawyers? Well, hell, they twirled their mustaches like Mexican bandits and went down to the Scapegoat for cocktails. Actually, Mac and I went with them, too. Mac expressed some disappointment that he never got to thank Lonnie Howell personally but Musselwhite wouldn't let him near the kid, and he didn't ask me to find him again.

But the lawsuits weren't completely over. The family of Doug Foley, the runaway kid, planned to sue Landry's estate, but that didn't concern me.

In spite of what I had said to the trio of cynical deer, I kept putting off my chores. I sat on Mac's veranda sipping Scotch and not thinking about Carrie Fraizer until the deer wandered back up the hill. Then I locked up, drove over to my office, where I turned on the television, supposedly to watch the late news, cracked a beer, and watched the set as stupidly as if it were a powerful fire.

Finally, I opened the blank envelope from my mailbox. I looked at Ritter's alarm code, security company password, and front door key as if they were artifacts from a lost civilization. Or a modern one. Ritter's key seemed to have electronic properties as well as physical, so just copying the key's grooves and teeth wouldn't be enough to open the lock. Smart key, wow. It seemed like a good idea to me. Except that I knew I would probably fuck it up and lock myself out of my house forever. Just like the time I told my new computer to kill itself, and it did.

Enough of that, I said to myself and thought about tearing myself out of my office funk.

Before I left, I called the paper to see if Pete Morgan, the reporter who covered the cop shop, was at his desk. He was. First, I asked him if he wanted to meet me for a drink, but he said he had to get a story out.

"What story?"

He told me all about it, then added that it looked as if Arno Biddle was going to be arrested for possession of drug paraphernalia, small amounts of marijuana and cocaine, and wrestling with the cops.

"And they're thinking he's good for pushing the girl off the balcony?" I said.

"Those two have a history of loud, violent disagreements," Morgan said, "but usually they limited their fisticuffs to bars. But I'm guessing more serious charges will be filed shortly. What's your interest, Sughrue? Domestic disasters again?"

"Only my own," I lied, hung up the telephone, and finally left.

But as I drove past the Scapegoat on the way to Ritter's house, my weaker self took over, parked, went in, and started drinking handfuls of single malt. So I sat there shooting the shit with old shit-shooting friends until nearly two o'clock before I caught my breath. I thought about calling Whit, but it turned out that I was just drunk, not stupid. I gathered my wits and left a fairly coherent message on her office voice mail. She'd check her voice mail in the morning. She was a professional. As I perhaps wasn't; I still had to go feed the cats. I settled my check and got a six-pack of Negra Modelo from the bartender, who insisted on calling me a cab.

Whatever had been keeping me from going to the Ritter place seemed to have disappeared. Hell, when the cab stopped in front, I was so happy just to be there that I nearly asked the two college girls in the backseat in for a drink. We'd just picked them up in front of the Deuce and they were drunker than fat ticks on a wino's ass. Alas, sanity prevailed. And they were afraid that my six beers wouldn't go very far among the three of us. Reluctantly, I agreed with them. When I climbed out of the cab, they asked to bum a couple of beers; I looked at them as if they had asked to hunt over my best bird dog.

"As my mother used to say," I said, "If you don't have time to stop in, don't bother stopping by." She used to tell that to prospective customers who stopped by our old shack to leave an order and wouldn't come in for coffee or a highball; then she would close the door in their startled faces. She wasn't a great Avon Lady,

117

but she was a hell of a lot of fun as a mom.

The young girls just looked blankly from the backseat. So I gave them the whole six-pack and wandered toward the front door, waving good-bye over my shoulder. As the cab pulled away I heard one of them squeal out the cab window, "We don't have an opener." But that was asking too much.

In spite of the fancy key, the Ritters' front door opened smoothly for me. I shut it and stepped toward the blinking alarm keypad, thinking I should punch in the code before I looked for the light switch. A drift of dusky moonshine from the skylight filled the ground floor of the house. Just as I reached for the keypad, two large white clouds came off a narrow table just inside the door. My heart stopped before they landed on my shoulders.

When I screamed, the cats fled so quickly that they left rips in my wind-breaker and my skin. I was surprised that I didn't shit my jeans. But not surprised that I couldn't dig the alarm code out of my head. After a moment the telephone on the narrow table rang.

"Aristophanes," I mumbled into the receiver, pronouncing it correctly, thereby and for the first time in my life justifying the government's expense for sending me to graduate school under false pretenses.

"Good night, professor," a tired voice answered.

As soon as my heart slowed a bit, I turned on every goddamned light on the ground floor, then began a serious search for something to drink. I was glad that the professional cleanup crew had been there before me because the place smelled of Pine-Sol rather than blood. The Ritters didn't have a bar that I could find, but the kitchen pantry was liberally stocked.

"Canadian Club and coffee," I said to myself as I took an unopened liter off the shelf. And turned to face a two-foot typed list. "Rules for House Sitters," it said. There was some admonition about staying out of the liquor cabinet, but I ignored that. I got the coffee started, then decided that I might as well deal with the goddamned cats. After what seemed a long time, I found the cat gear in its own private closet — better hidden than the booze — cleaned the litter pan, freshened it, then took a can of expensive cat food off the stocked shelf. When I cracked the lid, they were there, stropping my ankles and squeaking happily. They had forgiven me, but I was still withholding judgment.

I spent the next three hours carefully searching the house without finding a single thing out of place. No illegal drugs, no pornographic material, no caches of cash. Just shelves and shelves of ceramic frogs. I paused occasionally to have whiskey-fortified coffee and a smoke on the back steps. I also ignored the rule about bringing my own food and found the remains of a decent pâté in the refrigerator. But otherwise my search was wasted. I even got a ladder out of the garage to climb up to the heavy crossbeam beneath the skylight. Nothing. The only even vaguely interesting thing was an open window beside the laundry chute in the master bedroom that led to a steel fire escape, obviously a modern addition. An open window in a house with central heat and air? I wondered about that. Perhaps Mrs. Ritter just wanted to catch a breath of summer air before she killed herself. Or the cleaners left it open to air out the house.

Hell, I didn't know. I poured the last of the coffee and a splash of whiskey into my mug, then went into the television nook to catch the early news. The Ritters didn't have any ashtrays, so I used the empty pâté container, once Chloe and Charmaine had licked it clean. They were my buddies now. As I leaned back on the small couch, remote in hand, coffee and ashtray on the end table, Chloe of the one blue eye curled in my lap to have her head scratched with my free hand. Her sister stretched out along the top of my shoulders and proceeded to clean my neck, both of them purring happily, as if I were great cat furniture.

Looking for the local news, I stumbled into CNN on-site coverage of a Middle Eastern riot. When Chloe heard the first rattling burst of AK-47 fire, she turned under my hand and clamped on the web of skin between my thumb and forefinger, her teeth going all the way through, then she leaped away. I sucked blood out of my flesh until it stopped, then I finished the coffee and the cigarette, and rose to leave. But Chloe had come from behind the television console with a broken half of a small ceramic frog held delicately in her teeth. She had also picked up a small wad of duct tape that had attached itself to her back leg. A dust bunny had stuck to the tape. Chloe flipped the frog into the air, batted it, then chased after it as if she weren't trailing an embarrassing load of tape and dust. In spite of my blood that she had spilled, I decided to relieve her of the burden, which, upon closer inspection, turned out to be dust, duct tape, and a tangle of clear, heavy fishing line. I didn't know what it meant, or even think about it, but it was the only thing out of place in the whole house, so I stuffed it in my jeans pocket. Then I cleaned up my tracks, petted the sisters, and walked home in the dawn light.

About five that afternoon, I dropped off the roll of film at a quick-print place, waited for the photos, then drove about ten miles east of town to Tildon's Corners Hardrock Bar. I knew the bar would be almost empty at that time of day. Or any other. The new highway had missed Tildon's Corners, leaving it to die a slow economic death at the dead end of the old road.

The Meriwether Valley opened up here, and the glacial moraines stretched out into rolling pastures and hay fields sparkling beneath the circling thrust of irrigation sprinklers. Before I went into the bar, I stared at the valley backed by the tree-dark slopes and snow-spotted peaks of the Hardrocks glistening in the late summer sun. Then I called Johnny Raymond on his cell phone and told him where I was and how long I'd be there. He didn't want to take off from his family on Saturday so I said fine. He arrived before I'd finished my second cup of coffee.

"I didn't know you drank anything with water in it, Sughrue," he said as he leaned on the bar beside me.

"If you could spell, copper, you could write a book about what you don't know about me."

"But you look a little fuzzy around the edges," he said. "Hangover?"

"I never lie to officers of the law," I said. I guessed the quick nap, shower, and shave hadn't smoothed out the edges. "A mild hangover. Gathered in the line of duty."

"Well, it's Saturday afternoon; let's have a couple of beers," he said, smiling as if my pain made him feel better. "Two Raindeers, Freddy," he shouted at the bartender, who stood across the empty barroom in front of a keno machine.

"Don't fall off the wagon for my benefit," I said.

"I have a beer every now and again," he said. "I quit for a long time when I came back from Vietnam . . . well, not exactly *when* I came back, but eighteen months afterward."

"Went crazy, huh?"

"You better believe it, mister," he said, almost proudly, as if it made him a better human being to have gone crazy.

"I thought you were a hero," I said. "Purple Heart, Navy Cross, that sort of stuff."

"Two Purple Hearts," he corrected me. "But I had a little trouble making the climate change from the Mekong Delta back to Meriwether County." He paused. "You know, I grew up on a little ranch not a mile from here."

"That's why I thought we'd meet here."

"You know, I've asked around about you for years," he said. "Some people said you were good," he said. "Others said lucky."

"Does it make any difference?"

"Nope. One of the first things you learn in a firefight, right? Good is okay but lucky is great," he said as the bartender brought the Rainier bottles.

"You have to keep relearning it," I said. We sipped our beers for a moment.

"You come up with anything on the Ritters?"

"Not yet," I said. "But I'd make sure the pathologist makes a careful cut."

"No problem there," he sneered.

"Oh, and there's one more thing, Raymond," I said.

"What?"

"Your boys lock up Biddle?"

"Of course," he said.

"He lawyer up yet?"

"Of course, but he'll be locked up until Monday afternoon," he said. "The DA's probably going to go for murder two at the arraignment. What the hell's that got to do with anything?"

"I don't know, exactly," I said. "But I may have some evidence that might clear him. Who's his lawyer?"

"Just your style," he said. "Smathers."

"Shit," I said.

"That's all you're going to give me, right?" Raymond said. "Just a bunch of crap."

"Honest and straightforward exchange of information," I said. "Within the limits of the law."

"You sure like to play with words, don't you?" he said. "Keep in mind that an obstruction bust might be hard to beat. This is my hometown, mister," he added. "In my book, twenty years or so still makes you a newcomer." Our season of good feelings seemed to have been swept away on his irritation and my hangover.

"Hey, man, when I get through with this, you can run for fucking governor," I said.

"Or just run," he said, then stomped out.

I turned to the bartender, who was back at the machine. "Hey, Freddy, you know that guy?"

"He's my cousin," he answered without looking up from the beeping squares.

"Fucker's as sensitive as a girl when he drinks," I said.

"Meaner than your worst ex-wife," he commented, like a man who knew what he was talking about.

Lorne Smathers, known as Butch to family, friend, and foe alike, would not be happy at my weekend call. He wouldn't be happy anytime I called. Some years before, when I had been working another case entirely, I found a Kansas City runaway cleaning house for Butch's client, and I stumbled on a cache of overwhelming evidence in a basement in Big Fork, where the kid was staying, that proved without a doubt that Butch's rich client had butchered his wife. So instead of a long trial and years of appeals, the rich guy blew his head off, and his family stiffed Butch. They even stopped payment on his retainer. But I called him at home anyway.

126

He wasn't there. But his long-suffering wife knew exactly where he was.

Butch; one of his law partners, a hawk-faced Italian woman from Butte, whose name I always tried to forget; and Biddle père, who looked nothing like his dread-locked son, sat around one of the small tables in a private dining room on the third floor of the Mansion, a remodeled Victorian on a finger ridge south of town.

I arrived just before sundown, in time for their cognac and cigar moment. Even the woman had a cigar stub between her bright red lips. I flipped the chair around, straddled it, lit a cigarette, and set my Scotch on the table before Butch could protest. By then it was too late.

The hawk-faced woman, Claudia Lucchesi, streaks of silver winging through her coal-black hair, dark blue eyes glittering, smiled as if I had a hunk of raw flesh on my forehead. Butch wanted to break into screams, but not in front of his client's father.

"Who's your cowboy friend, Mr. Smathers?" Biddle said. I didn't know anything about him except that he reeked of money. His suit probably cost more than my first car, his tie more than my boots, and his smooth gray haircut more than a bottle of good single malt Scotch. "Maybe he needs a drink."

"I've got one, Mr. Biddle, thank you," I said.

"You've got me at a disadvantage," he said, reaching his hand across the table. Sometimes the very rich can afford to be polite. "Norman Biddle," he said.

"CW Sughrue," I said, shaking his hand. He was built like his son, but took better care of himself. "And I've got a deal for you."

"A deal?"

"I'm a private investigator, sir," I said, "and I may have evidence that your son didn't shove his girlfriend off the balcony."

"Goddamn it," Butch said. "What the hell's going on?"

"Who is this man?" Biddle wanted to know.

Butch and Claudia both started talking at the same time.

"Shut the fuck up, Butch," I said. Biddle glanced at Claudia, then shook his head. "Did you hear what I said, sir?"

"You're some kind of private detective, right? And willing to let me have this supposed evidence for a price, right? What is this? Some kind of shakedown?"

"I am a private investigator, sir; I leave

128

the blackmail to the lawyers," I said. "Even Butch, who hates me, will verify that." Butch nodded blankly, his eyes following the winged dollar bills flying into the darkness. "This can be yours," I said, then slid the photograph over to him.

Biddle glanced at the photo. In the background, his son's face was clearly visible over his shoulder as he held the screen door open. Fifteen feet away from Carrie Fraizer, who had just begun her fatal fall.

"How did you get this?"

"Pure accident," I said, then reached over to take it out of his hand.

"No accident is ever pure," he said.

"But this *was* an accident," I said, "and has nothing to do with your son."

"What do you want?" he asked, a businessman to the core.

"I want to talk to him tomorrow morning before he knows about the picture," I said. "Nothing more. Afterward, Butch gets the picture and a deposition."

"You know, Mr. Whatever-the-fuck-your-name-is," Biddle said, "I can have that picture taken away from you."

"You may want to think hard about that, sir; maybe even consult with your lawyer here before you think about something like that," I said as I set fire to the photograph.

"He's a lot tougher than he looks," Claudia crooned.

"This is a copy," I said. "My lawyer has the original and the negative. Chain of evidence is solid."

Biddle laughed loudly, throwing his head back. His dental work looked as if it had cost more than my second car. "I love you tough-guy cowboys and your bullshit," he said, smiling. "You've got a deal. Maybe a jolt of jail time will make Arnold think about his life," he said, but he really didn't believe it. Then to Butch, he barked, "Make it happen, son."

"Yes, sir," Butch said.

"And give me a ride back to the hotel," Biddle said. "Now."

"Yes, sir," Butch said, then turned to Claudia. "Get the check," he said.

Biddle stood up quickly and stepped over to me. I shook his hand. "Thank you, sir," he said.

"Butch would have gotten your son off," I said. "I'm sure."

Biddle raised his eyebrows in wonder, then led the fawning lawyer past the just desserts tray.

"You want another drink, Sonny?" Claudia said from across the table. "I've got the firm's gold card." She was chuckling gently as she waved at the waiter. "Lorne's going to try to kill you," she said.

"I'm laughing so hard I'm wetting my britches," I said. "Sure, I'll have another drink," I added. "Wife's out of town, so another cocktail to drive away the loneliness sounds fine." Claudia and I had always almost been friends.

"You're a shit, CW," Claudia said. "But a nice shit. I need a ride. My boss seems to have abandoned me in the search for foul Mammon," she added, then smiled. When she smiled, she was lovely in a predatory sort of way.

"Sure," I said. "But you have to promise not to attack me this time."

She promised. But it was a promise from an Italian lady lawyer from Butte.

It started with a simple refusal to follow her into her house for a cup of coffee or a drink. Then she wanted a hug, then a good-night kiss. Moments later I was defending not just my virtue, but also my life. She was as agile as a monkey and as strong as a great ape.

"Thanks for the lift," Claudia said suddenly, moving back to her side of the Taurus. "And the wrestling match, too. You're not in bad shape for a guy your age."

"Thanks," I said, sighing.

"I just wanted you to know what you're missing," she said. "Good luck," she added, then climbed out and walked slowly toward her porch light, giving me the full effect of her high heels, long legs, and swinging hips. I watched in spite of myself. She'd wrestled the whiskey right out of me.

When I walked down into the Goat, the Saturday night dining crowd had finished their after-dinner drinks, and the usual clutch of kids who worked at the place had migrated to a folkrock Irish band playing down at the Deuce, so except for a pair of guys who looked like Bible salesmen and a sullen Johnny Raymond, who gave me his best long hard look, the bar was almost empty.

"You get mugged, Sughrue?" he sneered.

"What?"

"You're bleeding at the mouth," Raymond said.

I picked up a bar napkin, scrubbed my mouth, then said, "Nope, mud wrestling with a lady lawyer from Butte." I tossed the lipstick-stained napkin on the bar down toward Johnny Raymond, then walked to the other end as Steve came out of the cooler.

Behind me, I heard a muttered curse, then the clack of an empty bottle on the oak slates. When I turned, Raymond tossed a twenty on the bar, then stormed out, the smeared bar napkin crumpled in his hand.

"What the fuck was that about?" Steve said.

"Who the hell knows," I said.

"He's been a prick all night," he said. "I think his new job is gettin' to him." I sat at the end of the bar. At least I could have a cigarette. Fuck, I was smoking again. Hard-core. I promised myself that when this idiot case was over, I would make Mac find a drug to make me quit again. Steve went back into the cooler, where he had been stocking and packing a bowl of weed before he cleaned up the bar and closed.

"Hey, boss, want a hit?" he said, holding the door to the cooler open.

"Can I bum a doobie?" I said.

"I thought you'd quit," he said, then glanced at the cigarette smoking in the ashtray and the half-empty pack in front of me.

"Some stranger left it here," I said.

But he just smiled, shucked the cellophane off the pack, and disappeared behind the bar for a moment. He came back with a thumb-sized bomber in the wrapper, stuck it in my windbreaker pocket, then poured me a large Macallan's. Living in small places had its benefits.

"Can I have one of the stranger's smokes?" he said as he picked up the pack of American Spirits. Steve cleaned and carried trash while I smoked and drank. He came back from his last trip to the Dumpster and asked, "It's still early. You want another one while I finish stocking?" It was his bar, so he could stay as long as he wanted.

"No, thanks," I said. "I've got some un-finished chores."

"Be cool," he said.

"Hey man," I said before he walked away. "You catch any part of the conversa-tion that Charlie Marshall, George Paul, and Ken Cole had last night?"

"They were talking about taxes, I think," he said. "But, if I remember correctly, we were being slammed that night, so I couldn't really tell."

"Taxes?" I said.

"Death and taxes," he said. "Be cool," he added.

"If only I knew how, man," I said, then grabbed a six-pack and went to feed the cats.

Six

After cat chores, I opened one of the beers, fired up the joint, then sat on the small couch in the Ritters' television nook while the white Persians settled into their usual places as I surfed the channels with the Mute on until I found a black-and-white movie. *Now, Voyager.* That seemed safe. I didn't remember any gunfire or howling. Bette Davis seemed to smoke a lot, though. And deeply, as if it were a sexual experience. It made me want a cigarette, but Chloe didn't seem to want to give me my hand back. She had my thumb in her mouth, gently, and shook it for a second, then settled in for the movie, gnawing on my thumbnail as if it were a Gummi Bear. Charmaine decided my neck was clean and started on my ear. In spite of the residual angry vibes that seemed to fill the huge house, and in spite of my own awful memories of that first moment when I'd stepped into the house, I was oddly peaceful on the couch with the cats.

When I dug into my pocket for my cell phone, I felt the tangle of leader, duct tape, and dust, but left it in the pocket. I called Whitney's cell, but she didn't answer, so I left a message. Bette Davis had nearly convinced me that nicotine was the gateway drug to heaven when the cell phone chirped in my pocket. The cats disappeared so quickly and quietly that I realized they must have been trained to flee when the telephone rang. By Charity Ritter, I assumed, the sort of fat woman whose social life took place mainly over the telephone.

"What are you doing?" Whit asked when I answered the call.

"You wouldn't believe me."

"With you, I'd believe almost anything," she said tiredly.

"I'm sitting on the Ritters' couch with their cats, watching Bette Davis chew the scenery, then roll it up and smoke it."

"On the job again, huh?" she said. "You're hard to get hold of, CW. How are you? I heard what happened."

"I'm hanging in there," I said. "Sort of."

"What's wrong?" she said.

"I found another dead body," I said.

"Oh, hell, honey. Are you all right?"

"I'm fine."

"You're not . . . ?" she asked. *Going crazy again?* was what she didn't say. After I'd been shot, I spent a long time filled with paranoid depression, terrified. In that state, I had food, water, and weapons cached all the way across West Texas to the Mexican border, ready to pick up my family and flee on foot if the *contrabandistas* came after me again. Until I went after them. "You're not stoned, are you?"

Wrong question. "I'm fine," I repeated.

"You haven't dealt with it yet, right?" she said. "Maybe you can talk to Mac."

"That's how I got in this shit," I said. "But I promise to deal with it." Then I added, "I hate to tell you this, but the new body belonged to Carrie Fraizer."

"Oh, my god," she groaned. "She was such a lovely woman. What happened?"

"It was an accident," I said. "She leaned on a balcony rail behind the Pacific Northwest. It broke. She fell six stories."

"I'm so sorry," she whispered.

"Why don't you have a couple of drinks?" I said.

"Thanks," she whispered. "But I just had an endless dinner with a client. And I've got to start looking at schools for Les in the morning anyway."

"Good luck," I said, but didn't mean it. I couldn't imagine Les in a private school. "I'll see you shortly." She did say that she loved me in a soft sad voice that hit me right in the gut, then hung up.

As I sat silently on the couch, Charmaine came from behind the television console, the other half of the broken ceramic frog in her mouth. This one was tangled in a bundle of clear fishing leader. I got off the couch and wrestled the console out of the corner so I could see what was behind it. A hole in the plaster and lath for the television cables, lined with white cat hairs. I went into the kitchen to pick up a flashlight I'd seen when I was looking for a drink. When I shined the flashlight into the hole, I was looking directly into the basement, so I went back to the kitchen and down the stairs to see what I had missed on my first search.

The tiled laundry room, a modern internal addition, was bright and clean, with a line of heat lamps above a clothesline, but the rest of the basement was full of the typical detritus of nearly a hundred years of occupants, as well as a fine layer of dust. Cat tracks led from near the bottom of the stud beside the hole behind the television to a canvas basket beneath a laundry chute. I'd missed that. The sheets and towels from the upstairs bedroom in the basket showed circular depressions where I suspected the girls had enjoyed secret naps. There were no bundles of leader, though. Just a few tiny metallic green ceramic chips. I went back up to the kitchen for a couple of Ziploc bags. I put the fishing leader into one bag, then went to the upstairs bathroom for a pair of tweezers. Down in the basement, I picked up as many chips as I could find without disturbing the laundry.

Then I spent the rest of the night trying to find out where the girls stashed their trophies. With the occasional stop for a beer or a catnap. Both girls followed me faithfully, as if I were searching for a mouse snack for them. But they didn't help. I finally found the two halves of the frog behind the last shelf of books I searched, along with a dozen mouse tails, a squirrel's skull, and a mummified garter snake.

"You girls are a wonder," I said to them as I put the frog halves into another Ziploc bag, and they seemed to agree. I wasn't sure why I was treating the ceramic pieces like evidence, but I thought I should.

I found an unopened can of French pâté in the pantry and gave it to the intrepid hunters, then went home for a much deserved nap before my one o'clock meeting at the county jail.

★ ★ ★

It took a long time to convince Butch and Mr. Biddle that I should be allowed to talk to Arno privately; then it took a call to Raymond to persuade the deputy who ran the jail to let me see the prisoner alone. In the middle of our call, he put me on hold because his call-waiting was beeping. Afterward, he sounded quite cheerful when he asked me to hand the telephone to the jailer.

"So who the hell are you?" Arno asked me when I stepped into the interrogation room, shaking his thick, dirty hair at me. In the old days, the jailers would have shaved his head.

"I'm the guy who just might save your ass," I said. "Didn't your father tell you that?"

"Hey, dude, my old man said I was supposed to talk to you just like you were him," Arno said, then paused. "Well, fuck you and the jackass you rode in on."

I sat down anyway and asked, "Why was Carrie seeing a shrink?"

"Fuck you," he repeated, glaring at me. "None of your goddamned business," he said, then clammed up, so I gave him one of my cards and let him. Before I could stand up or even regret the waste of time, the jailer came through the door, motioned me out, then told Arno that he had been kicked loose.

Out in the hallway, Biddle stopped me. "I'm sorry," he said. "Is our deal still on?"

"Sure," I said. "You make bail?"

"I'm sorry," he repeated, ignoring my question. "Why is it that the baby of the family goes bad so often?"

"Ask a shrink," I said, then turned to Butch. "Musselwhite has the picture and the negative in his safe."

"I'll still need a deposition," he said. "My office at ten Monday morning?"

"If I'm still alive," I said, then asked him if he had made bail, but nobody answered me, so I tried to leave it at that. But I'd never learned how to mind my own business. I walked across the street to lean against my rented car and have a cigarette, hoping to see where they went after Arno got kicked loose.

I should have known something was up when Pete Morgan showed up, the television news crews right behind him, with Raymond appearing a few moments later. When the Biddles and Butch came out the door, they were met by a clot of reporters there to witness Raymond's arrest of Arno

Biddle for capital murder. I stayed as far away from the circus as I could, but Arno spotted me and screamed, "That guy over there! He knows I didn't do it!" But the officers kept cuffing him anyway, then locked him into the back of their unit to take him downtown to book him again.

When it cleared out, I followed Johnny Raymond for a few blocks, then called his personal cell phone. "What the hell's going on?" I said.

"Who the hell is this?" he asked, chuckling like a broken-down farmer who had just plowed up a nest of baby rabbits, then he hung up on me.

I drove home to wait for the airport shuttle to pick me up, but my cell phone rang as I pulled into the driveway. The last person I expected. Arno.

"Mr. Sughrue," he said, his voice trembling. "I don't know who you are or what this has to do with anything, but I want to hire you."

"I've already got a client," I said, "and you didn't want to talk to me."

"Fuck that," he said, ignoring me. "Carrie never said, but I knew she was seeing a shrink to get up the courage to dump me. She said I was too much like her fucking father —"

"That speaks to motive, doesn't it?" I said.

"Hell," he whispered wetly, as if weeping. "I'm the one who should have been seeing a shrink. Man, I loved that woman. She could have left anytime she wanted to. I swear on my mother's head. Anybody who knows . . . who knew us can tell you that."

"Maybe I'll look into your case for a bit," I said. I didn't like the kid, but he sounded convincing.

"And there's this other thing, man," he said quickly, almost wailing. "I don't understand it. But that was my corner; that's the only place she'd let me smoke a bowl," he added quickly. I could understand that. "She never leaned on that part of the rail. Never. Said it stunk like a cowflop campfire. I don't know. Hell, maybe somebody was trying to kill me. I just don't fucking know."

"What was she doing home that time of day?" I asked.

"I don't know that, either," he said softly. "She came home madder than a wet hen, found some lingerie under my pillow, and started shouting at me about some chick whose name I'd never heard before. Hell, man, I don't know what's going on."

I heard rustling in the background as the cops informed Arno that his time was up. "Help me, man," he squealed just before the line went dead.

He'd wasted his single telephone call on me. I didn't know what any of it meant, but I sat on my front steps waiting for my ride out of town.

"What the hell was that race car bullshit about, Sughrue?" Mac asked breathlessly as we stood atop MacDonald Pass two days later, listening to the cooling engine click as if the little BMW were counting off the hard miles. Mac's flat cap had blown away somewhere outside Ovando, and the high-altitude sun drew beads of sweat out of his pale scalp. His face looked wind-blown, disheveled, his eyes a bit too big and too bright, his burly eyebrows un-combed. After he had picked me up in Lorna's little roadster at the Missoula air-port, we had popped over to Highway 200, then pushed hard up the winding two-lane all the way to the top of the pass. He hadn't said a word the whole way. Maybe he had been holding his breath. "I always knew you had a death wish," he huffed, "but I didn't know it included me."

"Believe me, old buddy," I said as I

grabbed a small beer cooler out of the trunk, "that didn't have a fucking thing to do with a death wish. That was an affirmation of life, man. Think of it as fishing for *fun!*"

"Forgive me if I missed the fun part," he said. I offered him a beer, but he declined, saying, "You drink, my friend. I'm driving home."

"No problem," I said.

"So are you going to tell me what this is about?"

"Quite frankly, I don't know where to start," I admitted.

"Try the beginning," he suggested softly.

"Or how much to tell you."

"Tell me everything."

"You can't see the plains from here," I said, pointing east. "But you can feel them. The Great Plains. The Great American Desert, actually. The Big Empty. You can't see it but you can sure as hell feel it, right?"

"Right," Mac said. "Growing up out there was like growing up on a frozen ocean. I always wanted a house by the living one; that's why I painted them, but what the hell —"

"You're missing the point," I inter-

145

rupted. "I can't see a thing that makes any sense, but I know something's there."

"You know how much I appreciate your taking on the job . . ."

"I know something is wrong, Mac, but I don't know what," I said. "The clouds are different out there over the Big Empty."

"And?"

"When's Garfield Ritter getting out of the hospital?"

"Not for a while. They did a bypass Friday."

"I don't have anything but a dumb hunch, a bunch of unexplained junk, and a couple of worthless witnesses," I said, "but I'm fairly sure that his wife didn't kill herself."

"How sure?"

"You couldn't take it to the bank," I said. "But you could buy a round of drinks with it."

"Who are these worthless witnesses?"

"Don't ask," I said. "The other odd thing is that I've got a photo of Arno Biddle with his back turned, going in the door fifteen feet away from Carrie Fraizer as she was falling."

"And?"

"Earlier today Raymond arrested him for capital murder," I said. "I don't have any idea what he's got, but it must be fairly solid. He invited the press to the arrest. This guy really wants to succeed at his job."

"That's crazy."

"Want to hear the craziest part?" I said. "Even before I searched the Ritter place, he was convinced that Mrs. Ritter's death wasn't a suicide. And he asked for my help."

"He asked for *your* help? Christ, he hates you."

"True enough," I said.

"Whatever reason could he have for thinking that the death wasn't a suicide? I don't understand," Mac said.

"Well, partner, if you don't understand, who the hell does?"

"I don't know," he said, then absently took a beer out of the cooler. As he drank it, wordlessly, his silence deepened as he drew further and further into himself.

I walked over to look at the sign marking the pass, took a leak into two oceans, then pulled out my cell phone to try to call Whit, but I was either out of range, out of battery charge, or simply out of luck. I went back to the car, grabbed another beer, settled into the passenger seat, then waited for Mac to come back.

"How was the visit with Whit?" he asked as he settled behind the wheel.

"Don't ask," I said. I'd been to happier funerals.

He didn't speak until we were parked in the sunset shadows in front of my house.

"Thanks for the ride," I said.

"What are you going to do?" he asked, breaking his silence finally.

"I've got a chore, I guess," I said.

"Maybe I'm wrong," he said. "Maybe there's some kind of blackmail going on here that I don't know anything about."

"What are *you* going to do?" I asked.

"Keep eating my liver, I guess," he said, his voice deep and soft as if he carried the burden and pain of all the poor mad people in the world. "I'll just keep gnawing away at my liver until it's all gone."

When he left, I drove over to take care of the Ritters' cats, then came home to wander through the house until the emptiness got to me, so I went out to the office. I sliced some sausage and cheese, cracked a beer, then found a black-and-white movie I'd never seen before — some Gothic groaner with Gene Tierney and Vincent Price — then leaned back in my La-Z-Boy and popped one of Mac's little white sleeping pills.

When I woke with daylight streaming into my window the next morning, it seemed that I had dreamed the same thing over and over all night. Whatever it was, I couldn't remember it exactly. But I woke with the taste of blood and cordite in my mouth. I wasn't happy about that.

I started calling Johnny Raymond every hour on the hour, enduring his laughing hang ups. Until I got his voice mail. "Tildon's Corners at three o'clock this afternoon," I said. "I'm in a bad mood, so show up, you dumb son of a bitch, or my next call is to Pete Morgan at the paper. I need to talk to you someplace out of your jurisdiction, asshole."

The bar was dark and the parking lot empty when I got there, but the door was unlocked. Johnny Raymond sat at the bar in work clothes and scuffed boots. As I stepped inside, Freddy locked the door behind me. Raymond came off his stool in a rush, his large face burning. I knew he had been a good cop and suspected he'd been a good marine, but he wasn't much of a bar fighter. When I got tired of his swinging and missing or slamming his large fists against my arms and shoulders, I hit him in the throat hard enough to kill an ordinary man. He hit the floor, gagging until he passed out.

"Is he dead?" Freddy squeaked from the door.

"I hope so," I said. "What's that in your hand? Your dick?"

Freddy looked at the short bat in his hand as if he'd never seen it before. "I told him you didn't look like the runnin' type," he said, then pitched the bat behind a bank of keno machines. "But I didn't think you'd kill him," he said.

"He's too fucking dumb to die," I said. "What the hell was this about? Did he think I fucked his girlfriend? Or do you people fuck your cows and cousins?"

"I don't think he's got a girlfriend," he said, either ignoring or not understanding the insult. "His wife's awfully churchy, you know, and she probably didn't appreciate your language. He's my first cousin and all, but he gets a little more batshit every year. It ain't too widely known, but he beat a guy half to death when they were on vacation in Mexico. Took all his money to pay it off."

I went around the bar to fill a pitcher with ice water and got a couple of beers. I dumped the ice water over Raymond's face. A couple of times between beers.

Finally, he climbed to his feet and stumbled to the restroom. He came back a few minutes later to flop on the stool beside me.

"You could have killed me," he croaked like a man who'd smoked Camel Straights all his life. "That would have been wonderful."

"I'm not going to apologize," I said. "I had to put you down, Johnny. You're too big and strong to handle any other way. Hell, I'm going to have to lean over to brush my teeth tomorrow."

"Then I guess I don't have to apologize, either," he said.

"Right. We wouldn't want to presume too deeply on our friendship."

"What the hell do you want?" he growled.

"I'm going to guess that when the pathologist took another look at Charity Ritter, he found enough Valium and alcohol in her to stun an ox, plus some other shit — ketamine, maybe — a needle mark somewhere, in the hairline or the belly button or the rectum, and some very thin bruise lines in her armpits."

"How the hell did you know that?" he asked.

"A couple of cats told me some shit."

"You're just guessing."

"Enough of a guess to keep the case open?"

"There's no case right now," he said. "The people I answer to don't see it that way."

"And I thought you only answered to God himself," I said. "You're sure that Biddle is good for Carrie Fraizer?" I asked.

"That's not part of our deal."

"Well, partner," I said, "you know what I know. Arno is clean. I'll be in touch."

"Don't bother," he said to my back as I walked away.

I went by the Ritters' to leave plenty of dry food out for the girls, then took off to see my family again. Maybe I hadn't stayed away long enough, or I had picked the wrong time to visit, because I was back in Meriwether the next night, when I slept in the La-Z-Boy again, drugged but not dreamless.

Late the next morning after a lazy breakfast and a stint of lackluster bill paying, I dug the pages out of the office safe, then went back to work. The name on the next page was Sheila Miller. Tuesday and Thursday mornings at seven. As far as I could find out on the computer, Ms. Miller lived in the Wagon Wheel Mobile Home Park, about ten miles west of town. She was the single mother of a seventeen-year-old high school senior named Marcy and worked three jobs. A personal health care aide in the daytime, she also delivered the *Avalanche-Express* every morning. Then she spent three nights a week just down the road from her place as a dancer-cum-bartender at The Phone Booth, a truck-stop paradise for longhaul drivers and other bits of random lust, a place that sported overpriced drinks, overrated tits, and soundproof telephone booths. A cursory search through courthouse records didn't turn up a marriage or divorce, or a birth record for her daughter. I couldn't picture myself hanging around a group home, a topless joint, or following a paper carrier through the predawn morning. So Sheila would have to wait for another day.

I put that one aside and looked at the next page. Mrs. George Paul. Georgia Germaine Paul, known as GG, a quiet, tall former nurse who looked a great deal like her husband: too many teeth in a mouth too wide, too much forehead, and jug ears that not even her hair could hide. She didn't have a beard, though, just a crop of wispy bleached hairs on her upper lip. I hoped she was still in Seattle because she knew me, and I just couldn't face hiding under a cap and sunglasses again.

The next three names were a complete mystery. Angie Cole. Janeanne Reynolds. Elwood Studer. Mr. Studer had a one o'clock, Monday, Wednesday and Friday. I thought I'd start there. I didn't even bother finding out who he was; just drove over to Mac's office to wait for whoever came out of the back door at two o'clock that Wednesday afternoon.

A soft, flabby man, seemingly aimless, stepped slowly out of Mac's back door just after two. Elwood Studer, I assumed. He looked around as if death, disaster, or personal humiliation waited behind the hedges, and he walked like a man who had just discovered his feet. He climbed into a new gray Buick and drove slowly away. I followed him into the flats of Hell Roaring Canyon, where he pulled into the driveway of a three-car garage beside one of the oldest and largest houses in the neighborhood, a rambling brick mansion that took up a small block with the remains of a small orchard behind it. A tall white-haired woman leaned on a cane with both hands in front of the garage door, a woman as hard as Elwood was soft. She had a tan, wrinkled face; a nose that could have split logs; and a grim mouth that wouldn't have smiled even after the kindling was cut and stacked. She lit into Elwood before he could get out of the car. I didn't have to wonder why he was seeing Mac or how he paid for the sessions.

In my guise as a real estate scout, I checked around the neighborhood. Elwood's mom had a reputation for chasing small children off her lawn with her cane, for accusing neighbors of stealing fruit from her backyard orchard, and was suspected of poisoning cats and dogs who wandered onto her property. Elwood had never been involved with anything more nefarious than the Boy Scouts or the stock market. He spent his days either working in the yard or watching soap operas with his mom, his nights doing jigsaw puzzles with her, and, after his mother went to bed, playing the market on the Internet. As far as the neighbors knew, he only left the house three times a week for what he claimed were allergy shots. I wondered how he'd found the bottom to call Mac the first time. And I was fairly sure he had never broken into anybody's office or hired anybody to do it.

It was past five by the time I finished, too late to pick up Janeanne Reynolds when she left Mac's office. She saw him three days a week at four. Nobody seemed to be home at Charlie Marshall's house, or at George Paul's when I drove past. The machine picked up at Mac's office, he wasn't answering his cell phone, and Lorna said that she didn't expect him home until seven. So there I was, a terrifically expensive PI with nothing to do. I thought about drinking, but decided to put that off until good dark, which was hours away. I went into my makeshift gym, lifted for a while, worked the bags — light and heavy — until my arms dragged, then showered, then idled again. Finally I called St. Vincent's to see if the professor was receiving visitors.

He was receiving, but not happily.

I could tell that he wasn't receiving visitors happily the third time he raised his flaking eyebrows and said, "Once again, sir, who are you?"

"Dr. MacKinderick's friend," I said. "I've been taking care of your cats."

"Those irritating little freeloaders," he said. "At least I'll be rid of those pests."

"What's that mean?" I asked.

"The first thing I'm going to do when I get home is hire somebody to take them to the pound," he said. "If I felt better, believe me, I'd strangle the little shits with my bare hands."

"You want me to take care of them?" I asked without thinking.

"How much will you charge?"

"Part of the regular service," I said. "I'll bill Dr. MacKinderick."

"Who are you again?"

"It doesn't matter," I said. "Just think of me as the guy who's going to do you a favor. Of course, I want a favor in return."

"What's that?"

"You recognize this?" I said, pulling the Ziploc bag holding the two halves of the broken frog out of my jacket pocket.

"Where did you get that?" he demanded. "How did it get broken?"

"You recognize it?" I said.

Ritter looked at me as if I were an idiot, then blushed. "It belongs on my bedside table. It's like a worry stone. I picked it up in China. I sometimes hold it when I'm reading before I go to sleep. Charity always made fun of . . . Did she . . . ? Oh, no, I guess not. I forgot."

I knew there wasn't a chance in hell that the killer had left a fingerprint on the frog, but I put it back in my pocket anyway. "Maybe I can have it fixed," I said, then started out the door. But I stopped to ask, "You don't happen to be a fisherman, are you?" He looked confused. "No? I didn't think so."

Ritter wanted to know who I was again, but when I didn't answer, he grabbed the telephone, and when I left, he was shouting at Mac's answering machine. I found myself thinking more kindly about Charity Ritter than I had in the past.

If I was going to move the girls, I needed a couple of cat carriers, so I headed for the mall. On the way I called Whit. She wasn't answering, so I left word on her voice mail to let her know that I had finally broken down and decided that we needed a cat. Two cats. Two girl-detective cats. I hoped it would be all right.

After I scored two cat carriers, it occurred to me to drop into the Ginger Snap Dragon, hoping Little Davy was working. He was dealing with the dinner rush, so I nursed a couple of beers while I waited for a chance to talk with him.

"Were you working last Friday?" I asked him when he finally paused long enough to chat.

"Sure," he said. "Is this about Carrie?"

"The police have already been here, right?" I said.

"You ain't workin' an open case, are you, Sughrue?" he said, grinning. Thanks to television, everybody on the street knew more about my job than I did.

"Just curious," I said.

"Yeah, right," he answered. "I took the call. It was a girl. A very young girl by the sound of her voice. She asked for Carrie. They talked a minute, no more, then Carrie grabbed her purse and stormed out. That's all I know, man, and unless you're working for Arno's lawyer, I didn't even say that."

"Thanks."

"I've got your beer," he said.

It took thirty minutes of *Jane Eyre* and two cans of pâté with truffles to lure the girls into the cages. All the way to my house they howled like mad women racing the winds of unrequited love across the moors. I hadn't heard back from Whit, so I stashed the litter box, the cat food, and the girls in my office, found them a romantic black-and-white movie, then sat down. My client wouldn't return my calls; my wife wouldn't return my calls; and I didn't know what the hell was going on. But I couldn't sit around watching movies with cats all my life, so I hooked it up and braved the damp, depressing climes of The Phone Booth.

For a twenty-dollar bill and a promise not to beat him half to death, Lamar, the bartender, an old if not fond acquaintance of mine, stuffed the bill in his pocket, smirked, and told me, "Sheila's the ugly one with the big tits. She'll be up in a while. Calls herself Sherlynn." I took my two warm Rainiers into the lounge, my two-drink minimum fulfilled.

Meriwether wasn't on the high-dollar Las Vegas-LA-SeaTac topless dancer circuit. More like the low-rent Tacoma-Yakima-Boogertown one. So I didn't expect much in the way of prime meat. I wasn't disappointed. I'd worked in topless bars when I was younger. Even then, I found them sad, ugly places. The last thirty years hadn't made them any better. So when the bartender announced "the lovely Sherlynn" and cued up Meatloaf's "I'd Do Anything for Love," I didn't know what to think. An odd choice of music for a topless dancer, I thought. When Sheila Miller came out, the small crowd of truckers growled, and I was even more confused.

She had an ill-fitting straw-colored wig,

too little forehead, too much nose for tiny eyes set much too close together, a small pursed tube of a mouth that never smiled, and no chin at all, but she had the moves of a professional dancer and a body worthy of pagan sacrifice. She seemed to love the music and gave herself completely to the song. But at the same time, she exuded waves of contempt and raw sexuality, a dichotomy, I assumed, that had probably destroyed her life. I could understand why she needed Mac's guidance and approval. Hell, I was aroused so quickly, I was embarrassed, so I finished my beers quickly, then left the lounge.

As I passed the bar, Lamar beckoned me over. "Hey, Sughrue," he hissed, "for another two twenties, I can talk the lady into a private lap dance."

I started to say something ugly, then decided maybe I could find out something if I spent some time in a small room with Sheila. But it was another bad idea. She wouldn't stop dancing her hard, heavy breasts in my face, and she avoided even the most general question, fluting vague answers in her tiny, soft voice. The bouncer wouldn't step far enough away, either. So all I proved was the weakness of my flesh.

Embarrassed again by the ease with which she had aroused me, I paid up, tipped, then slunk out of the close room like an egg-sucking dog.

On the way past the bar, Lamar motioned me over, whispering wetly, "For a couple hundred, Sughrue, I can arrange something even more private." I grabbed Lamar, my thumb deep into his armpit, squeezing until he squeaked.

"Don't ever say my name again, you shit weasel, don't even think it."

"What the hell's wrong —" he started to say, but a little more pressure cut off the words.

I couldn't have answered the question anyway, so I just left.

Seven

I hadn't been lodged in a dark corner booth at the Goat bar more than five minutes when the Marshalls and Pauls came in from the Missoula airport and gathered at the booth behind me. The women, I assumed, had just arrived on the often late last flight from Seattle. The women were rollicking drunk, the men surly. Charlie and George had probably been sitting in the dull, uncomfortable airport bar for a couple of hours, sucking down bourbons as they waited for the delayed flight, while the women dallied happily in the Crown Room at SeaTac. I was too close to them not to overhear their loud conversation clearly

A striking young couple draped in black leather with ink-black hair shrouding their metal-studded faces came into the bar, then sat at a table beside us. They looked as if they were a couple of rock stars who had wandered off MTV and into the wrong bar. A string of young dandies lined up to buy them drinks.

The wives didn't know what they wanted

to drink. The husbands grumbled while the wives dithered. Finally, the women decided on gin and tonics, then changed their minds before the cocktail waitress got to the bar. "Frozen margaritas!" the women shouted in unison. George muttered a curse, stormed to the bar, insisted on two bourbons before the bartender started the frozen drinks. Back at the table with the drinks, George and Charlie clinked glasses, ignoring the women. It went on like that for some time. They argued about what kind of snacks to have; complained about the price of Seattle hotel rooms and the constant construction downtown. The women switched to stingers, the men to Wild Turkey; the hot wings grew cold. Bitter laughter garnished with cynical bitching.

Then disaster. During one of those unexplained silences that strike through noisy crowds as suddenly and unexpectedly as heat lightning, George said, his voice deep with amusement, "If you goddamned women charged more for your blow jobs, your shopping trips wouldn't be so fucking expensive."

The silence in the bar spread wide and deep, like a crack in the earth's crust.

"Bastard!" Ellen screamed, then threw

her glass into George's face, grabbed her purse, and rushed out. Followed shortly by the punk-rocker girls as their band of hopeful suitors dispersed like foam peanuts in stiff wind.

Everyone at the table sat very still. The glass had opened a small cut on the bridge of George's nose. The drink and the blood dribbled down his face and through his beard. Without wiping his face, George said very calmly to Charlie, "Hey, buddy, maybe you should monitor your wife's drug intake a bit more carefully." GG shook her head slightly, then handed her husband a napkin. He wiped his face, finished his drink, then stood up, holding the napkin to his nose. Charlie and GG started to stand up, but George motioned them back to their chairs, then waved at the cocktail waitress for another round. "She'll go home and cry herself to sleep, right?" he said. "She left us afoot, right? So let's have a couple of drinks while we wait for the taxi, okay?" Then he walked toward the restrooms while the other two sat as if paralyzed.

GG murmured to Charlie, "She's been seeing this shaman, you know, one of those Native American women, and she's been teaching Ellen to chant her way into some sort of spiritual center of peace." Then she paused, "And it really seemed to be working. All the way back from Seattle. She came home as if she were in a great dream. Now all this happened. I don't know what to think."

"I hope George is all right," Charlie said.

"George is happy," GG murmured. "Raucous emotions turn him on. It'll be a rough night all around."

"I'm sorry," Charlie said, as if it might be his fault. He grimaced as if expecting a box of hot coals in his lap.

After George came back from the restroom with a piece of toilet paper stuck to the bridge of his nose, everything was quiet for a long while. I thought I might beat Charlie Marshall's cab home. Perhaps the ensuing conversation might be interesting and loud enough for me to hear outside the house. The Marshalls lived just off the Ridgeway Golf Course in the foothills of the Bluestones south of town, and I knew I could slink up to the side of the house. I waited until George told the bartender to call a cab, then I settled up and took off.

The Marshalls' house had been built into the hillside, two stories stacked above a daylight basement where Charlie had his woodworking shop beside the garage. As I drove past the house, I saw the Lincoln Navigator parked crookedly in the driveway in front of the closed garage doors. Except for a dim glow behind the shutters of the workshop, the house was completely dark. Taking a chance, I parked two houses down the street, then slipped through the yards and up the driveway to the south side of the house and knelt behind a shrub beside a dirty basement shop window.

After a few minutes, I could hear faint music drifting out of the shop, something ethereal and exotic, like a snake charmer's flute. And under the music, an even fainter hum that I couldn't identify, and a low chant, slowly repeated, softly compelling. I sat down, leaned against the south-facing concrete wall, and waited for Charlie's cab to arrive, wondering if I could get away with a cigarette, but decided against it, quickly caught by the flute and the soothing rhythms.

Sitting there in the midnight dark, the sun's warmth seeping out of the concrete into my back, I tried to unravel the past ten days. Nothing made any sense. Why would anybody stage such an elaborate death for Charity Ritter? Unless my joking guess was right. Somebody wanted Ritter to see what he thought was his wife's suicide. And what did Johnny Raymond know about Carrie Fraizer's death that I didn't? I could ask Claudia Lucchesi if I could catch her in the daylight. Too much blood, too many drinks, too little sleep. And my woman was a thousand miles away . . .

I would never know if I drifted into sleep or just into a confused stupor, never know if it was the arrival of the taxicab or the flurry of gunshots that brought me back to reality. The basement window flared with the muzzle flashes, and the walls shook with the blasts and the thuds of the rounds into the ceiling and walls. Taxicab doors slammed loudly from the street. I rolled to my knees and leaned over into the window well to scrub at the dirty film covering the pane with my handkerchief.

Except for a pair of black lace gloves, Ellen's naked body was as pale as the inside of an apple in the dim light as she swayed to the music, standing next to the humming band saw, the metal teeth a blur. When the slide on the semiautomatic in her right hand locked back, she took it away from the side of her head, looked at it as if she didn't know what it was. Then with a terrible motion both graceful and inevitable, like a move learned from an ancient religious dance, Ellen swept her right arm into the saw blade. The hand popped off just above the wrist with a tear of flesh, a snap of bone, and the blood splashing like water from a hose. I couldn't take my eyes off the hand as it bounced off the saw table, then out of sight, still holding the pistol. Darkness flashed across my vision. Then Ellen swayed languidly, like a poplar bending in the wind, back into the whirring blade to slice off the other hand.

Suddenly, the workshop was full of drunken people screaming. As I scrambled to my feet, thinking to go help, jerked out of my stupor by the horror, I tripped over my feet or slipped in the grass or something, then crashed forehead first into the basement wall. The last thing I remembered was a sharp sting in the back of my neck, as if I had cracked a cervical vertebra or torn a muscle.

I was out long enough for the police and ambulance to arrive. When I struggled to my knees, I was still groggy, but through the clear space in the basement window, I could see that Ellen was being taken out on a gurney, Charlie was slumped in shock, and George was shouting drunkenly at a patrol cop. I found a bloody scrape and a bone-deep gash in my forehead. Much dizzier than I should have been, I sat back down to lean against the wall until I seemed to have my wits halfway about me, then I called Johnny Raymond on the cell phone. Probably the first smart thing I'd done all day.

Even with Raymond not pressing too hard and Musselwhite standing behind me, it was noon the next day before the police kicked me loose into the ER. The doctor cleaned out the scrape and stitched up the furrow in my face. He said he didn't like the way my eyes looked. I told him it looked pretty much the same from the inside, so I took a cab down to the station to sign my statement, and went home in a cab, too. I didn't seem to remember where my car had been left.

That night while I had been in an interrogation room, Ellen Marshall had died of blood loss and shock.

The next day, Mac placed Charlie in a rest facility outside of Whitefish, supplied me with enough tranquilizers and pain pills to keep me fairly normal, then he canceled his appointments for a week, and he and Lorna flew to Seattle so he could see his analyst at some length. We hadn't exchanged more than ten words during our good-byes. And even those ten had worn us out.

When I was able, I moved the girls out of my office and into the house. They hadn't been there more than an hour before they owned the place. When the graduate students who house-sat for us came to take care of things for a while, Chloe and Charmaine decided that they owned them, too. Then I climbed on another crappy flight.

This time instead of staying at her parents' house, Whit and I spent the night at an airport hotel. We had dinner and drinks in the room, made love, then had another ragged conversation.

"Are you going to keep working for Mac?" she asked.

"If he wants me to when he gets back from Seattle," I said.

"How long?"

"As long as he keeps paying," I said. "I have to make a living, too, remember."

"Maybe you should take some time off," she suggested.

"That's what I'm doing."

"Can I ask you something, CW?"

"What?"

"How would you feel if I had an affair?" she said.

"Are you going to sleep with a prosecutor to get a deal?"

"Be serious," she said. "What would you do?"

"I'd kill somebody," I said.

"Me?"

"Of course not."

"My lover?"

"Only if he had a skinny mustache, slicked back hair, and never took off his black socks in bed."

"Be serious."

"Killing somebody," I said. "That's about as serious as I get."

"Yourself?"

"I don't think so," I said. "I'd just drive up and down the street until I found an asshole I didn't like, then I'd drop the hammer on him."

"That would be just like killing yourself, honey," she said. "You're smoking cigarettes again, and I know you're smoking dope, too. Living on beer, sleeping pills, and coffee. That can't be good with one kidney. I'm worried about you. And us. Are you going to be all right?"

"If I'm not, you'll be the first to know," I

said. "Don't worry, okay? That just makes it harder."

"I'll try," she said. "But it'll be hard."

"Nothing else to do," I said, slipping away from the conversation like a coward in the night. "What would you do if I had an affair?" I asked, a hollow laugh in my throat, the flickering image of Sheila Miller in the front of my mind.

"You mean you're not?" she said, good heart that she was, trying to laugh, too.

"Nope," I said. "I'm married to a lawyer, and I'm afraid of her."

"You damn well better be," she said, then snuggled next to me. "I hope Mac's going to be all right," she added. "I know how he feels it when one of his patients is in pain."

"Hell, he hates it when they have a hangnail," I said. "But how the hell do you know how he feels?"

"Just guessing," she said, then closed my mouth with hers.

Janeanne Reynolds was the anchor and news director for the local television news I didn't watch. Which is why I didn't know the name. She had been an anchor in Denver until she'd become the latest trophy wife of the local station owner, whose family owned a dozen small stations across the West. As far as I could gather from a couple of days' work, all she wanted out of life, besides the mansion on the hill, was to continue her job covering the news in a small western Montana city, but her husband wanted to start a third family. Don't marry the boss; it's a bad idea if you want to keep working. I made a point of watching her work a few times. She was too good for our small market, but she seemed to honestly enjoy her work.

Angie Cole was the daughter of Meriwether's most successful real estate developer, Abe LoRusso, but she had married beneath her. She and her college-dropout husband had borrowed money from her father to open an upscale coffeehouse and bistro in an already flooded market. They lost her father's money bean over biscotti instead of producing grandchildren. The word was that she hadn't left the house since the bankruptcy.

Neither of the women were serial killers, having affairs, or indulging in a secret life as degenerate gamblers.

Garfield Ritter, on the other hand, was doing one of them. As soon as he was mobile, he spent most of his time away from the college sitting on stools in front of

174

keno and poker machines in every small town within thirty minutes of Meriwether, feeding the machines twenty-dollar bills as if he had printed them. He never won. Hell, he never even had a free drink.

Charlie Marshall came back from his week of convalescence looking even unhappier than he had when he left. Since GG Paul never left the house these days, I tagged her husband a few times out of boredom — a waste of time since he probably had the computer skills to hack into Mac's system and wouldn't need to break into the office. He spent the occasional afternoon visiting with Charlie Marshall, and sometimes in the evening he visited The Phone Booth, sitting on the edge of the stage. Between the same two truckers, twice. Particularly when Sheila Miller was dancing. But as far as I could tell, he just looked.

Sheila seemed so fragile and busy that I hated to follow her. I knew that she turned the occasional trick, but she was very circumspect about it. I did dig up a bit of her past. She'd been fifteen and in high school when her daughter had been born, and they had left Medford, Oregon, shortly afterward. In spite of her looks, Sheila turned so much money at The Phone

Booth that she had avoided being shoved around the topless circuit. Her daughter, Marcy, was a stoner who hung with the local high school Goths, her classic beauty hidden beneath too much dark makeup. Unlike her mother, she had the face to go with the body, even if the body was a bit skinny, but the kid had never been in any real trouble. She went to school regularly in her little Miata, even met with a math tutor two afternoons a week, and then with Mac's eating-disorders group afterward. She and her mother seemed close, except for the occasional shouting match, closer than most mothers and daughters might have been given their lives and backgrounds.

It was all too normal. Hell, even Elwood Studer, denied his afternoon sessions with Mac, still left the house three times a week at the right time, and drove aimlessly around for a couple of hours, aimless but following exactly the same route, until the time he normally came home.

Unlike Mac, who didn't come home. He extended his Seattle visit indefinitely and asked me to come over to talk to him.

Finally, I called Claudia to see if she'd let go of some of her inside-the-police-force information. For decency's sake, we met late one night at The Bluestone, a roadhouse twenty miles south of town with a large dance floor and a small bar. And log cabins with fireplaces located conveniently behind the place along Bluestone Creek. I got there early and tried to hide in a dark corner, but she made an entrance like she always did. Tonight, instead of her usual tailored business suit — she liked to play the gangster's daughter, but her father was a famous Butte tailor — she sported black jeans, a white cowboy shirt, red boots that matched her mouth, and an attitude as sharp and sparking as a straight razor. I gunned my drink before she could get to the table.

She sat down, ordered for both of us, then brushed back the black-and-silver wings of her loose, thick hair.

"Here to pump me, Sughrue?" she asked, then laughed huskily.

"Give me a break, will you?"

"Not until you give me one, cowboy."

"You want to dance?" I said with a sudden, twisted inspiration. Patsy Cline was singing "Crazy" on the jukebox. Blame it on Patsy.

"What?"

"Let's dance," I said as I grabbed her

hand and led her onto the dance floor.

Thirty minutes of dancing and a few drinks later, we sat down, winded and sweating. We had fit well together. I had grown up hanging around dance halls, and Claudia, who had been around country music herself, followed with an aggressive grace.

"Thank you," she said when we sat down. "I really enjoyed that. I feel young and properly depraved, and so grateful that I have to tell you that the DA's office is slow-pitching discovery on the Biddle case."

"The trip hasn't been totally wasted," I said. "I enjoyed the dancing, too. Although I feel old and wasted, ready for a nap."

"Well, not totally wasted," she said, her eyes sparkling like the moonlight on the creek behind the roadhouse. When I flinched, she laughed at me. "Stop being so damn sensitive," she said. "When I really want you, CW, you won't have a chance."

"I thought you said I was tougher than I looked," I reminded her.

"Lawyer talk," she said. "I don't like slow-pitch," she added. "And the DA really wants to hang this kid out to dry, so I took things into my own hands."

"Butch in a dither?"

"No more than usual," she said bitterly. "But I came up with a copy of the crime scene inventory. That was all I could get, but it looks like enough."

"Interesting," I said. I knew better than to ask how she had gotten it.

"One thing really stuck out," she said. "A red crotchless teddy. Carrie was a big girl, CW. It might have fit on one of her thighs. But nowhere else."

"That's all?"

"Not quite," she said. "Down in the basement, behind a loose brick, they found a small stash of two kinds of acid — liquid lysergic acid diethylamide and hydrochloric acid — one to rot your brain and one to weaken the mortar around the screws holding up the railing."

"Could've belonged to anybody in the building."

"The hydrochloric bottle had one perfect thumbprint on the bottom," she said. "Arno Biddle's."

"What made them look in the basement?"

"Your usual ubiquitous anonymous call," she said. "What's your interest in all this?"

"Justice," I said without thinking about it, had the last of my drink, then set my empty glass down. "And protecting my client. I'll tell you about it someday."

Claudia reached over, lightly scratched the back of my hand with her long, red nails and said, "How is it that we never got together in the old days?"

"In the old days, sweetie, you wouldn't date me because I was a struggling hippie PI instead of a rich lawyer," I said. "Also, you were as mean and ambitious as a spitting cobra."

"Oh, that," she said, then broke into a soft, sad smile that made her face young and lovely again. "You mean back before I threw my life away on a married man who was meaner and more ambitious than I was?" She didn't want an answer to that question. "What now?" she asked.

"I've got to go. An early flight to Seattle," I said. Claudia knew what that meant. Either a drive to Missoula for a 6:30 a.m. loop through Salt Lake, or a small plane bouncing around the mountains. Another gift from the Reagan deregulation years. "To see a client," I added.

"How's Mac holding up?" she said. "He's certainly had a string of bad luck lately."

"He's always taken his patients too seriously," I said. "I don't know how he ever held up." Then I stood, saying, "Thanks, Claudia. You going to hang out?" I nodded at a trio of young guys leaning against the bar.

"Wouldn't be quite the same," she said, then stood up, too.

In the parking lot, we hugged each other, said good-bye like parting friends, then climbed into our rides.

Thanks to a delayed flight and a canceled one, it was after four by the time I got to the Surry Park Hotel in Seattle, and I felt like I'd spent the day in hell instead of the Salt Lake airport. I must have looked like it, too. The snooty desk clerks wanted to know what I was doing in their hotel.

"I'm Dr. MacKinderick's assistant," I said. "Igor."

They weren't amused. I guess Lorna wasn't, either. When the desk clerk called up to the room, she didn't bother talking to me, just told them to tell me that the doctor was on his way down to meet me.

When Mac stepped out of the elevator, limping, he said, "Leave your bag behind the desk, Igor, and walk this way." His grin was as sketchy as a wave-washed gull track, but I did as he said, followed him out through the revolving door, limping into the afternoon sunlight. We were all the way down to the Market before he said, "You can stop limping, my friend. I got drunk and twisted my ankle coming out of the Bistro the other night."

"You got drunk?"

"Same thing my analyst said."

"What was your answer?" I said.

"You damn betcha."

"Can't say I blame you," I said.

We walked through the Market as the tourist crowd ebbed and flowed like an errant tide. Summer was nearly over, but the vendors wouldn't be breaking down their stalls until much later on this long summer afternoon. The fruit and vegetables gleamed as brightly as postcard replicas, the flowers glowed, and the seafood glistened in their shaved ice beds.

"How's your head?" Mac asked when we stopped in front of the elevator down to the bay front. It wasn't just the limp. Mac looked twenty years older than the night we'd won the Old Farts championship. "Still seeing double?"

"I guess I had a little harder knock than I realized," I admitted. "Never saw double, just didn't see right. If I didn't know better, I'd swear I had a couple of acid flashbacks that night in the interrogation room."

"Thanks for holding out," he said. "What were you doing outside Charlie's house?"

"Just doin' my job, boss," I said. "Either that, or I had an especially stupid idea."

"Speaking of ideas," he said. "Any notion who copied the disks?"

"No more now than I did when I started," I said. "But I can guess who didn't."

We crossed Alaskan, then turned north along the bay front, walking slowly until Mac stopped to lean against the rail to stare at the water, calm except for the passing wakes of freighters and ferries and rich folk's follies. He stared at the scene so hard it looked as if he wanted to paint it. Gulls and crows scrabbled among the litter with dead seriousness, as if looking for something more important than a snack. It was a fine, brilliant afternoon, the only dark cloud hanging in my head.

"Are you going to tell me?" he finally said. "Who didn't do it?"

"Sheila's too frightened," I began, "Janeanne's too self-absorbed, Angie's too timid, Garfield's too selfish, Elwood's too dominated by his mother, Charlie's too sad . . . and poor Carrie is too fucking dead. That's all I know. So, what's so important on the disks?"

"There's a . . ." he said sharply as he turned to me, then sighed, turned back to the water, and apologized. "I'm sorry, CW. You know I can't tell you how much I appreciate it. You've done a great deal of work, haven't you? God, and you've seen the deaths. I don't know how you stand it."

"Bad habits, I guess."

"All habits are bad," he said bitterly. "What's the police angle on Ellen Marshall's death?"

"The police aren't talking to me these days," I said.

"I thought Raymond was your new best friend."

"Not exactly," I said.

"So you haven't heard what the note said?"

"Note?"

"*I've always hated my hands on my body,*" Mac said sadly. "*If I can't kill myself, I think I'll trim them.* That's what she wrote."

"Charlie told you?"

He nodded, then said, "This is the most awful part of my life. And here I am breaking a sacred trust. Shit."

"What are you going to do?"

"What do you think I should do?" he said.

"Walk away from your practice, retire, leave Meriwether forever."

"Sounds like denial," he said. "I'd never advise denial. Of course, my analyst says the same thing. Except with a sweet Swedish lilt to her voice. How the hell did I end up with an analyst who sounds like my mother?"

"I don't know, Doc," I said. "You're the shrink."

"Sometimes your friends know more about you than you do yourself," he said.

"And sometimes they don't."

"Whatever," he said. "How's the separation going?"

"We're not calling it a separation, yet," I said, "but it's not going worth a shit."

"I'm sorry."

"Not your fault."

"Thanks for saying that, but I fear some of it is," he said without explanation. Then he paused, turned inward again. "I don't know. I'm coming back to town, going back to work, and, even though I agree with your assessment of my clients, I want you to stay on them. And if you can stand it, I want you to work it even harder."

"Why?"

"Ron's got another twenty grand in an escrow account, plus another thirty that belongs to you, my friend, when we work this out."

"Fuck the money," I said. "What's the real reason?"

"I just know something terrible is going to happen," he said, "and these people need my help."

"I don't know how much more terrible it can be," I said.

"Trust me," he said.

"I don't know," I said. "I just don't know. And Mac . . ."

"What?"

"I've stopped remembering my dreams."

"And?"

"I think I'm dreaming about the war again."

"Don't worry about it," he said. "Trust me."

And I did. I had no choice that afternoon. Even though, standing among the bright, clean tourist throng, I felt like one of the turkey buzzards that lived in the abandoned steam-rig oil well derrick in the cotton field behind the shack where I had grown up, mostly. They were dark birds covered with old blood, new vomit, and rotting roadkill guts. Sometimes in the night, when my father was off into his own madness and my mother was too deep into the vodka to notice, I slept rolled in a quilt under the stars in the backyard. Before I slept, I listened to the mockingbird who had fallen in love with long distance. From her nest in the salt cedars along the road, she hooted like a passing freight long into the shining midnights. But sometimes, too, I could hear the gabble of the vultures as they ate their carrion meals over and over again into the dark of the moon.

When we got back to the hotel, I saw Lorna briefly on the way to my room only because Mac insisted that I should say hello. She looked as fresh as a rose blooming in a spring shower, a flower with a death beetle hidden so deep in the blossom that it only showed in the soft quiver of her throat.

Afterward, I walked up to Belltown, had a plate of pasta at the bar of the Queen City, then drank myself into the sort of stupor that ensured I would miss my flight the next morning and spend the day drifting between Salt Lake and hell.

I went back to work, slowly, and Mac

and I avoided each other as if we were guilty conspirators in some heinous crime.

I thought of him often in the early evenings as he sat on the veranda with a large Scotch and a cigar watching his small herd of deer, probably speaking to them more politely than I had.

But I made no effort to contact him as I continued my search, which felt like a hunt for an unused heroin needle in a South Central alley. Nothing worked, though, and I felt as if I had worn out all my options, so I made up my mind, then called Whit at her office to let her know that I would be sleeping in the rent car for a few days.

"Serious surveillance, huh?"

"Dead serious," I said.

"Is this nightmare ever going to end?"

"I don't know, love. I'm not even sure it's my nightmare," I admitted. "Whatever, I'll be back among the living in three or four days. Then I'll fly out for a long visit. We'll sit down and work something out."

"I certainly hope so," she said. "You haven't been here much when you're here."

I apologized, then went out to the topless bar.

For three days I stuck to Sheila Miller like a cocklebur on a long-haired dog. I haunted The Phone Booth, both inside and in the parking lot. I wandered around the neighborhood where she worked at a group home. As far as I could tell, she treated her clients with a great deal more smiling respect than she did the customers at the topless joint. I parked outside her trailer-house and watched her help her daughter with homework, interrupted by the occasional fight — with Marcy sneaking away in the station wagon one afternoon — but nobody interesting ever visited and nothing untoward happened. I even followed her on her paper route two mornings. I couldn't figure out when the woman slept. As far as I knew, Sheila Miller, part-time topless dancer and hooker, was one of the most decent, hardworking persons I had ever trailed.

I was about to give up and bother somebody else, but that last morning, a Thursday, I followed her to Mac's office, then parked behind her old Chevy station wagon. I thought I'd catch a short nap, but I collapsed into dead sleep and didn't wake until ten. Sheila Miller's old car was still there, though. I was halfway up the walk to the back door when muffled but clearly horrified screams leaked out of it. I didn't pause. I had a copy of the key but couldn't find it quickly enough. It took five or six kicks to break the lock out of the door frame. When I crashed inside, Mac's secretary stood in the opposite doorway, shrieking like a madwoman. The office was a shambles, the aftermath of a bar fight or a grenade explosion. Sheila Miller's naked body lay on the couch. She would never have to worry about her face again. It had been beaten into a bloody pulp. After the first glance, I didn't look back. Mac's favorite softball bat lay bloodstained on the floor beside her. And Mac was nowhere to be found.

Eight

Lorna had a block on her telephone at the Surry Park, a block that the desk clerk wouldn't let me budge no matter what I tried, and when she didn't return my calls, I finally decided to grab a quick flight to Seattle to tell her in person. Ron Musselwhite caught me on the cell when I changed planes in Spokane. His news wasn't all that good. Johnny Raymond had just called to tell him that the Washington State Patrol had found Lorna's car in the lot at the trail leading to the edge of the world — Cape Flattery, the very northwestern tip of the continental United States. The interior of the roadster was covered with blood, especially the driver's seat. A pile of bloody clothes and shoes, presumed to be Mac's, had been found at the end of the trail where it overlooked the Pacific. Because Raymond had issued an APB for the car, the WSP office had impounded the car.

I told him I was going to need some help getting to Lorna's room, and I asked him to call the desk at the hotel to see if he couldn't get me past the clerk, "Or any-body who can get me past the desk clerks there," I said. "They're tougher than your Aunt Edith."

"My Aunt Edith teaches Sunday school in Ponca City," he said, then apologized. "I'm sorry, man. I'm sittin' here in Mickey's suckin' a double Turkey rocks in the morning. This shit is making me cra-zier than a hoot owl. I can't believe Mac would . . . Well, you believe the same thing, don't you?"

"Right," I said. "I've got a can of snoose in my pocket if I can't get to Seattle with-out a nicotine fix."

"Call me when you get back," he said.

"If I get back," I said. "If . . ."

The FBI agent caught my elbow just as I leaned on the counter and asked for the hotel's manager. He looked about sixteen with his sheared light red curls, pug nose, freckles, and an all-American gap-toothed grin, but his tailored dark-blue suit, white shirt, and rep tie shouted FBI. As did his warm, dry handshake. He had the thick neck, deep chest, and bulky shoulders of a serious weight lifter, so bulky he had to wear a cross-draw belt holster on his slim hips. He moved with a runner's easy grace.

"Mr. Sughrue, I assume?" he said. "I'm Special Agent Charles Cunningham. My partner's inside the office clearing things with the manager." His voice was as fresh and youthful as his face. I kept expecting it to crack like an adolescent's.

"I hope he has better luck than I did," I admitted.

"She," Cunningham said, "she. Agent Morrow usually gets her way."

Agent Morrow came out of the office with a thin, dapper man in tow. The hotel manager, I assumed. The woman could have towed a freighter. She was built like a tug. She must have been on the verge of minimum height and maximum weight for that height, with a body as square as a ton of bricks set on the legs of a power lifter. Even her plain, unadorned face was square, framed by short black hair brushed back in an almost military fashion. When I shook her hand, I could feel the thick callus that covered her palms.

"Agent Pamela Morrow," she said. "You must be Chauncey Wayne Sughrue."

"CW," I said. "I'm a friend of the family and a legal representative of Dr. Mac-Kinderick's lawyer. What's the FBI doing here?"

"I know who you are," she said sharply

193

as she led us to the elevator. "In fact, Mr. Sughrue, I know everything about you." Then the four of us stepped into the elevator, as she continued, "I've seen your army records — for some reason the record of your court-martial was sealed then destroyed in the interest of national security — and the records of your years of service in the late sixties and early seventies with the Department of Defense Intelligence Agency. Also, your name pops up in some interesting DEA files."

"That's wonderful," I said as the elevator lifted to the top floor of the hotel. "So you must also know that I've never been convicted of anything, lady. Maybe you know one other important thing?"

"What's that?"

"The hotel manager's name," I said. "We haven't been introduced."

"Folger," the thin man said nervously. When I shook his hand, it was as cold and slick as a deepwater eel.

"I assume Mrs. MacKinderick is still in her room," I said, and he nodded sadly.

Cunningham answered for him, "As far as the hotel knows, she's been in her room for the last few days. Hasn't left once. Telephoned out for food and drink. Hasn't let the maid in to service the room, either."

"Thanks," I said to the big kid.

When the elevator doors opened, I motioned for Morrow to exit first. She shouldered the manager aside and headed down the hall. We followed at a respectful distance to Lorna's suite door. She ignored the DO NOT DISTURB sign and pounded on the door with that insistent knock that only a cop can muster. After a few moments, we heard Lorna's frail voice through the door, telling us to get the hell away from the door.

"FBI, Mrs. MacKinderick," Morrow boomed in a voice so powerful that the rock would have rolled aside even without the password.

"Fuck off!" Lorna screamed.

Agent Morrow turned to Folger. "Open it," she ordered.

"Maybe if you won't tell me why you're here," I said, "you might show me a warrant or something like it," I said. Morrow looked at me as if I were something dirty on one of her shining low-heeled pumps.

"Open the door," she ordered again.

"You might want to wait a moment," I told the manager, then pulled out my cell phone and started dialing.

"Who are you calling?" Folger asked nervously, the card key in his hand.

"A friend of mine at the *P-I*," I said. "It might make an interesting newspaper item that a hotel with your reputation let the FBI into a room without a legal right."

Folger glanced at Agent Morrow.

"Do it," she said.

"Do you have any reason to believe a crime is being committed?" I asked Folger, "Or that Mrs. MacKinderick is in any danger?"

"Only in danger of breaking our single-person room service record," Folger said, almost giggling.

"We're going to interrogate that woman," Agent Morrow said.

"After I've told Mrs. MacKinderick that her husband is missing," I said, "and she recovers, I'll give you a call. *Then* you can talk to her."

Morrow raised her hand to knock again. I touched her hard shoulder. "Touch me again, Sughrue," she said, "and Agent Cunningham will take you down."

"I'm sure he can," I said. "But, believe me, my lawyer can kick your lawyer's ass. So let's do this the easy way."

"Agent Morrow," Cunningham said quietly as he handed me his card. "He does have a point. Let's do it the easy way, okay?"

Morrow looked betrayed, but she gave up and stalked down the hallway back toward the elevator. Cunningham gave me a sick grin, then followed her.

Folger sighed, "Good luck," then handed me the card key. I opened the door a crack and shouted, "Lorna! It's CW! We've got to talk."

After a bit, Lorna's face appeared at the crack, her eye smudged with sleep, her hair flying every which way. She was obviously naked beneath one of the hotel's robes — one of her rosebud nipples peeked at me. "What?" she sniffled. "What the hell is going on?"

"I told you," I said. "I've got to talk to you."

"Oh, hell," she muttered. "Let me get some clothes on." Then she disappeared, leaving the door slightly ajar.

The living room was empty when I stepped inside. The bedroom was in an upstairs loft. I heard the television click on to CNN, then the shower started, but neither sound covered the hissing bundle of whispers. I stepped over to the coffee table, which had been hastily and badly cleared, opened the small drawer in the center of the table, and wasn't surprised to find a silver straw, razor, and snuff box, and a small smudged mirror. The snuff box contained a goodly portion of great cocaine. Or so the small taste I touched to my tongue told me. I set everything back on the coffee table, then opened the drapes and a window. Not to enjoy the view of the bay but to smoke. The coke had numbed my mouth all the way to the back of my tongue.

I dug a quick Scotch out of the service bar and sucked that down along with four cigarettes before Lorna came down the stairs, her wet hair snugged to her head. She was wearing jeans and a sweatshirt — designer jeans and a cashmere sweatshirt — with thick-soled flip-flops.

"Honey," she said lightly. "I do believe this is a nonsmoking suite."

"Nonsnorting, too?" I said, which she answered with a small squeal. "I'll go down to the courtyard for a moment," I said. "You better tell your friend to get the hell out of here —"

"Did Mac send you to spy on me, you son of a bitch?" she interrupted.

"If I have to go up to get your friend," I said, "he won't like the way he lands when I throw him out. So fucking do it, lady."

Then I walked carefully out of the room without breaking anything. Made it all the way to the lobby without breaking anything, too. I didn't even speak loudly to Folger when he came up to me.

"Is there a problem with Dr. MacKinderick's room?" he asked. "I don't think we've ever had the FBI here before. Well, perhaps once before."

"Everything's fine, sir," I said in my best official voice. "There's been an accident, and I just have to talk to Mrs. MacKinderick. No problem at all. Nothing to worry about. Mrs. MacKinderick is just composing herself." Then I added, "It would be a great help if I had a copy of her telephone calls and messages, sir."

Folger stepped over to the desk for a moment, then he came back with the printouts. "I know you work for Dr. MacKinderick," he said. "I found your name in our records. He paid for your room the last time you were here."

"Thanks for your help," I said.

"I hope everything is all right," he said softly, like a man who knew it wasn't.

"Thanks again," I said.

Once outside, I walked over to one of the benches around the hotel's patio bar, then had a peaceful cigarette. Until I saw Cunningham standing in the shadows of the stairway up to the street. When he saw me see him, he walked over without a greeting.

"She's gone for a warrant?" I said, and he just nodded slightly. "But she won't get it, will she?" I said, and he just shook his head. "I'll call you tomorrow," I said.

"Thank you, sir," he said, then started back to his niche.

"What do you bench-press, Charlie?" I asked.

"You don't want to know, sir," he answered, smiling, then walked slowly back to his position.

As I watched the revolving doors, a tall, skinny young man dressed in black leather, silver earrings, tattoos, and Doc Martens hurried nervously out of one of them. I managed to bump into him. He didn't seem to have stolen the silverware. I looked him over very carefully. In case Lorna needed an alibi, he probably wouldn't be too hard to find.

Back up in the suite, the door was ajar, so I stepped inside. Lorna was sitting on the couch, straw in one hand, the razor in the other, idly chopping two lines, pulling them into a pile, then chopping lines again.

"What in the livin' hell is up, CW?" she demanded before I could say a word. "You show up here with the fuckin' Feds —

what am I supposed to think?"

"I'm sorry to have to give it to you this way, Lorna," I said. "But your telephone line was blocked, and the desk wouldn't let me through even when I told them it was an emergency."

"It's a good hotel," she said, suddenly senseless.

"And you wouldn't return any of my messages."

"I wasn't picking up messages," she said, then leaned over to snort the line. "An emergency?" she said, rubbing at her nose.

"Mac's been missing since last Thursday," I said.

"Last Thursday?" she said, then her eyes rolled up in her head, and she fell over on the couch in a dead faint.

When I checked, she hadn't swallowed her tongue or stopped breathing, although she seemed to be panting like a tired dog. Her pulse was strong and rapid, but not dangerously so, I guessed. I straightened her on the couch, propped her feet on a couple of cushions piled on the arm of the couch, then found a blanket in the closet to cover her. Within minutes, the panting stopped and the snoring started.

"Jesus fucking wept," I said, then looked at her other line. I hadn't forgotten a thing about the white lady. Once she was in law school, Whitney had made me promise never to do cocaine again. Which wasn't too hard since I'd always sort of been a dope-smoking fool. I started to dump the rest of Lorna's stash into the toilet, but decided not to. She was going to wake up to enough loss. I chopped a couple of lines on the back of the upstairs toilet, filled a small bindle, then stuck it in my billfold.

Then I searched through the bedroom until I found Lorna's jewelry box. The bedroom looked as if a mad child had moved in with a punk rock band. Stuffed animals occupied every space not covered with party debris. I didn't know what to think. Except I knew I had to cover Lorna's ass, so I put the stash, the straw, and the razor into the jewelry box; then I took it down to the desk and had them put it in the hotel safe. Just in case Agent Morrow did get a warrant. Then I went out to talk to Cunningham.

"She passed out when I told her," I said, "but she's sleeping quietly now. I'll call you when she wakes up, so you can get off your feet for a while."

"Not on your life, sir," he said. "Pammie's coming to relieve me, so I'd best be here."

"Pammie?"

"Agent Morrow," he said, blushing.

"I understand why she has such a hard-on for me, Cunningham, but why does she have such a hard-on for this poor woman?" I said. "She doesn't even know her. You guys don't even have a crime yet."

"MacKinderick's name rang some bells in Agent Morrow's head. Something she heard when she was still in Washington. D.C., that is," he said. "And Cape Flattery is one hell of a place to jump into the ocean. We can also claim jurisdiction on the Makah reservation."

"Well, tell her I wish her the best of luck getting back to J. Edgar's house," I said, then headed back into the hotel.

On that terrible morning when I finally got Mac's secretary to stop screaming and sit down, I told her to call 911 as soon as she stopped sobbing. Luckily that gave me a few minutes to poke around with my hands in my pockets. As far as I could tell by just looking, the hard drives had been jerked out of Mac's computers. The drawers labeled current files were completely empty. The older files seemed undisturbed. I heard sirens in the distance, so I slipped out the back door to wait for the law.

The law, in the form of Johnny Raymond, wasn't happy. "What the hell happened here?"

"You know as much as I do, Sherlock."

"Wrong time to get smart," he said, putting one hand on his cuffs and the other hard on my shoulder.

Resistance was out of the question completely, in spite of the fine moment in the bar watching the hardheaded asshole nearly choke to death.

And this time I'm going down, I thought, until I saw Claudia's deep maroon Jag coming down the street. Ron Musselwhite was out of town, so I had his secretary call Claudia for me.

Usually in that sort of situation, Claudia would arrive on the wings of an ill-tempered harridan, whipping the air with the poisoned tongues of the Medusa. But she worked Johnny Raymond the other way that morning — all sweetness and politeness with legal icing. Raymond didn't want to bite but she kept finding reasons to release me. Until he stuck his big, strong, white teeth into the cinnamon roll instead of me.

We climbed into Claudia's ride and headed for the nearest bar, Mutt's, a bar that almost exemplified the phrase *low dive*. She looked as if she had just stepped out of the bad-butch edition of *Vogue,* and I looked like a guy who had been sleeping in his car while somebody died in his friend's office. The woman I'd been tailing, no less.

"Jesus," she said, "I've seen bar rags that looked better. What the hell happened? What were you doing there?"

I gave her a five-dollar bill and got a receipt back. "As far as I can tell, somebody killed the stripper. Then for some reason, he stole patient files, the hard disks, the floppies, and most of the paper in the place."

"That doesn't answer why you were following the woman there."

"Mac was convinced that somebody had stolen his patient records — just the ones in long-term analysis," I explained as if I understood it.

"You think he killed this one? Or any of them?"

"Of course not."

"So what can I do except keep your bail low?"

I waited a long time to answer. "Claudia, my dear, when I finish saying this, you can hit me, walk away, never speak to me again,"

I said, "but it's an ill-kept secret that you've got a line right into the department. You've jumped ahead of your peers every time. And something keeps you here."

"I like the weather," she said calmly, my five-dollar bill still in her hand, leaving me afoot among low companions. "My favorite place."

"Without your help, Mac's going down for this," I said. "Without it, he's meat. I know you've got somebody in the department by the nuts. You got to squeeze for me, honey."

"Be careful what you ask for, Sughrue," she said as she folded up the five-dollar bill and slipped it between her breasts, "you might not like the answer. And don't tell anybody but Ron or me where Lorna is until you talk to her."

"Would you please give me a ride to my car?" I asked. "I need about three days of sleep." She left me in the dive, where I had to bum drinks from Mutt until Johnny Raymond found me.

Once I had given my statement to the police, with Ron's assistant standing over my shoulder, I slept for two days. Except for calling Lorna when I woke up to pee.

Before I could get in the elevator, my cell

phone buzzed in my windbreaker pocket. Ron Musselwhite. More good news. The early blood work on Lorna's car revealed only one blood type. Mac's. And a man fitting Mac's description had stopped at the emergency room in Moses Lake to have twenty-six stitches put into the side of his skull. An accident with his tire jack was the explanation. I thanked him, then steeled myself to face Lorna, half hoping she was still asleep or, perhaps, had even disappeared.

But Lorna was awake and tearing up the suite searching for her cocaine when I unlocked the door. Perhaps she had a little bigger nose-jones than I had suspected. "Where the hell have you been, Sughrue," she hissed. "And where the hell is my stash, you bastard." All the southern honey seemed to have dripped right off her tongue.

"Mrs. MacKinderick," I said calmly, "you'll find two fat lines on the back of the downstairs toilet, so roll up a bill and help yourself."

"Could I borrow one of your bills, hon," she purred. "Dr. MacKinderick doesn't care for me to carry cash money." The south had risen again in her voice.

I didn't know what to say about that, so I

rolled up my most crisp bill, and handed it to her, accepting her simpering smile as thanks. I suppose I should have realized it before: Lorna had not the slightest touch with reality; she seemed completely insane.

But when she came back from the bathroom, after a couple of fat line bumps, she seemed perfectly normal. She sat on the couch, cupped her hands together on her tightly clenched knees — a good little girl — then asked brightly "What was it you said about Mac?"

The afternoon went to hell after that. Lorna went through the small makeshift bindle in the first hour, so I had to go down for the jewelry box. Then she jumped into the shower to wash off the evidence of her first hysterical sobbing. She was into the service bar white-wine stash by the time I got back. I made a quarter-ounce bindle, hoping it would last, then got some very strange looks when I took the jewelry box back to the front desk. There were rivers of tears, road miles of cocaine, and a couple of showers; then she decided she had to get out of the room — she'd been in that room for five days, dammit, she had to get out. I agreed with her, but I didn't know it was going to take another shower, much blow-drying of her thick hair, and three changes of clothes. Finally she decided that none of her colored outfits matched her nail and toe polish, and, dammit, her hands were shaking too badly to do the work herself. So she hit the bindle a couple of times with a long fingernail, then folded it up, and tossed it to me, saying, "Could you tote that for me, CW. I don't have any pockets."

The fact that Lorna was even upright and moving was an amazing feat of insane will, the fact that she was talking fairly lucidly surely a result of the great cocaine; but the fact that she looked like a million dollars as we stepped out to the hotel's patio bar had to be a miracle.

Dressed in loose white raw silk pants and jacket over a black tube top, clicking along on black high-heeled sandals, a floppy hat in one hand, heavy sunglasses in the other, Lorna glowed in the watery sunlight of early afternoon. I could see Cunningham's eyes shining from the shadows where he waited. Lorna and I sat on the sunny side of the patio bar. Of course, nothing would do but a bottle of Cristal. As we waited, Cunningham slipped out of the shadows to sit at a table on the edge of the patio, as if he was trying to catch our conversation.

After the waiter filled our flutes, Lorna raised hers and said, "You must think me a horrible person, CW. Absolutely terrible. To be drinking champagne on such a day."

"You're a real bitch," I said, "and you're talking like some character in a fuckin' novel. Nobody knows what happened to your husband, who also happens to be my best friend, so let's get serious."

"You don't understand anything, do you?" she said, then drained her champagne. "Mac knew how I was when he married me."

"And just how the hell are you?"

"I take things," she said, then motioned the waiter to refill her flute. "I've always been a *taker*. Mac is a *giver*; I'm a *taker*. That's how we are. So tell him anything you want to about me. He already knows it."

"Didn't you hear what I told you up in the room?"

"I'm crazy, sir, not deaf," she said.

"I'll agree with that," I said. Every time she opened her mouth, another woman popped out.

"He's just missing, darling, not dead," she said. "He won't be dead until I see the body."

"Is there any particular hospital you'd

like me to check you into?" I said, but she just smiled sweetly. "Or can I recommend a shrink?"

"Thanks for your concern," she said calmly. "I'm sure it's well meant, but it's misplaced, CW. I'll be fine."

"You need a professional keeper," I said, then waved Cunningham over to the table. He approached very carefully. I pushed out a chair for him as I stood up. "Sit down, Agent Cunningham," I said. "And show Mrs. MacKinderick your credentials. Lorna, this young man wants to talk to you. If you're as fine as you think you are, you'll keep your mouth shut. I'll be right back."

"Where are you going?" she asked, as if suddenly afraid. She flopped her hat on her head and slipped the dark shades on her face. "And why?"

"Just inside for a few minutes," I answered. "I've got a few things to take care of. You're in good hands." I left before I could hear her offer Cunningham a drink. Although I might have been interested in his answer.

Folger met me at the front desk. He had already sent the maids to Lorna's room. He apologized for not having a room for me, but he promised to find me something nearby and he graciously let me use his office telephone to make half a dozen calls. He also promised to carry out the favors I asked him to do.

By the time I got back outside, the patio was completely in shadow. The sky was still blue, the sun still shining, but in the shade I was quickly reminded that Seattle sat on the edge of a deep, cold finger of the Pacific. Lorna slept quietly in her chair, the hat over her face, the shades slipped down over her nose.

"I'm glad you're back," Cunningham whispered as I sat down.

"You two have a nice chat?"

"She fell asleep almost as soon as you left," he said. "Poor lady."

"Poor lady," somebody growled behind us. We didn't have to turn around to see who it was.

"You missed your chance, Pammie," I said over my shoulder. Then asked Cunningham to give me a hand getting Lorna up to her room. He was only too glad to help, if just to get away from Morrow's glare.

After we had laid Lorna on her bed, Cunningham looked at me, then stammered, "What now?"

"Well, buddy, I'm going to undress the

poor woman and put her to bed," I said. "You want to watch? Or help?"

He turned and walked quickly down the stairs and out the door. But not quickly enough. I saw his face. You could have painted a barn with his blush.

As she slept in the loft, I waited down-stairs with a pot of room service coffee, a sandwich, and the television. About seven, Folger tapped on the door. He handed me my package and a pair of card keys.

"We had a cancellation," he said. "It's two floors down, I'm sorry to say, but it's with our compliments." Then he paused. "Do you have any idea how long . . . how long you will be staying?"

"Until I can get her to go home," I admitted.

Nine

At ten o'clock the next morning, Lorna looked as if she hadn't moved since I'd covered her up the night before, so I let her sleep on. I ran into Agent Cunningham on the patio. He offered me a cup of coffee, and I accepted. Yesterday's sunshine had become today's normal Seattle weather. Raindrops as slow as Chinese water torture, and as effective, dribbled on the canvas awning over our table. A cloud of fog, thicker than last week's slumgullion stew, flowed and eddied across the space, leaving everything it touched wetter than the rain. You couldn't see the Market half a block away or Elliott Bay beyond. Hell, there were moments when I almost couldn't see Cunningham.

"How is she doing, Mr. Sughrue?" he asked.

" 'Mr. Sughrue'?" I said. "Does this mean I'm no longer the scumbag of the day?"

"That's not my department, sir. How's Mrs. MacKinderick?"

"A sleeping doll," I said.

214

"A piece of work, as they say in Kansas," he said.

"You can say that again," I said.

"A piece of —"

"Just kidding, Cunningham," I said. "I've got an errand to run that'll take a couple of hours. Perhaps while you're making sure she doesn't leave town, you can make sure she gets some breakfast. Or at least some tea and crumpets."

"There's a crumpet shop just down the street," he said eagerly.

I wished him luck. Then went down into the garage for my car.

An hour or so later I was winding through the dripping woods of Bainbridge Island across the sound. I had some idea of where Mac's ex-wife lived, but nothing exact. We'd been over to catch a Mariners-Yanks series a few years back, and on the last afternoon, when we had several hours before our flight back to Meriwether, he had taken me out to see the house where love had died. It was large enough to be a hunting lodge, a glass and Alaskan cedar monument shining on the upper edge of a meadow that sloped down to a pond, but I suspect that the only hunting that went on was for rising stocks on the Internet.

"I'd show you the inside, pal, but the divorce wasn't exactly pleasant," he had said, "and I don't want to start it up again. You know what they say: marriages are sometimes over, but divorces never end."

A phrase that trickled like rainwater through my head as I searched for the place.

Turned out, though, that we did see the inside that afternoon. As we U-turned, a great hound lumbered from the roadside, trailing his lead and baying to beat the devil.

"Shit," Will said. "One of Lindsey's puppies is running wild and free. And, God, she hates that."

So Mac coaxed the large bloodhound, Rexford, into the backseat of the rented Caddy, then drove back to the gate while Rex snacked on the leather armrest. At the gate he pushed a button below the mike, and was greeted by a rather timid voice.

"Lindsey, it's Will, honey," he said. "I found Rex in the road, and you might want him back in the house."

Then came a muted exchange I very carefully didn't overhear. But the gates opened anyway.

Inside the lovely house, it looked as if an insomniac, an alcoholic, and a speed freak shared a house. Lindsey was a pale blonde, thin almost to the point of translucence except for her large, heavy breasts, which she leaned over as if to hide them. They seemed on the verge of pulling her off her tiny, dirty feet. The bloodhounds lounged like a pride of lions, chewing on the bones of abandoned pizza boxes and the skins of french-fry bags. And the smell: an insane asylum-cum-zoo. We had a quick warm beer, then fled.

Mac didn't say a word until we reached SeaTac. Instead of turning into the parking garage to return the Caddy, he turned into the first strip bar he found, parked, then turned to me.

"Let's see some titties, pal," he said.

It wasn't a particularly pleasant evening, and it lasted long past our flight and into the next day. Mac and I climbed onto our flight heavily burdened with guilty hangovers. We never spoke of the evening again. Not to our wives, not to each other, and, I suspect, not even to ourselves during those dark nights of the soul.

After looping and twisting and turning through the backwoods of Bainbridge, I finally found the gate. But I wasn't sure that I'd found the right woman. The voice that answered my buzz was anything but timid. Or reluctant to let me in when I explained who I was.

It was as if I had stepped into a different house. The glasswork glistened like stainless steel in the gray light. Everything was neatly in place. Lindsey seemed a different woman; she seemed to have gained both weight and stature without making herself larger. Her hair seemed the same pale blond I remembered, but somehow thicker, glowing instead of fading. And she carried her breasts as if they were new muscles, decently earned. She led me to the breakfast bar where we perched on stools.

"The dogs?" I said.

"They were killing me. Can you imagine that? Something I loved and treasured and enjoyed for most of my life was killing me with allergies," she said. "Jesus, I had to go into an asthmatic shock and nearly die to discover it."

She sounded so happy I hated to tell her the bad news. "There's no easy way to say it, ma'am, but it looks like your ex-husband killed himself last Friday."

"Bullshit," she said, then laughed. "That arrogant prick wouldn't kill himself."

I told her the circumstances, but she

didn't seem either bothered or particularly convinced.

"You haven't heard from him lately, have you?" I asked.

"Not a word since that day you were here," she said. "My checks come through the lawyers just like the others'. A small enough recompense for what he cost me."

"The others?" I asked, not thinking about what she had said about cost.

"His first four wives," she said, "that I know about. One lives in Marin, one down in Colorado, another one in La Jolla, and I think the first one's in Seattle, but her name never came up." Then she looked at me slowly. "You didn't know, did you?"

"Sure," I lied.

"Bad liar, buddy," she said grinning. "Will has a bad habit of marrying one of his patients about every five or six years. Especially the ones with money. Sometimes I think he loves money more than women, and boy does he love women. Of course that means divorcing the last one, which is always nasty and expensive."

"He never said anything —"

"He was like that," she said.

"You don't happen to have the other women's phone numbers or addresses?"

"I do. All but the one in Colorado," she

said, "but leave your card, and I'll see if they want to talk to you."

"I'd rather —"

"I'm sure you would," she interrupted. "But we'll do it my way. We're sort of a close-knit and protective group, the ex-wives of Dr. Will MacKinderick. Except for the first one. She's a mystery."

"All right," I said, then dug a card out of my billfold.

"You want a beer?" she said suddenly. "Might make this all go down easier."

"Why not," I said. "But I'd really like a cigarette."

She went around into the kitchen, then came back with two bottles of Bohemia in one hand, a business card in the other. I looked at the card before I put it in my pocket. LINDSEY PORTER, ARCHI-TECT.

"He told me you were a stockbroker," I said as she handed me the beer.

Her smile was very much amused. "I'm sorry," she said. "You are his friend, right?"

"Right."

"Then I'd advise you not to look too closely at him," she said. "Let's go out-side."

We sipped our beers and watched the fog

butting at the glass walls. Then I told her what had happened. Or at least as much as I knew. It took two beers. Her smile faded but never completely disappeared, flickering around the corners of her mouth like a curious butterfly.

"Mr. Sughrue," she said, "I can tell you a couple of things that might help. Will MacKinderick didn't kill anybody, including himself."

"How can you be sure?"

"Are you married?" she asked.

"I was the last time I looked," I ventured.

"You don't look married," she said. "Listen, Will MacKinderick is a fucking coward. He arranged to get sent back from Vietnam because he couldn't stand the pressure in the OR. He picked his ER jobs very carefully, then when he couldn't stand it, he went back to become a shrink." She paused, took a deep breath, then added, "And that's all I've got to say about that, mister." She paused to watch the wisps of fog filter through the evergreens, then roll back on themselves like playful puppies. "I should have kept painting," she said as she stepped over to a work in progress propped on an easel, a view of the meadow much as it was but lashed with sunshine. Something about the painting bothered me, but I couldn't place it. "I enjoyed the painting," she continued, "but Will always said I was no good. Maybe he was right. He was better than I was and never lost a chance to tell me about it. He could be a mean son of a bitch. But I loved him until he left me. And perhaps a little longer."

"You want me to call you when I find out what happened?" I asked.

She came out of her foggy visions to say brightly, "You call; I'll let you know if I want you to tell me."

"It's a deal," I said. We shook hands, firmly but briefly. "You're quite a remarkable woman, Ms. Porter."

"It was a long time coming, mister," she said, grinning, "but I certainly am."

We smiled our good-byes; then I walked out into the cool, wet air. As I put my hand on the door handle, I realized what had bothered me about the painting: she was painting sunshine onto a dark photograph.

Back at the Surry Park Hotel, I decided that I needed a drink and a smoke, so I sat down under the awning and collared one of the hotel's snotty waiters. Cunningham wasn't around, and even though I had counted on it, I almost hoped he'd had the sense to stay away from Lorna. I had had plenty of experience listening to husbands and wives telling stories about their spouses as if they were people I'd never met. Lindsey's story bothered me, but not too much. And lots of people don't like to talk about the ex-spouses.

As it turned out, I didn't have much time to think about it before the riot broke out behind me. The famous studied elegance of the Surry Park Hotel lobby was suffering mightily from Lorna's assault on the front desk. Naked under a hotel robe, she was screaming and pounding on the desk as Mr. Folger huddled behind it. She picked up the registration pad and bounced it off Folger's sweating forehead. Then she went for the pen. Cunningham tried to grab her arm, but she screamed for him to keep his hands off her, then buried the pen deeply into his forearm. I hustled inside, grabbed her robe with one hand and slapped her with the other. Lorna went completely slack, as rubbery as a snake. She slid out of her robe and hit the floor naked and unconscious. Either she had never been slapped before, or perhaps I had let loose weeks of frustration and coldcocked her.

"My god, man, you've killed her," Folger squealed.

"She's fine," I said as I checked her pulse and covered her with the robe. "She just needs a little rest. Call an ambulance. Now." Then I turned to Cunningham, whose face was as white as if he'd been shot, and handed him my card key. "I'll meet you in my room in a minute. Go now." He had the sense not to argue and to keep his bloody arm hidden from the crowd gathering in the lobby.

It took me two runs through the psychiatrist list in the yellow pages to find Mac's shrink's name. By pleading life or death, I got through during a session, explained the problem, and left it in her calm, capable hands. Dr. Cassilli had such a soft, lovely voice that I felt like a better person just for having listened to her.

I told Folger what the shrink had said, then asked for a pair of pliers.

"What?"

"Man, don't fuck around now," I said. "I fixed your problem, now you get into the junk drawer behind the desk or the bell boy's pants and get me a pair of pliers." Folger hustled like a man worried about a bomb. But when I took the pliers and headed for the elevator, he suddenly panicked.

"What if she wakes up," he stammered.

"Slap the shit out of her," I said. "Or let those guys take her." I motioned over my shoulder at the paramedics coming up the stairs from the street.

I stopped by Lorna's room for a second, cleaned up, and grabbed a few things. Cunningham was sitting on the couch in my room, holding his arm wrapped in a towel. "Jesus," he moaned, "if Pammie finds out about this, she'll insist on charging the woman. Assault on a federal officer. My God, the paperwork."

"No shit," I said. "What happened? Lorna want some blow, then another bang?"

Cunningham looked as dazed and confused as a child. "I can't pull it out," he complained. "It's stuck."

"Does it hurt?"

"Like the very devil," he said.

"This is going to hurt worse," I said.

"What?" he said, glancing at the pliers in my hand.

I tossed them on the couch beside him, then a big-eyed monkey with a stupid grin, a stuffed toy. "No," I said, "this."

"What?"

"Nanny-cam, asshole," I said.

225

"Oh, shit," he said, suddenly an adult in a world of shit.

"I guess you don't want to see the tape?" I said. "Since you've been there, done that, and brought back the hickie."

At least he had the guts not to deny fucking her. "That won't be necessary," he said. "What do you want?"

"Well, lover boy, right now I'm going to fix your arm, then smuggle you back to wherever you live, so you can come back in a clean jacket," I explained. "Now I'm going to cut that one off you."

"And then?"

"We'll get to that."

I'll give him this: he didn't faint when I jerked the pen out of his forearm, poured vodka into the wound, stuffed cotton balls into the hole, then, for the final touch, tied it down with a pair of Lorna's thong panties. Then I got him a windbreaker out of my closet — his shoulders would have burst through one of my shirts — mailed the tape to myself at Musselwhite's office, called his secretary, told her what to do, then took Cunningham down to the garage, bypassing the lobby, then up to the duplex on Swedish Hill, where he lived and where we were able to do a little better job binding his wound.

"How long has it been since you've had a tetanus shot?"

"A couple of years," he said.

"Got any antibiotics?"

"Never been sick," he confessed.

"I'm pretty sure I've got some in my Dopp kit," I said, "and some Lortabs."

"I don't want any pain pills."

"Don't be an idiot," I told him. "Your arm is going to be as sore as a boil for longer than you have any idea, and without pain pills you won't have a full range of motion, and believe me Agent Morrow will know, and she'll get it out of you —"

"No," he protested.

"Buddy, she'll open you like a rotten tomato."

"So what do you get out of this, Sughrue?" he asked, hanging his head in shame.

"What happened to the 'Mister'?"

"Screw you. Don't push it too hard," he said, more sad than angry. "Just tell me what you want."

"Even without a body, the Bureau is still carrying Dr. MacKinderick's death as an unexplained death on an Indian reservation, right?" I said, and he nodded. "And we've got what? Interstate flight to avoid prosecution, right? I want copies of the evidence photos, forensic reports, case files, and then I want you to walk me through the crime scene. You people are still treating it as a crime scene, right?"

He shook his head.

"Closed it down already? Well, tonight you copy the files, and tomorrow you take a personal day. Are you clear about that?" I said.

"Clear as a bell," he said. "And I can see my return to the Kansas Highway Patrol as clear as a bell." Then he turned his drooping face up to mine. "What kind of criminal are you, man?"

"Criminal?" I said. "Man, think of me as Dr. Justice. I can get it done. And I've never been charged with anything that stuck. So just be as smart as you're supposed to be, kid, and everything will work out," I said. "Now let's get back to the hotel, and act as if nothing happened."

"What about the tape?"

"Finder's keepers, kid," I said. "It'll be in my lawyer's safe by this time tomorrow."

"You're a smart old bastard, aren't you?" he said.

"And highly trained at government expense, just like you, bud," I said. "But keep in mind that I'm a couple of years short of old and that I loved my parents, so the next time you call me a bastard, you'd best be smiling."

Cunningham looked mildly confused. He had thirty pounds and twenty years on me, but I had put the snake bite of doubt in his eyes.

"We ain't gonna be buddies, kid, but we're gonna get along."

When we arrived in the hotel lobby, Agent Morrow was almost as close to a fit as Lorna had been, and Folger looked even more distraught. Of course, if I had slapped Pammie, I probably would have broken all my fingers and my wrist, then she would have jerked my arm out of the socket and gnawed it like a chicken bone.

Luckily, her anger was directed at Cunningham. "Where have you been, Agent?"

"Chasing down a lead," he said smoothly. "Mr. Sughrue got a call from a CI who thought he had spotted Dr. MacKinderick."

"*Mr.* Sughrue doesn't have any confidential informants," Morrow said sharply. "In fact —"

"Hey, good point, Agent Morrow," I interrupted. "But the lawyer I work for has clients."

"In fact, he's on the verge of an obstruction charge."

"Here, Agent," I said, then handed her two card keys. "Dr. MacKinderick's room. My room. Search to your heart's content." Then I turned to Folger. "Have I got a couple of faxes back there?" Folger dug them up quickly. "Legal waivers of our rights," I said, as she scanned the documents. "But of course no questions for Mrs. MacKinderick until Ron Musselwhite is here."

Morrow looked up quickly, the muscles in her jaw working out. "Is he that asshole in the braids?"

"I'll pass on the compliment," I said.

"Why would I want to search your room, Sughrue?"

"I just want you to be happy, Pammie," I said.

But she wasn't too happy.

Later that evening, I called Whitney to fill her in about the events of the last couple of days. She had always been good about helping me work out what I thought by talking to me, but she seemed distracted that night. Finally, I asked her directly what she thought.

After a long pause, she said softly, "CW, for a man in your profession, you seem to have a bad habit of trusting the wrong people."

After a pause even longer than hers, I said, "Thanks for that little gem of wisdom, Whit. Believe me, I'll keep it in the front of my head for the rest of my life." Then I hung up, switched off both phones, dug one of Lorna's battered bindles out of my billfold, and without thinking, chopped two fat lines. I did one slowly, then the other more quickly. Just like riding a bicycle, you never forget. Then I wanted a double handful of Scotch, some aimless conversation, bright lights, big city, strange women, all that shit.

The next afternoon, later than I'd meant to be there, I stood in the cold wind off the sound on the ferry from Edmonds to Kingston, hoping it might wash the wasted evening out of my head. I ignored the pile of messages on my cell, just as I refused to look at the case file and the photos that Cunningham had offered, but nothing seemed to help. So I rattled off the ferry and put my nose to the rain-wet highway, following my old buddy around the corner of the Olympic Peninsula toward the end of the world.

On a wet and foggy weekday at the end

of summer, the Cape Flattery Trail parking lot on the Makah Indian Reservation wasn't too crowded. In fact, it was strangely empty. Except for Cunningham and a tribal police unit. I grabbed my Old Goat windbreaker out of the trunk and followed Cunningham the three quarters of a mile to the last lookout on the trail, the place where Mac's clothes and shoes had been neatly piled next to his bare footprints at the edge of the cliff. In the distance, Tatoosh Island seemed to be sailing away into a gray darkness. The Pacific front had stirred huge rollers out of the cold ocean. Below me, I could see the vicious currents sweep up the coast to collide with the rollers, then scramble with the outrunning tide sweeping around the curl of Neah Bay and the long stretch of the Strait of Juan de Fuca. Nobody ever swam out of that.

"Fucking melodramatic bastard," I whispered by way of memorial or admiration, and I almost believed that he had done it. But I wondered why Mac had stopped to have his head stitched halfway across Washington. Maybe he was afraid of losing too much blood to make his exit. Then I dug into my pocket for a cigarette. I had open packs stashed in all my jacket pockets now. I found an unfamiliar box of Swan matches, too. When I opened them, I found the bug. Short range, short battery life, but state of the art. I couldn't recall the last time I had worn that particular windbreaker. And couldn't think of a reason for anybody to bug me.

Walking back down the trail, I didn't bother looking for clues. I knew that the cleaning crews had already been out with everything in their power to wash away the blood. The whole world was frightened of blood these days. And the steady drizzle had done its work. There was nothing here for me. Back at the parking lot, Cunningham handed me a plastic envelope, then left without saying good-bye. He looked like a man who had lost his buddy. But he had lost something even more precious: his innocence. I feared that he'd keep losing it until he became just another bureaucrat with a gun.

So I took the case files and photos back to Port Angeles; bought a jeweler's loupe, a bottle of Lagavulin, and a six-pack of PBR; then checked into a motel and cleared off the desk.

First, the paperwork. The FBI had never been my favorite public agency, but you had to admire their organization. They had done a month's work in three days. There were no surprises in the Meriwether PD's preliminary report. Sheila Miller's daughter, Marcy, didn't have much to tell the detectives. And my bare admission that I had been cooping in my ride while the murder took place was hard for me to look at. Blood types in the office were consistent with both victim and perp, Sheila and Mac, DNA pending. Everything that might contain any information — hard drives, floppies, minidisks, and the back-up Zip drives — were gone. The paper files were mostly intact but out of date. The interrogation of Moses Lake hospital personnel was consistent with the arrival of a single male with a large but superficial head wound. There was no evidence of concussion, he was a doctor, and he had checked himself out of the ER against doctor's advice. Nothing much in the reservation police report. A BMW Z car abandoned overnight in the parking lot at the trail head. Gouts of blood discovered at daylight. Drops of blood along the trail, some on the log sections used as flagstones along the trail. Others on boardwalks and bridges across the wet areas. Bloody handprints on some railings, more on the railings of the lookout. Blood on the clothes and shoes.

Then the pictures, where I found nothing out of the ordinary until the first shot of the interior of the little car. On the passenger-side floorboard, a single manila file folder, empty, the name *Landry, Turner* typed on the tab. Well, I couldn't chase him into the grave again. There was also a typed, bloodstained note on the passenger seat. It took the jeweler's loupe, but the words rose off the page clearly. *Lorna, love, so sorry, so, so sorry — is this darkness all we can know of love?* It all sounded crazy to me. After my last telephone conversation with my wife, I didn't much care to think about love and darkness. In fact, I didn't want to think about anything at all. I had a couple of beers and a room service burger, rented a couple of thrillers on the television, and popped a couple of sleeping pills. I didn't have any trouble sleeping after that.

Dr. Cassilli couldn't see me during the day to talk about Lorna, but she managed to meet me for a drink at the Four Seasons for a few minutes before a dinner meeting she couldn't miss. If the name and the softly accented voice suggested a Botticelli, the actuality was something completely different. Miriam Cassilli stood six four in heels, with a sculpted storm of gray hair swept back from her large striking face. She had a nose that made Claudia's look like a sparrow's and softly intelligent eyes that deepened with her voice. As they used to say, she looked like she could play horseshoes with horse collars.

Her large hand cradled the glass of merlot, and she smiled sadly at me. "I don't know what I can do for you, Mr. Sughrue. I can't tell you anything that might help in your search, if that's what it is, as long as Will MacKinderick isn't declared dead, and I can't force Mrs. MacKinderick to take her medication or stay away from alcohol and cocaine. She'll be stabilized in a few days, then she's your problem, not mine."

"Thanks," I said.

"I'm sorry."

"No, please don't get me wrong, ma'am," I said. "I meant thanks for your help. It's going to be easier to get her out of the hospital than the jailhouse."

"Mac thought very highly of you, Mr. Sughrue," she said. "Often it seemed you were his only friend, and since you were, I think I can safely tell you in my professional and personal estimation that Will MacKinderick was capable neither of murder nor suicide."

"Well, Dr. Cassilli, you're the second woman to tell me that in the past few days," I said, "and, I suspect, the second ex-wife, too." She didn't deny it. "Computers are snakes and Whatcom County isn't that far away. Just a few more miles to Canada, and I'd never have found it."

"I've tried to erase that part of my life," she said grimly, then switched the conversation to me. Shrinks. "You have trouble trusting women, Mr. Sughrue?" she said with a tiny smile.

"According to my wife, I'm too trusting, period," I said. "I guess it always seemed easier to think that people were telling me the truth than to assume that they were lying. A lazy man's response to a troubled world, maybe."

"A trusting heart is a precious thing, I think," she said. "What are you going to do now?"

"Maybe I'll see if her parents won't take her in for a while."

"Given what I know about her, I don't think that's a very good idea," she said seriously.

"Oh, shit," I said. "Excuse me."

"If she'll agree, I'd suggest a month or two of convalescent care, and detox might be the best choice," she said. "I can make some suggestions."

"I'll see what I can do," I said, then sighed so hard it seemed that the buttons might pop off the overstuffed lobby furniture.

"Are you going to be all right?"

"Who the hell knows?" I admitted.

"What are you going to do?"

"Well, I guess I'm going to find out what happened," I said. "That's what I do. Nobody ever knows why, Doc, but I do 'what' really good."

"Good luck," she said.

"I'll be in touch," I said.

"I was afraid you were going to say that," she whispered, finished her wine, then left me at the table.

I finished my drink, walked outside, then dialed Musselwhite's private cell number, the one reserved for the most serious emergencies. "Chief," I said when he answered, "I don't know where you are or what you're doing, but you best tie up your braids and get your ass to Seattle."

"What's up, Dog?"

Ten

Three days later, most of it spent lecturing me about fucking with the FBI, Ron had Lorna in a nice convalescent facility north of Seattle. I never found out what he said to her to get her to commit herself for sixty days, but whatever it was, it worked. When Agents Morrow and Cunningham showed up as the hotel people were packing Lorna's room, I was standing in the middle of the downstairs room with the cocaine-loaded jewel case like a large piece of dogshit in my hands. I quickly stuffed it into the nearest bag, probably behaving in a guilty manner. Ron stepped in front of Morrow, his large hand extended, a huge grin on his face.

"Hey, chubby," he said, "I'm the asshole in the braids."

Cunningham and I left them to their conversation as we slunk into the hallway and down to the patio bar. It was one of those fall days that make people forget the rainy days. We sat down like old friends. He ordered coffee, but I told him to have a drink. "She's going to be so mad, man, she couldn't smell blood on your breath."

"Well, fuck it," he said and ordered a vodka tonic. "How long are you going to keep me on the hook?"

"Actually, kid, if you'll find out one thing," I said, "I'll think about destroying everything."

"What's that?"

"Why she's got such a hard-on for MacKinderick?"

"That's easy," he said. "She used to be on a high-level task force investigating money laundering. And MacKinderick's name came up once on a computer search of offshore transactions, then disappeared. Along with about ten thousand others. She knocked out all the computers on three floors and blew out the backup files. Five years of work. She blamed a short, bad wiring, a hacker — but somebody had to take one for the team, so she left the task force and came into my life."

"That's the only name she remembered?"

"It's her mother's maiden name," he said. "She didn't have a first name — Dr. MacKinderick's name never appeared on any drug files — but when she saw it out here, she went batshit."

"So she's just a loose cannon?"

"You could say that," he said. "Now what about me?"

"Maybe you can tell me what this is?" I said as I showed him the bug I'd found.

"Probably another federal offense," he said, holding it, "but I'm sure that doesn't bother you."

"You didn't bug me, did you?" I asked.

He laughed. "With our budget, man? This is some bootleg ultrahigh-tech shit. For about thirty-five hundred dollars you can pick up conversations within a quarter of a mile until the batteries go. The DEA might have some they picked up in a raid. And maybe the Israelis. I've never seen one except in a catalogue. I can only promise you that you're committing a felony just holding it."

"Thanks," I said. "You're a nice kid. I've got your number. Relax."

Then I dropped the device into his watery drink. I think he called me a dirty word as I walked away but I wasn't listening.

When I told Ron about the exchange as I drove him to the airport — he was flying home first class; I was driving Lorna's luggage back to Meriwether — he warned me, "You keep fucking with those people,

Sughrue, they'll get you."

"Bureaucrats with guns," I said. "They've been trying to get me for years. Besides, I'm not the one who called her chubby."

"Slip of the tongue," he said, laughing quietly.

"At least now we know for damn certain that things aren't as they seem," I said. "He left me that one lead."

"The Turner Landry thing?" he asked as I pulled up to the departure curb. "How the hell does that connect?"

"Well, old buddy, those bodies didn't just drop out of the sky," I said. "At least not all of them."

"Beautiful, Dog. There's still all that money in the escrow account if you need it," he said.

"I'll let you know."

"Good luck," he said, stepping into a limo, while I pulled Mac's Range Rover into the construction nightmare of downtown Seattle, heading for my home chores.

The first morning back in Meriwether was spent unloading Lorna's luggage, having an extra set of house and office keys made, and finding another young couple in graduate school to house-sit until Lorna was able to come home. Then I spent the early afternoon teaching the Garfield sisters to fetch a catnip ball and playing phone tag with my distant wife. It was hard to tell who won. Even our successes were strained.

When Whitney finally caught me, I was sitting on the front porch lolling in the sunshine like a fat hog. And it went to hell, immediately.

"Les won't tell you, CW," she said sternly, "but I will. He'd appreciate it if you didn't call so often."

"What?"

"He says it embarrasses him in front of his friends," she said, then paused.

"What's the rest of it?"

"All right," she said, "he's having nightmares again about that time in the desert."

"What time?"

"When you killed those men on the steps and around the trailer," she said.

I had the *contrabandistas'* dope and money and they had Whitney and Les. Years of paranoia and preparation had worked. *Ollas* of water, extra moccasins, knives, and pistols buried at five-mile intervals. It was meant to help me escape, but it worked the other way. Twenty miles from the Rio Bravo to the trailer. I took my family very seriously. I ran twenty miles across the desert, gutted two men, cut one's head off, then drove the Bowie all the way through the last one. Then washed in the horse trough before I opened the trailer door.

"Honey, I don't want you to think that I've forgotten all you went through during the bad times," I said, "but please remember that I got you out and made them pay."

"That's the problem," she said. "Remember? They paid with their lives. My God, couldn't you have found some other way?"

"Like what?" I asked. "Like fucking what?"

"You son of a bitch, we saw you through a crack in the blinds, saw you ass-deep in the freezing horse trough, washing at the blood — as if it could ever come off." She paused. "You were smiling. And Lester saw you, too. His nightmares come back under any kind of stress, and Mac said it has something to do with you. I love you, but we can't live that way ever again."

"Mac?" I said, sick with waiting for the answer. "He's been seeing Mac?"

"You've got to make a choice," she said, ignoring my question, "and soon."

"There are a few things to clear up," I said. "Then I can come out."

"Just a few things," she said, sarcasm throbbing in her voice. "Right."

The girls, perhaps sensing my sadness, climbed into my lap and began to chew on various parts of my body. "You know where I fucking live," I said, the anger slipping back into my voice. "You're welcome anytime," I said. "The blood has all washed away."

"I don't think so," she said quietly.

With no answer for that, I hung up the phone. I hated to admit it, but those deaths were the end of my madness. Who knows why? After I got shot, I had a tickle in my heart, and I knew that tickle was fear. Maybe I was stupid, but I wasn't used to living with fear. Once the drug smugglers were dead, I was no longer afraid to die. So to hell with it. I went back to work. Something I understood, carefully not thinking about Whitney or Mac.

Then I called Claudia Lucchesi and badgered her into meeting me at the Bluerock Lodge, which wasn't easy, but she finally agreed. That done, I drove out to the Wagon Wheel Mobile Home Park to call on Marcy Miller, Sheila Miller's daughter.

The young lady who answered the door

had lost the Goth clothes and makeup, and removed the metal from her face. She had a power suit on, high heels, hose, and a new short haircut. She could have been a junior executive in training.

"What can I do for you?" she said. Her voice was harder than her mother's but softened by an overbite and a slight lisp. "I've got a job interview in thirty minutes."

"I thought you were in high school," I said dumbly.

"I graduated this summer," she said. "What do you want?"

I handed her my card, explained who I was, expressed my sorrow, and told her that I wanted to talk to her about Dr. Mac-Kinderick.

"Listen, mister, I've spoken to the police until I'm sick at heart," she said, "and the only thing I've got to say to you is fuck off." Then she tore my card in half, threw it at my feet, and slammed the aluminum door in my face, leaving me standing there feeling like an idiot, stupid, lost, and vaguely sad.

Things didn't go much better with Claudia. When she showed up straight from the office in her rat-killing clothes that night, she found me drooping over a watery Scotch at the half-empty bar. She stopped beside me, her hip cocked as if she were standing at the side bar.

"Okay, where're the candlelight, champagne, and room keys?" she said. "You look like a man trying to decide between sex or death."

"Don't tempt me," I said.

She threw a twenty on the bar, shouted to the bartender, "A double tequila shooter with a Corona back, and get my friend something festive."

"Thanks," I said.

"What the hell's wrong with you?" she said, then gunned the tequila.

"Don't ask," I said. "Please."

"Then what the hell do you want?"

"I need the name of the guy who lost the Turner Landry blood and tissue work," I said.

"Turner Landry?" she said. "Old news. What's in it for me, cowboy?"

"Anything your hard little heart desires," I said, more sadly than I meant. "Anything."

"Jesus," she said, then sipped her beer, you're not kidding."

"I'm not kidding."

"Sughrue," she said, "for reasons that don't even make sense to me, I've always wanted to fuck you. But not like this. I want you whole. I'll give you a call. Next time let's meet someplace where the most expensive item on the menu isn't an over-cooked bacon double cheeseburger."

She was gone before I could say thank you or good-bye. The bartender came back with Claudia's change, and shyly said, "Actually the bacon double cheeseburger is pretty good." Then she smiled as if that might cheer me up. "And we'll cook it however you want," she added.

"You're a darlin', darlin', but I think I'll have a double tequila shooter," I said.

"Worked for her," she said. "You want another beer?"

"I'll just finish hers," I said, which was a mistake. When I finished the shot and the lime, I nipped at the beer bottle, still sweet with Claudia's lipstick. As if to prove my strength of will, I did another, then slipped into the john to finish the last tiny bit of Lorna's bindle.

Which in no way explains what I did next. The crime scene tape was off Mac's office doors, and the cleaning crew had come and gone. When I flicked on the lights in the empty office, it was all there, just as real and intense as a combat flashback. I just waited it out, waited until it became an empty office again, full of nothing more threatening than the sharp odors of the cleaning solvents. The room was completely bare; everything had gone into police storage somewhere. The only thing out of place was the open door of the file closet. For no good reason, I walked over, stepped inside. Either the passage of the air or my weight caused the door to swing shut behind me. When the door latch clicked, the hair on the back of my neck rose straight up.

When I turned, the ventilator panel, opaque from the outside, was completely clear from the inside, offering a perfect view of the space where Mac's couch had rested. This time I had no control over the flashback. Images of Sheila Miller's body, alive and dead, swept over me like a passing freight. Without remembering a single movement, I was suddenly outside in the middle of the dark street, sweating, trembling with the adrenaline rush. A rush that lasted all the way to the Goat, through a dozen Scotches, then all the way home, and through the night. I suspected that I was drunk because I broke into Whitney's house even though I had a key. Maybe I felt like a thief in Whitney's house because of the separation. I quickly gathered up the cats to take to the office to watch all-night television with me.

Well, I'd had my mystical experience, so I paid for it with two solid weeks' worth of stupefying legwork. I spoke to everybody in every house within a hundred yards of the Ritters', spoke to them three or four times, then spoke to them again until one old lady called the cops on me. Then I moved on to the Marshalls' neighborhood, which was a hole almost as black as that horrible night I'd watched Ellen Marshall slice her hands off on the band saw. I saved the Pacific Northwest Hotel for last because the residents there, even with the assurance of Arno's father, weren't likely to have light conversations with anybody resembling a cop. So I spent four days humping up and down the stairs at all hours of the day and night, usually with a twelve-pack under my arm and a fat doobie in my pocket.

About six on the last afternoon, I found a police unit parked next to my ride. As I opened the door of the Outback, the cop hit his horn and motioned me over.

"Chief Raymond wants to talk to you, Sughrue," he said.

Raymond's office was as neat as a galley on a sailboat, and I didn't think he had cleaned up just for me. Only two things weren't department issue: a framed picture of his wife and three little girls in their Sunday best and one of his SEAL team in cammies and face paint ranged in front of a hooch in the Delta like a badass, post-apocalyptic street gang. Raymond looked straight and stern, his back to me, his uniformed figure dark against the afternoon sun. His desk was bare except for a pencil and a single legal form. I sat down without being asked.

"I wanted to do this personally," he said as he turned and shoved the legal form toward me with the pencil's eraser. "Just so there was no confusion."

I glanced at the restraining order issued by a district court judge, then said, "Hey buddy, this ain't necessary. All you had to do was ask."

"This way I'm sure," he said.

"I thought we were friends," I said.

"Don't push it," he said. "Just keep your nose out of this case. You've got no client. An obstruction charge might take time to prove, but contempt of court doesn't. I've got you by the gonads, you worthless piece of . . . I wouldn't wipe you off my shoe."

"That's unprofessional, Johnny, my boy," I said as I stood up, "asking for my help was the smartest thing you ever did. This shit's the dumbest. I don't know the who or the why about these killings yet, but I know how it went down and, believe me, I'll fill in the blanks. I've got a complete witness file on each death. I've got eleven people who saw housepainters at the Ritters' house."

"Anybody recognize anybody?"

"White hat, white pants, could've been ice-cream men," I admitted, "and ten witnesses at the Great Northern who saw oversized Girl Scouts with cookies of an unusual brand."

"What had they been smoking?"

"Whatever I gave them," I said. "These are kids, you dipshit." That almost brought him out of the chair and over the desk. Heaven knows, a bad idea but entertaining. "And I've got five women who studied under the dancing Shoshone shaman, who just might have talked Ellen Marshall into clipping off her meat hooks."

"You've got shit. You are shit. In my jurisdiction, sir," he said, "shit rates a little higher than marijuana dreams. But not much."

"Hey, man," I said, picking up the restraining order. "You're getting confused. We're the good guys."

"God help us," he said, but not with a great deal of conviction.

Just as I'd hoped, Ron Musselwhite had gotten wind of this ugly turn of events and was sitting behind his antique cotton broker's desk sipping a Negra Modelo, the bottle tiny in his bear's paw of a hand. Ron might dress like a Native American cowboy museum piece, but he collected Braque drawings and pre-Columbian Spanish furniture, so his office had the easy grace and comfort of a gallery. He nodded his huge head at the under-the-counter refrigerator, so I grabbed a beer, too.

"I'm sorry, Dog, but this all came out of left field," he said. "What did you ever do to Judge Trupin?"

"You don't want to know."

"Actually, I need to know," he said seriously.

"I did his ex-wife and his daughter one weekend up in Whitefish," I admitted. "Hell, I didn't know who they were. Or that they'd babble about it in group, then rat out each other."

"And what did you do to Johnny Raymond? Nail his wife?"

"I don't know what happened there," I said. "One minute we're holding hands, and the next he's got his dick in my pocket."

"And?"

"Well, there was a little ruckus," I said. "But he didn't seem to take it too personally."

"You kicked his ass?"

"Just a little."

"I don't know how the hell you do it," he said.

"Do what?" I asked unnecessarily. "So what the hell happened?"

"Nothing good, Dog," he said. "I hate to be the fountain of foul tidings, but I don't think you want to try to get the judge to release the injunction. It would take more money than you can spare, more time than I care to spend, and cause more hard feelings among the wrong people than either of us can afford." He paused, sipped the beer, and seemed to be staring into the cubist maze of a Braque print. Then he said, "And that ain't all. The DA blindsided me with a sealed grand jury murder indictment of Mac, plus they froze all his bank accounts, including the escrow he put up for you."

"What the hell is going on?"

"Hell, I don't know, but when they froze his accounts . . . well," he said, "that's where it gets really interesting."

"Yeah?"

"Except for your escrow, which the court effectively locked up, too, Mac's bank accounts were empty," he said. "Maybe if you send me a bill, I can unlock some of your money."

"None of this shit makes any sense."

"You're telling me," he said. "And guess who's on the hook at Lorna's loony bin."

"How did that happen?"

"White man speak with forked check," he said. "I should have realized something was up when Lorna's last check, covering the uninsured part of her stay, bounced. Of course, it gets crazier."

"How?"

"The day after Mac disappeared, all his bank accounts were transferred into privately held shell corporations with offshore accounts."

"Did he do it?"

"With the correct account numbers and passwords," he said, "anybody could do it by telephone or computer."

"What the hell does it mean?"

"Either he's running, or somebody killed

him and stole all the money. There's one more little thing."

"I hesitate to ask."

"You didn't look at this, did you?" he said, then opened his safe to take out the nanny-cam tape.

"No, why?"

"You should have," he said ominously, then punched the tape into the player, fast-forwarded to a spot he had marked, then let the soundless, jerky tape run. At first, I couldn't tell what was happening. I expected to see Cunningham on his hands and knees, begging Lorna, but instead I saw Lorna on her hands and knees as she was being butt-fucked by a broad-shouldered, muscular man I didn't recognize. Lorna pitched forward, exhausted, then the man backed up and turned around, and I nearly fell out of the chair.

Lorna lay on her side against the pillows, her face contorted with pain or pleasure — I wasn't sure I wanted to know which — and on the end of the bed sat Agent Pam Morrow, her crotch sporting a large double-barreled pink dildo. Then there was some other sordid action that I didn't watch.

Ron paused the tape. "Old J. Edgar is either spinning in his grave or spanking his monkey," he said. "But they sure have lowered the bar — spies, perverts, and drug fiends."

"Consenting adults, as they say," I said.

"Not necessarily," he said. "Before it started, Pammie gave Lorna a hypo. Don't know what it was, but it woke her up, and kept her loony at the same time." Then he fast-forwarded the tape again. "This is consenting adults."

Agent Cunningham stood beside Lorna's bed, crumpets and tea neatly arranged on a tray, saying something. Before he could finish, she had rolled over, unzipped his pants, and had his dick in her mouth. The fact that Cunningham didn't drop the tray was amazing. When she was through, he set the tray carefully down, then began tearing his clothes off. But Lorna ran to the bathroom for her stash before he got undressed. Then it was consenting adults.

Later, she stormed out the door in only her robe, as Cunningham threw his clothes on.

"I don't know what to think," I said, honestly. "But I own these fuckers."

"You don't want to own them, Dog," he said quietly. "Forget them."

"I'll think about it."

"Don't think, do," Ron said. "Since you're out of a job, why don't you do me a terrific favor."

"Do I want to know?"

"No."

"What do I get out of it?"

"Butch owes me a favor," he said. "I'll see about getting you an interview with Mr. Biddle. With a client, you're back in business, and maybe we can find out what the hell's going on around here."

"And I have to . . . ?"

"Drive over to get Lorna before I go broke," he said.

"Send an ambulance, man."

"She insists on you," he said. "And in fairly lucid terms. Make sure she stays on her medication. Don't let her drink. And keep her out of the blow."

"When?"

"She's expecting you day after tomorrow. And she wants to go home. The house belongs to her, thank god, and there's enough money in her accounts to keep things running for a little while."

"This is what I deserve for thinking a lawyer was my friend," I said.

"Right now, Dog, this lawyer is your best friend," he said, grinning broadly. "Send me an inflated bill, and perhaps I can get the judge to turn loose some money. Lorna sounds fine. Or at least fairly sane. I'll set up some kind of round-the-clock nurse help. For a few days. She'll be fine."

"It's me I'm worried about," I said. "Lorna's tougher than ancient lizard shit."

Eleven

But she seemed as delicate as a snow flower on the long drive back from Seattle. Perhaps being drugged, raped, and then enduring a couple of athletic tumbles with Agent Cunningham had taken some of the starch out of her. But, lord love a duck, she was still completely lovely, a shining beauty seemingly untouched by the recent past. She tilted the seat back, settled a pair of large shades on her face, then curled up in a comforter I'd taken from her bed, her rattiest stuffed animal, an elephant, clutched in her arms. She took a leak and got a Coke in Ritzville but fell asleep before she'd finished it.

When I pulled into the MacKindericks' driveway, the three does stood blind in my headlights. The fawn's spots had faded, and the winters were showing on the old doe's snout. She looked as old as I felt. The nurse met us at the door as I carried Lorna across the threshold as if she were a dead bride. She helped me put her to bed, then I fled into the night. Where I found Claudia Lucchesi sitting on my front porch, leaning on a backpack, flanked by the cats, looking for all the world like the devil's foundling.

"What's up?" I said.

"There seem to be people living in Whit's house," she said.

"Cats, too. It happens. They sneak in during the night," I said, "just like it belongs to them. Little bastards."

"You got someplace we can talk?"

In the office, I could see the fatigue in her face, so I put her in the La-Z-Boy, poured a couple of fingers of Scotch into a dirty glass, and opened a beer for myself. The cats had to survive on deer sausage, which they had to kill again to make sure it was dead before they gnawed it. Something about that I liked. "What's up?"

"I heard about the order," she said. "That's what happens when judges are elected —"

"Or they marry out of their league and spawn passionate daughters," I suggested. "Or at least women who can't keep their mouths shut."

"I was hoping that story wasn't true."

"Hell, I should have tried to get a mike into the group session," I said. "But I did hear that the size and nature of my apparatus changed as the evening wore on," I said. "Final judgment: like a tomato worm without a brain."

"That's what they say about you, Sughrue," she said sadly.

"Give me a break, hon," I said. "Nobody was married or even engaged. Consenting adults." Although the line stuck in my throat.

"So why are you here, darling?" I said. "You disapprove of my morals."

"Such as they are."

"You know I'm married, and I wouldn't fool around with my second-string lawyer."

"What about Ron?"

"I suspect that Mr. Musselwhite, since he's six inches taller, sixty pounds heavier, and a fifth-generation killer, could have his way with me," I admitted. "So what the hell are you doing here, Claudia?"

"I thought you might want to pack for the trip," she said.

"The trip?"

"I'm sick of this damned little town," she said. "Sick of so-called justice. Sick of myself, if the truth be known."

"I'm on your side, love, but I don't know what you're talking about or why you're carrying a duffle."

"Robert Guilder has relocated south," she said flatly.

"And who's that?"

"You'll find out when we get there."

"We?"

"I sat there this afternoon and listened to that arrogant little turd treat Ron like a red-headed stepchild," she said. "And believe me, the little bastard owes him big-time." Then she sighed, and added, "So I threw it all away. All those stupid fucking years."

"Threw it away?"

"Butch was thinking with his dick when he drew up my partnership contract. So he'll spend the rest of his life scrambling his hairy ass off to pay me."

"You quit?" I was still somewhere on Interstate 90, highway miles like a snowstorm running into my eyes. I couldn't get my mind around it. "You quit?"

"It feels great."

I poured two more drinks, watched the cats decide that perhaps the deer sausage had a bit too much pepper for them, then they dashed out the cat door, heading for their water bowls in the house. Somehow my glass was empty, so I had another.

"How long have you had cats?" she asked.

"What?"

"The cats? Where'd they come from?"

"Cat detective school, I guess. Hell, I don't even remember when I last slept or sat down at a table or leaned on a bar," I admitted. "I don't have any idea what the hell you're telling me, and I'm not sure that I want to. I don't even know where I'm going to sleep."

"We could break back into my place."

"Break back in?"

"Butch owns my condo, even the damned furniture," she said, then laughed. "He had the locks changed, hoping I'd have to come to him to get my things. Stupid asshole, thinks a Butte girl can be foxed by a sliding glass door. I got all my clothes. I'll have to sue for the rest, the controlling son of a bitch."

"Who the hell is Robert Guilder?"

"He's the guy that lost Landry's blood and tissue work," she said. "You said you wanted the guy's name."

"That I did. So why won't you tell me where he is?"

"If you knew, you wouldn't take me along," she said shyly.

"Claudia, love, I don't know what's happening with my marriage," I said as calmly as I could. "But it ain't over yet, and I don't want it to end in somebody else's bed."

"No problem," she said. "I promise."

"Do you have any idea what you're getting into here?" I said.

"Tell me. I listen like a professional."

"Johnny Raymond is looking for any excuse to lock me up," I explained, "and the FBI ain't all that happy with me —"

"What did you do to them?"

"Don't ask," I said. "And there's a good chance you could get disbarred just for hanging around with me. And I might do some things you don't want to know about. So I'd suggest that this is a really bad idea."

"Just what I need right now," she said. "I think. Besides, it would take you a month to find out what I already know, and I won't tell unless I can come along."

"You can be a bitch, darlin'," I said. "And sometimes you enjoy it, don't you?"

Claudia's happy smile was all the answer I needed. I settled up with the house sitters from fetching Lorna, engaged them for a longer sit, then got down to business.

"Here's the deal," I said as I opened the floor safe. "Dump all your credit cards, IDs, cell phone, and anything with your name on it in the safe." The safe was where I kept my best fake IDs, gathered and carefully maintained over the years. And real passports, live credit cards, cash, and current driver's licenses. In case I had to run, I was ready. I'd been ready for years. "And I do mean everything."

"What's that about?" she asked. "If I don't stay in touch with my mom, she'll have the National Guard out looking for me."

"Use pay phones," I said, closing the safe. "I don't want anybody but Ron to know where we are or what we're doing, okay?"

"What about your car?"

I opened the office door to the back garage and turned on the lights to reveal a gray four-wheel-drive Chevy short box pickup, not too old, not too new, not too clean, not too dirty.

"We're going in that?"

"Well, it ain't your Jag, sweetheart," I said. "But it'll leave your ride in the dust. The engine isn't exactly stock — it'll do an honest one forty — and the shocks aren't standard either. Plus, the guy who owns it doesn't know he owns it."

"Jesus," she groaned. "I've always known you were a criminal. What do we do if we have to check into a hotel?"

I pulled a set of almost perfectly good fake IDs, live credit cards in assumed names, and all my running cash out of the safe, leaving the perfect ones inside, and said, "I'm always ready to run. We'll figure out something for you on the way. Lost purse or something. It'll be fine. Fake IDs are easy for good-looking women."

"Thank you, I think," she said.

"Guys are always looking at your tits," I said. "Women at your hair. You think Chinese people all look alike? Just look at any bunch of good-looking women all at one time. They all look alike."

"Even me?"

"There ain't nobody like you," I said, meaning it. "You got any cash?" I asked.

"A couple of thousand in mad money," she said, "and I can hit the ATM on the way out of town."

"That'll help," I said.

"You want to tell me again why we're running like thieves in the night?"

"Because we are," I said. "If I'm right, we don't want to leave any sort of trail. Unless you just tell me where he is."

"Not a chance, cowboy," she said, her smile young and happy again.

The pickup was a bonus. I grabbed my traveling gear, the bag with the laptop but without the Browning 9 mm or the

Walther .22 — if I needed a piece, I could pick it up along the road — a Dopp kit with some legal meds and some illegal, and said, "Get your bags, lady, and let's look at some highway."

We swapped cars in the garage, then headed south in the middle of the night. That's all she told me. Head south.

Since time didn't seem to be a factor, we hopped over to Missoula to pick up Highway 93, then headed south. We got as far as Hamilton before exhaustion overcame us. We got one room with two beds, already so tired we fell into the beds without even saying good night.

The rest of the trip was calm and companionable, a long easy drive through the Nevada desert fall, listening to Vivaldi and Zevon, drifting through along miles of the real Old West, the sort of country where jackrabbits carried water bags and gophers stood by the side of the highway, their little paws raised, waiting patiently for the brief breeze of a passing car. Les's favorite moments when he was a nubbin. I told him we were holding the tiny animals up for gopher pee to get across the desert. Of course, I had to show him a bottle — a warm Pabst passed for gopher pee as far as he was concerned. But he barely chuckled when I mentioned it on the cell. I stopped for a beer, slammed my fist into a dead cottonwood, and let it pass.

"We need to go back?"

"We've just started."

Ron was on a double murder trial in Billings, and he didn't have much time for our shenanigans. But he did arrange for a bundle of cash to be delivered at Cactus Pete's on the Idaho-Nevada border.

"Jesus," she said, "what do people do out here?" She was in one of her rodeo queen outfits, lovely enough to sell to a passing rustler. "What can they possibly do?"

"Survive is about all," I answered. "My dad cowboyed and Indianed out here when he came back from the war."

"What?"

"About half the time he thought he was an Indian — sometimes a Cheyenne, sometimes a Sioux or a Comanche — but mostly he was just a saddle tramp, breaking horses, cutting wheat, and baling hay. I never saw much of him. Except in the summers. Hell, sometimes I didn't even recognize him when he came home."

"What happened to him?"

"Nobody knows," I said. "Maybe he just

drifted off into one too many sunsets."

Claudia wouldn't give me a hint about where we were going, but I didn't much care. A road trip without a point, down one of the most peaceful bits of highway left in the country. Of course, from some of the roadside turnouts where we stopped, we could hear the distant thump and crunch of the bombing range beyond the distant mountains.

Whit left several messages, but I was too confused to respond to them. My son didn't want to talk to me, which hurt like a broken rib, but I left him alone as much as I could and kept the few conversations as short and mundane as possible. We'd driven this highway together, but he didn't remember. But I wasn't too worried. I knew that the first time I saw Les again, the love and laughter would rush right back. Each time I checked with the house sitters, the cats were more and more in charge. Lorna seemed to be asleep every time I called, which was fine with me.

Outside Vegas, Claudia directed me over to Kingman, Arizona, where we picked up I-40, then over to I-17 down to Tucson, where we turned left on I-10 across the bottom of Arizona and New Mexico. When we turned right at Deming, I guess my face changed because Claudia asked me what was wrong.

"Let's find a drink," I said.

"I'm with you now, cowboy."

When we got settled on bar stools at a motel lounge, I admitted, "I've been here before, and it wasn't particularly pleasant." I didn't think she needed to know about how my partner was tortured and forced to dig his own grave between Anapra and Columbus, then kill two men with a shovel and flee naked across the desert. When I finally found him in a Deming motel with a heroin monkey on his back, he still had a dead man's hand under his pillow.

"So Robert Guilder lives in Columbus or Palomas, huh?" I said. "Ain't nothing else down here."

"Columbus," she said. "In a house built next to an air park — runway and hangers and the whole nine yards."

"So what do we have on him?"

"Very little," she said. "He was allowed to resign with a full pension, but about the same time, his mysterious great-aunt in the Bahamas died and left him with a couple of million bucks. Maybe three. So he traded his little Cessna for a used Beechcraft King Air, a C90B, I think. He takes up the occasional sight-seeing group, but mostly he just flies around alone. Oh, and he traded his old wife from Havre for a blond giantess from Ukraine, an ex-officer in the medical corps."

"Any place to stay in Columbus?"

"One motel, a bed and breakfast."

"Shit, I'd rather sleep in the car," I said. "Maybe we should hang here a couple of days while I check him out, and you can put all your lawyer shit to use and hit the courthouse. Then I'll pay him a little visit."

"Don't even think about leaving me behind."

"Right," I said, but started planning a way to do it. "Let me have the address, okay?"

She hesitated, but finally turned loose of it.

We checked in at the motel where we were drinking — two rooms this time — and I rented a dusty brown Jeep so I wouldn't show up in the tiny town of Columbus wearing Montana plates.

We had flat enchiladas and half a dozen drinks for dinner, then a sweet tequila-laced good-night kiss, which almost became something else. But just sealed the friendship.

Because I couldn't get hold of my hacker friend in Boston, I had to spend most of the night chasing Robert Guilder around the cyberworld, spending money I didn't have, loading my credit cards until they squealed like gored oxen. But he was boring as a lab coat. He had his work; he had his plane, which seemed the center of his life.

Early the next morning I tried to send Claudia on a separate chore, but she refused. The day before, I had picked up a U.S. Geological Survey map of southern Luna County, a set of desert fatigues, and an aviation radio, so by good daylight I had my spotting scope settled on the back door of Guilder's sprawling fake adobe house. He came out, a tall, pear-shaped man with a bad black toupee that glistened like a grease puddle on his round head. The light morning breeze didn't wiggle a hair on his head. Hell, even his mustache looked fake. He went into the hangar and wiped down his aircraft with the loving care of a proud father, then checked the engines as carefully as if he were about to fly across the Atlantic. But as far as I could tell from the radio, he had filed a flight plan to Fort Stockton and back, without any stops. An old boy wouldn't mess with dope smuggling this close to the border. The airfield's only advantage was its closeness to the border, which was a singular disadvantage unless he wanted to run. He could run in moments.

Guilder was the first one in the air, his craft lifting across the bottom of the Florida Mountains, but as the morning brightened, his neighbors drifted out to their hangars or pools, raised their American flags, and drank coffee while talking to the postman. I swear, though, that one old lady in a bright pink jumpsuit came out into her sculpted concrete backyard with a handful of little flags and proceeded to put them into little holes. Then she returned to the house for a cup of coffee, a golf ball, and a putter. She had a miniature golf course in her backyard. And by damn she was having a hell of a time. Every time she hit a hole in one, I could hear her laughter crackle through the clear desert air.

Then the major event of the morning arrived, striding out Guilder's back door. Larise Grubenko Guilder must have been well over six feet, slim but well muscled like a professional swimmer, with broad shoulders and thick, solid, beautifully sculpted thighs. Just about as much bad woman as a good man could want, and not wearing enough clothes to cover a mouse. The tiny suit almost perfectly matched her walnut tan. She had about four feet of golden, almost white, blond hair hanging across her broad tan shoulders. Breasts like high explosive nose cones rose proudly above washboard abs. Bulging calves and slim ankles completed the picture, slightly outlined by flashes of red on her lips, fingernails, and toes. I wondered what sort of nursing she had practiced.

I let Claudia take a look. "My God," she said. "What's that?"

"Probably a couple hundred grand's worth of pussy."

"Don't be crude," she said, then I led her back to the Jeep and took her complaining mouth back to the motel.

"Trust me," I said, "you don't want to be around this. Or know about it."

She accepted it, but she didn't like it.

Assuming that the desert fatigues gave me a slightly official look, I worked my way around to the front of the house, parked, strode officiously up the walk and hammered like a cop on the door. The old lady golfer stared at me through her window, shaking her head sadly. A sign I should have perhaps heeded.

Larise opened the door wearing a loose, transparent wrap over her tiny suit and holding a pair of panty hose draped over her shoulder. The rest of the room was filled with Western movie paraphernalia.

"What do you want?" she said sharply with only the barest hint of a husky accent.

"I'm a private investigator from Montana," I said, "and I'd like to talk to your husband."

"And I'd like you to sit down very carefully in that chair," she said, nodding to a deacon's bench along the foyer wall. But I didn't do it.

"Lady I don't know who the hell you think you are," I said, "but it's been a long goddamned time since somebody holding a pair of panty hose told me what to do."

She hit the side of my head with the doubled foot of the panty hose, which she had filled with sand and bird shot. She might as well have shot me. I hit my knees like a God-sodden nun the first time she hit me. Then the second time I tipped over like a sack of loose sand, sand that ran in pretty puddles out of my head. My last thought was that she could hit pretty good for a broad on four-inch heels.

Twelve

I suppose I thought I was going to wake up to the dulcet tones of a nurse or an angel, but the first words I heard were a sharp command: "Hold still." Then the too-familiar feel of a suture pulling tight on my scalp. I opened my right eye slowly only to find myself blinded by an erect nipple behind the swimsuit top.

"Don't get any ideas," she demanded. "Blood is so hard to get out of silk."

I shut my eyes and seemed to drift away. When I came back, it was because she had popped an amyl nitrite capsule under my nose as she finished. Maybe I went back out because she popped another under my nose and shoved what tasted like three bitter Lortabs into my mouth. I came up like a snagged fish to discover that I was tied naked, spread-eagled, to iron bedposts. Larise had her wrap back on, for all the good it did.

"What the fuck?" I said.

"You've got a very hard head, my friend," she said softly. "I'm sorry, but I had to hit you twice. I expected you to be out for several hours. You're a wonderful surprise."

"You're not the only one who's surprised," I said, glancing at my naked body.

She smiled like the evil witch she was, then said, "Don't complain. The stitching is very good, except for the ear — I had a little trouble with the ear — but the bleeding has stopped, and your ear won't flap in the wind. Clean the wounds twice a day and leave them uncovered. I tried not to cut too much of your hair."

"How nice," I said, "but you've gone to a lot of trouble for nothing. There's nothing I can do to you or your husband. You should know that. You're clean, green, and perfectly legal with the INS, and nobody can track his money past his dead great-aunt in the Caymans. You're completely safe."

"*Safe,*" she sneered. "Such a stupid American word."

"I just wanted to ask him a few questions. That's all."

"Questions," Larise spit. She didn't seem particularly interested in anything I had to say. She just walked around, examining me like a boar trussed for the fire pit. "You know, this will be a first for me," she said, still smiling. "First time unprofessionally that is," she whispered. "Professionally I've beaten generals until they pissed blood from their eyes. I've shit in their greedy mouths, peed on their fat faces. But now I'm free. And you're the whore with questions." Her laugh tickled my spine like a line of army ants.

"My wife and I do this all the time," I lied, sweating. "Nothing new to me."

"You have a wife?" she asked.

"Wonderful lady. Happily married for years."

Larise's smile said it all. *You'll never be the same.* She dropped her wrap, discarded her suit like quilt scraps, then leaned over my crotch, her hair like smooth golden sand sweeping across my hips, her shaved crotch in my face. "You've got lots of scars," she whispered. "I love a man with scars." Then her tongue, soft as a feather, touched me. Somewhere in the distance, a doorbell rang, the washing machine throbbed like a sore thumb, and an aircraft took flight. "Lick me," she said, "or I'll bite your dick off."

There wasn't a second when I didn't believe her.

Fear the fantasy that comes to life, my friend, fear it like death.

It was only the middle of the afternoon when Larise helped me out to my Jeep in front of the house, but it felt as if years had passed, as if I had become a very old man recently. Even my freshly washed fatigues — bloodstains scrubbed desert tan again — felt as soft and cuddly as hospital pajamas.

"Are you sure you can drive?" she asked as she patted me on the cheek and gave me a soft friendly kiss. "Remember, no questions for my husband. Never. The next time I won't be so nice." Her smile suggested whips, chains, and stiletto heels on my nut sack.

"Right," I whispered, then drove into the blinding sunlight. The old lady golfer gave me a look, but I don't think it had anything to do with sympathy.

Claudia wasn't exactly sympathetic, either. In fact, she laughed all the way back to the border until I threatened to punch her. The only person who had any sympathy was the druggist across the border in Palomas who, for a ridiculous price, provided me with enough Vicodins to keep moving for a few days.

When Claudia stopped laughing, she

asked, "You resisted with all your heart, didn't you, CW?"

"I seem to remember something about that."

Claudia's giggles became uncontrollable again, so I left her in the Jeep and huffed back to my room. She was right behind me. "I don't know why I never thought about trying that approach," she said between her fingers. Then she had a moment of control before it started again. "You didn't come, did you?"

"No," I lied. Actually, the last time I'd come, I was convinced I'd come blood, but it was just tired postignition exhaust. My dick was so sore I had to buy a jock and sit down to pee. I felt as if I had been recircumcised. "Absolutely, not," I added. "And I can do without that fucking smile."

"Take it easy, cowboy," she said. "No regrets. Come on, I'll buy you a drink, maybe even dinner."

"In El Paso," I said. "Pack up. We've got to go to El Paso."

"What the hell's in El Paso?"

"A friend," I said, "a man I need to talk to before I go back into that house."

"You're serious, aren't you?" she said, and her smile faded like the sunset.

★ ★ ★

Somehow the life seemed drained out of El Paso. Maybe it was the new fence or the border patrol units lined up along the *rio,* perhaps the whore of NAFTA. Sometimes it seems as if the whole world is becoming a third world country.

We checked into the Holiday Inn at Sunland Park. I grabbed an overpriced halfwarm beer out of the room's minibar while Claudia took a long shower. I'd seen all the naked women I wanted to see for a long time, so I stepped outside. Sundown still hovered along the horizon. The ranges of the Potrillos and the Floridas rose in sharp relief against the fading pink. I knew that if I could see around the motel, the Thunderbird would be growing into flight across the face of the Franklin Mountains. As the air cooled, the rocks released their heat as softly as the breath of a sleeping child. A magic moment. But I knew better than to look east to the Asarco towers or south to the ever-burning dumps of Juarez — the desperate poverty, the murdered women from the *maquiladores,* the tons of drugs waiting to move. There must be a better way to run the world.

Or perhaps I had just fallen into an abyss of dishonor, ruined and dirty. By a bought

Ukrainian whore. Now I wanted a shower. Fuck the stitches. Like the lady said, I have a hard head.

Claudia was nearly dressed when I came back in, dropping a soft, green jersey that held her like an embrace over black panty hose. Then she slipped into green suede heels, her green eyes glittering. I felt like a rat on the run.

"I'll meet you in the bar," I said, perhaps more curtly than I meant. But I wasn't into my apologetic mode yet.

I washed the blood out of my hair and watched the bloody foam course down the gutshot scar and the rest of my ruined body. There should have been tears, too, but I was still angry. If I lived long enough to become an old man, I was going to be a mess. But they hadn't got me yet. I'd been older a few hours ago, but now those old Scotch-Irish redneck genes had taken over. Plus a couple of Vicodins. I was a fistful of random trouble again.

Claudia was sitting at the corner of the bar, surrounded by horse trainers and horse turds, as I walked up. She excused herself, picked up her purse, and headed for the bathroom. I shouldered through the clot of middle-aged boys and took Claudia's seat.

"Hey, buddy," the biggest one said, "somebody's sitting there."

"No fucking shit," I said over my shoulder to the big one.

Then I added to the bartender, "You might as well call the ambulance now, 'cause I'm gonna kill the big one first."

The chicano bartender turned white, and I spun my stool to face the big one. He was wearing one of those polyester western suits with fake stitching and a pair of cheap cowboy boots. I felt a drip of water, or blood, drift down the side of my cheek. I guess that made my point. The group muttered and nattered and stuttered back to the tables.

"He's just crazy," I heard somebody say.

"No fucking shit," I repeated, then stood up off my stool. Chairs scraped, but nobody moved toward me.

Claudia stood suddenly before me, wiping the blood off with a bar napkin. "What the hell are you doing?" she said. "Sit down before we get thrown out."

"Separating the shitheels from the shit-heads," I said, but I sat down. I ordered us shots of Patrón tequila and bottles of Tecate.

"Should you be drinking like that, with

your head, you know?" she said.

"What is today?"

"Saturday, I think," she said, and the nervous bartender nodded quickly.

"Well, I've been humiliated, lied to, fucked over, and run around," I said. "My wife is living in fucking Minneapolis, my best friend is either dead or a murderer, and I've got a very bad headache. Nothing I can do tonight can fix it or fuck it up. So let's find me a hat, hire a limo, and paint the town."

Claudia smiled like a teenager contemplating her first night out, clicked my glass, and agreed.

It wasn't a stretch, but it was a classic Lincoln Continental with suicide doors, and the driver took us places we had never dreamed of being in. Back and forth across the border, dancing and drinking and eating and singing. Julio's, the Kentucky Club, del Norte, some salsa place. Then he brought us back at daylight after a *menudo* breakfast.

We slept in the same bed that day and spooned, both occasionally shivering through bad dreams. We were shy with each other that afternoon, oddly without hangovers, but still pals, and still on the hunt.

I knew that Hareem, the bail bondsman I had worked for when I was hiding down here, would be in his office in downtown El Paso on a Sunday, bonding out the Saturday night bad guys. But I never expected his receptionist, Lila of the blue hair, harridan extraordinary, would be there, too.

"Lila," I said as Claudia and I came in the door, "you still stealing doobies from your kids?"

"You mean the doctor, the lawyer, and the computer geek? Or the Holy Roller housewife?"

"Yeah," I said.

"And why would you want to know?"

"It's just the way I am," I said.

"CW, you idiot, how the hell you been?" she said, then scrambled out of her chair to hug me so hard my head ached. "What's up? You back in the business?"

"Sort of."

"Who's this?" she said. "This is not your wife," she said sharply. "I know your wife."

"She's my lawyer," I said.

"Well, you were always the sort of saddle tramp that needed a lawyer in his bedroll," she said. Then to Claudia, wearing a black lawyer suit, "Honey, I wouldn't sit down anywhere in this shithole." The calendars hadn't been changed since Carter and the dust hadn't been disturbed since the last drug dealer had had a fit over the price of his bail.

"Thanks," Claudia said.

Then to me, "Hey what do you want? That ain't your social face, not with that ear and a streak of blood on your face." Somehow we'd lost my hat the night before.

"Claudia, would you please wait outside?" I said. She gave me an odd look but complied. "I need a piece," I said to Lila. "A big son of a bitch. And a roll of quarters."

"Don't cuss in my office, CW," she said. "I'm the only one who can cuss in my office."

"Sorry," I said, then dropped a dollar bill into the pickle jar on her desk. I suspected Lila sent her kids to school out of that pickle jar.

"Did you try the newspaper?" she asked, as she pitched me a roll of quarters.

"Too much of a trail," I said. "I want something that can't be tracked back to anybody."

"You want one of the clean pieces out of the safe, don't you?" She was talking about guns whose history had disappeared shortly after they'd left the factory.

"On the money, my dear."

"Well, you go get it," she said. "I don't want to know."

"What about Hareem?"

"The old fart's asleep," she said. "You could steal his pants." I slipped into Hareem's office. The old man snored as if a kazoo had been stuck into his shrunken mouth. His teeth rested in a flyspecked glass of warm vodka, and his small hands were tucked into his stretched waistband. I opened the unlocked safe and slipped out a piece — a Colt short-barreled .357, the numbers burned off — took out a handful of rounds, then left the old man to sleep. He had done me many good turns during the hard times. Lila and Claudia were standing in the dirty downtown street, as out of place as angels dancing on the backs of tarantulas.

I kissed Lila good-bye, told her to tell Hareem thanks. And handed her a bundle of cash.

"Keep your cash, Sonny," she said. "I ain't even gonna tell him you were here." Then Claudia and I climbed into the rented Jeep.

"I'll bet she was a piece of work in the old days," Claudia said.

"Shit, she's caught more bail jumpers than most people ever see," I said. "Says it's the grandmother thing, and the .44 Bulldog she carries in her girdle."

As we drove west on Mesa, I stopped to pick up a couple of roses from a street vendor, then a six-pack of beer.

"You taking flowers to your girlfriend?"

"To Lester's mom's grave."

"Whitney's not his mom?"

"No," I said. "And I'm not his dad. I got his mom killed. I fucked up. I killed his dad, too, but that wasn't a fuck-up. That was on purpose. So we adopted Les, and ran with him from the people who were trying to kill me."

"Drug smugglers?"

"And some Hollywood types," I said.

"He looks so much like you two," she said, then added, "but I suspect you don't want to talk about it right now."

"Thank you," I said.

I drove across the valley of the Rio Grande, up the old western banks to the place we called the eighth wonder, where I had thrown Winona's ashes into a whirlwind of desert dust, then tossed the flowers off the cliff and drank the beer until it was warm backwash. I was never going to be whole, but some of the holes had been filled. As I've always said, anybody who doesn't believe in revenge never lost anything worth having.

"I'm sorry," Claudia said softly. Then added, "I'm a little worried about what you're planning."

"Don't," I said. "They're the bad guys. They can't call the police."

This time I did it right: showed up at the door before Robert Guilder took off, displayed only a fake badge at the peephole, and when Larise opened the door, I hit her with a short uppercut on the point of the chin so hard I knocked her right out of her silk robe and her fluffy mules. The roll of quarters burst, scattering across the fake calfskin rug. I was way beyond caring. I slipped a roll of duct tape out of my small backpack and whipped a couple of wraps around Larise's wrists and ankles, then I met Guilder at the kitchen door, slapped the toupee right off his head, and tossed him into a captain's chair by his flying coveralls.

"Put your hands in your pockets and don't say a word," I whispered, then tapped him on the nose with the .357 just hard enough to raise a tiny bump and a small cut. "Sit down in your chair, and don't move. If you move, I'll strangle you with her guts." Then I strapped him to the chair.

I think he believed me, so I went back to check on Larise. She hadn't swallowed her tongue, and her jaw wasn't broken, just a few chipped teeth. I grabbed a couple of poppers out of the medicine cabinet.

It took two bursts up her nose to bring Larise back to the world, but she was tough. She came back with a smile and an invitation, "You came back for more?" The accent was a little deeper, with a slight lisp.

"Listen," I said quietly into her ear. "You've got a good life here and as long as you keep your mouth shut, you can have that life. I don't want anything from you. I just want to talk to your husband."

"You've already hurt me," she said, smiling now. "You're leaving and never coming back, aren't you?"

"I'll think of you now and again," I said, then closed her mouth with her thong panties and a piece of duct tape. "But not too fondly."

Her eyes still smiled as if she knew better.

I took the piece and the pack into the kitchen. Then motioned Guilder toward the back door. The golf lady was placing her flags, and she waved brightly. Then I muscled Guilder into the hangar, right next to his plane, his baby, his beauty. I closed the doors and put a couple of wraps of duct tape around his body, pinning his arms to his side, his hands locked in his pockets. Then I took something odd out of the backpack. A plastic liter soda bottle stuffed with cotton puffs and steel wool. I stuffed the revolver barrel into the opening.

"Asshole," I said, "I'm going to ask you one time, and one time only . . ."

"And you're going to kill me," he stammered. "Is this something Larise did? I didn't have anything to do with it. This is all her fault."

Okay, I lost my patience and slapped him hard enough to knock him down, then had to help him up. "I don't know where you got that woman, you nitwit, but she's worth a dozen of you."

"Off the Internet," he babbled. "I didn't know the people she was involved with —"

I slapped him again, gently this time, and said, "All I want to know is who paid you to lose the Landry blood work?"

"What?" he screeched.

I put a round through the left cowling of his aircraft engine. It was even quieter than I'd hoped, but the silencer disintegrated.

"My god, man, you can't shoot my air-plane!" he screamed.

"Wrong answer, asshole," I said, then took another makeshift silencer out of the pack. "Oh, look, it happened again," I said. Another hole about two inches to the left of the other, and a shower of debris.

Guilder fell to his knees, babbling, "Some blond woman in big shades set it up. I'd never seen her before, never seen her again. Just that one time in the Caymans. Shit, she even told me how to wash the money. And what the hell difference did it make who killed who, who was fucked up, and who wasn't, where the piece of stove wire came from, I mean who cares —"

"Where'd you lose it?"

"Steel locker, deepest part of Flathead Lake, just like she told me."

"What'd she look like?"

"Look like?" he whined. "Christ, I don't know. A woman, dark glasses, a scarf, a wig; hell, it could have been anybody."

I know it was mean, but I used the third silencer to put another round between the other two. Guilder fell to the hangar floor, a sodden mess now, covered with tears and engine oil, dotted with bits of white plastic, cotton balls, and gray scribbles of steel.

"You better hope your wife loves you," I said. "At least a little."

"She doesn't love me," he whined. "She beats me up all the time."

"Learn to love it, man," I said, then walked back into the blinding desert sun, just as blind as I'd been when I came.

The old lady waved, shouting, "You boys not going up today?"

"Engine trouble," I answered.

I didn't really have any hope that Larise would go out to take care of Guilder before he died like a snake left in the sun, so I cut her loose. She rubbed her jaw briefly, as if being hit wasn't that unfamiliar for her. Then she scrambled into her mules. She liked the height advantage. She looked as if she might take a swing at me just for the hell of it.

"I'll knock all your teeth out this time, honey," I said, and she relaxed. "As long as you keep your mouth shut, and make sure the worm stays quiet, your life will go along just like always. But if any of this comes back on me, you'll pray to get back to that army whorehouse."

"I'll make no problem for you," she said, sweetly, "and the worm will not . . . roll over?"

"Don't let him die out in the hangar," I said.

"What did you do?" she asked, worried for the first time.

"I put a couple or three rounds into his toy," I said, "so you be nice to him for a little while, okay?"

"Mama will be nice," she said, but I didn't like the look of her smile.

I wasn't sure how long Larise had to stay married for full citizenship, but I sure felt sorry for Guilder when it happened. I bet myself that she would make him pick up the spare change scattered around the room.

On the drive back to Deming I wiped and dismantled the revolver and tossed the pieces in dry washes where the next rain or wind would cover them with sand. When I got back to my room, Claudia was waiting, thoughtfully. She looked into my crazed eyes and didn't say anything for a long time. "What happened this time?" she asked.

"I persuaded Mr. Guilder to talk to me."

"And his wife?"

"She was enjoying a little beauty sleep."

"You know, this may be a little rougher road trip than I was planning," she said.

"It spite of my years with Butch, I sort of enjoy practicing law."

"I can put you on a plane this afternoon," I said. "Just say the word."

"Maybe just tell me what's happening," she asked. "I am your lawyer."

"As much as I can," I said. "I don't know, exactly," I admitted, "but somehow all this shit started way back with the Turner Landry case. I don't know how or why. But I do seem to remember that the kid who died with him, one Doug Foley, was from somewhere down in southern Colorado. I thought perhaps I would talk to his folks."

"Talk?" she said. "Just that?"

"Just that."

"No more Miss Ukraine?"

"That never happened."

"You sure?" Claudia said, her smile back in place.

"We came to a mutually agreeable agreement."

"Did you get her to sign it?"

"In blood," I said, and the smile slipped off Claudia's face.

"Yours or hers?"

"Mine," I said. "All mine, I'm afraid." A decent human being would have blushed or cried or told the truth, but I didn't have the guts to be decent. Or live in Minneapolis.

After we dropped the rental off, we drove over to Las Cruces, then picked up I-25 and headed north, stopping only for a green chili cheeseburger at the Owl Bar in San Antonio. Then we went on to Albuquerque, where we stopped for four days at a Best Western Suites Hotel, which had plenty of telephone lines and a modem connection. We tried everything we knew to try to get a lead on the Foley family, but they proved surprisingly difficult to locate. None of my investigative search engines had more than the slightest information, and that was mostly bare-bones court records of lawsuits. The post office box in Colorado Springs that they had used while suing the Landry estate was no longer in use. The express mail came back stamped NOT AT THIS ADDRESS. There was a rumor that they had taken their sealed settlement from the Landry estate in cash — two suitcases full of cash. A rumor from a bar: their lawyer told another lawyer who was sitting beside another lawyer who had gone to school with Ron Musselwhite. But there were no listings for Edgar or Della or Doug Foley in any telephone book in the

West. We did find that Della Foley had had an earlier successful lawsuit against a gas station in Fort Collins — more than fifteen years ago — also sealed and settled out of court. But my hacker was still unavailable. He was either drunk and homesick in Boston, or his liver had finally given out. He didn't respond to my e-mails, and I didn't want to leave a telephone record. So I stopped in Colorado Springs, dumped Claudia by the pool, then went to work.

The hard part about getting to Fort Collins was driving around Denver, battling traffic and signs that either lied or joked about the directions. But the trip to the library went perfectly The *Coloradoan* was on disks, and the story popped up immediately. The writer must have been working on a novel because he wrote it like a mystery story: the air vent along the gas-filler tube had cracked with age or pressure from the load of tools behind the seat; the nozzle switch had bent so badly that when the tank filled, the gasoline poured down the air vent, puddling under the seat; investigators suspected that a spark from the old radio started the fire; Della screamed, the attendant jammed the emergency shut-off valve, but it was blocked by a bit of candy — an Almond Joy to be exact — and she was only saved because an old farmer carried a chemical extinguisher. Della lost her legs, but they saved the baby, Doug Foley.

I copied the story, got a receipt, then stopped by the cop shop. The one cop who had worked the case had had his head smashed in an alley in Denver. Mugging there. Accident at the gas station. All the cases old news.

When I got back to the room, I cut the stitches out of my ear and scalp with Claudia's nail scissors and made my head presentable. We went out for dinner instead of ordering room service and found a quiet Mexican place in a strip mall, a place recommended by the night clerk. I got a pack of smokes when I ordered the drinks.

"I didn't know you smoked," Claudia said.

"I don't."

"I don't either," she said, then shook one out of the pack. As I lit it, she said, "You know, CW, you may have forgotten, but if you've still got the receipt, I am your lawyer. You can occasionally tell me what the hell is going on. As long as you're not planning a criminal act."

"Okay," I said. "What the hell do you want to know?"

"Like what you got from the airplane geek?"

"He said that a woman who looked a lot like anybody gave him a bale of cash to lose the Landry blood work and all the other evidence, plus instructions on how to wash the money," I said. "You ever been to the Islands?"

"What?"

"Just kidding," I said. "I've got a good hunch who the woman was, but I can't make it fit."

"What are we going to do about finding the Foley family?"

"Time to be a real detective again," I said. "Put away my laptop and return to artful lies and fancy footwork."

"Are you ever going to return your wife's calls?" she asked casually.

"I don't know," I said. "Maybe when this shit's over. If it's ever over."

She didn't smile, but she didn't have to. She still had her eye on me, but she hadn't looked closely enough to see that I was damaged goods. We'd slept in separate rooms since that night in El Paso, careful not to touch each other even by accident.

"But thanks for asking," I added.

"No problem," she said, stubbing out her cigarette. "This cigarette tastes like mouse turds. Don't ask how I know how mouse turds taste."

"Probably a lot like rabbit turds," I said, and we laughed, easy with each other again.

Thirteen

Since the last time I had driven through, Colorado Springs seemed to have exploded, spread into the foothills and across the high plains, metastasized like Denver, complete with cheaply built but expensive condos, minimansions, strip malls, smog, and recklessly snarled traffic. We extended our stay at the Sheraton — I hate a motel without a bar — just off the interstate, where we checked into two rooms again with one of my several fake but clean credit cards. I'd begun to feel that even by paying cash, I'd been leaving too many tracks. I thought of it as laying a false trail. Over the years I had gathered several sets of IDs that were as solid as gold, and another few that would do in a pinch. Since I'd been gutshot, I'd been ready to flee, to drop this life and assume another.

Claudia had her legal career to consider, so except for some general advice I left her out of this part, the part where I went to a copy shop, faked a letterhead and a business card from the Landry estate's legal

302

firm, and gave myself a job. Then I was off to a novelty shop out by Fort Carson where I had a fake tabloid printed. I called the Foleys' lawyer, William Minster, and made an appointment for late that afternoon.

Minster hadn't seemed to prosper since the Landry settlement. He shared a receptionist with a bail bondsman, a credit counselor, a sex therapist, and several empty offices in a small modular building just off Bradley Boulevard. The list of specialities on his door under his name included everything but blackmail and murder for hire. The man sitting behind the desk, though, looked as bland as a flat beer. Neat blond hair matched a thin mustache, and rimless glasses framed a pleasantly plump face split by a smile as innocent as the first martini. Something about his light blue eyes, though, made me think of gimlets. His suit was off the rack but a fairly decent one. Only the faint odor of cheap bourbon sullied the scene.

"So what can I do for you, Mr. Grubenko?" he said. I had decided Larise's name sounded properly thuggish enough to go with my dirty jeans and steel-toed boots. "Your message was quite vague."

I didn't say anything; just laid out my

303

fake papers: a business card identifying me as a licensed investigator from Denver, the letter of inquiry from a fake law firm, and a copy of the *East Bay Guardian* open to an article alluding to rumors about leaks from the sealed settlement with the Turner Landry estate.

"What's this got to do with me?" he said after he looked over the papers, pushing them back toward me. "Why didn't they just call me? Instead of sending a hired thug."

Perhaps I'd dressed down too far. *Thug?* I thought, but still didn't say anything.

"If you're looking for the Foleys," he said, "you're wasting your time talking to me."

"How much is your time worth?" I asked in my best thuggish voice.

"More than you can afford, Mr. Gruber," he said. "Why don't you just find the Foleys yourself. You're supposedly an investigator."

"That's Grubenko," I corrected him. "And I'm not an investigator. People pay me to go away. The question is, how much can you afford."

"What?"

"My speciality isn't finding people, buddy," I said. "My speciality is earth moving. And lawyers."

"What?"

304

"Dirt," I said. "They turn me loose on you, buddy, and I'll bury you. Nobody, not the cleanest, purest lawyer in the world can survive once I start. You'll lose your practice, find yourself overwhelmed with malpractice suits, and be lucky not to do time."

"You must be out of your mind," he squealed, but he grabbed his hair, like a man who had trouble thinking.

"Law school has its benefits," I said, then picked up my papers and started to leave.

"Look, you," he said suddenly, a man afraid, a man whose lost chances showed in the red splotches glowing on his face. "I don't know where the Foleys are, I swear. They're a couple of old hippie maniacs. Really. I mean what kind of people walk away with more than two million five in cardboard suitcases —"

"People without bank accounts," I said. "Drug dealers."

"No, as far as I can tell, they deal in chickens, eggs, and ham," he said. "Fresh vegetables in the winter."

Now it was my turn to say, "What?"

"Free-range chickens, naturally nested brown eggs, and the best smoked ham and bacon you can buy," he said. "No kidding.

I think they've got a place way the hell east of town, but I don't have any idea where. And when I say they're maniacs, man, I'm not exaggerating. Mr. Foley looks and acts like some Old Testament prophet, and the woman . . . Jesus, the woman looks like a crippled witch."

"Crippled?"

"She's got no legs, man, I mean nothing below midthigh."

"She lose them in the gas station accident?" I asked, as if I didn't know.

"I always assumed so," he said. "But they never said anything. Hell, they almost never said anything. The suit was a slam dunk once the one against the shrink was settled. We never even got as far as a court date."

"What happened to your piece of the money?" I asked.

"What happened?" he said, then snorted. "Well, if you take a drive up almost to the Garden of the Gods, about halfway up on the right at the top of the ridge to the south, you'll see an adobe hacienda where a fucking bottle-blond chicana bitch and a baron of tortillas live quite well on the remains of my piece."

"It might be worth a piece of change if I can find the Foleys," I said.

"I see their truck around town occasionally," he said. "A black Ford panel truck with their name in small print on the door. And I'm pretty sure they've got an unmarked stake truck, older and more beat up. I've seen the old man driving it at night. Their shit brings a pretty good price in this town. Fucking rich people are crazy. Even my ex, Yolanda, uses free-range chicken when she makes her shitty enchiladas. As if you could tell the fucking difference." Suddenly, he reached into his desk for a pint of Old Crow. "You want one?" he said hopelessly, holding up the half-empty bottle.

"No, thanks," I said. "I'll be in touch."

"Sure," he said, sighing as he lifted the bottle to toast my departure.

Back at the motel just as the shadows of the Rockies stole across the lawn, I stopped at Claudia's door. I could hear her talking but couldn't make out the words. But when I knocked, I heard her hang up. She came to the door in black jeans, black cowboy boots, and a black leather vest over a white cashmere sweater. Her black hair drifted in long curls to her shoulders, her face framed by the white wings. I was reminded once again of what a striking woman she was.

"How'd it go?" she asked.

"He collapsed like a bad soufflé," I said. "But he didn't know much."

"Ron called on your cell," she said. "Your wife called him. He didn't know what to tell her. I didn't know what to tell him. You're going to have to deal with this, CW. You can't just let it hang."

"I know," I said. "I called Les when I was stuck in traffic. Even he said I needed to call his mom. But I don't know what to say. I told her we'd talk when this was over."

"Perhaps you should try again," Claudia said as she moved around me. "I'll meet you in the bar." Then she walked down the balcony.

Whitney went into her kindness mode. She wanted to know how I was feeling, how the case was going, that sort of thing.

"Look," I said, "I told you that when this was over, I'd come to visit, and we would see if we can work something out. But something really strange is going on here."

"You need some help?"

"No, I need some luck," I admitted. "Mac has left me with a ball of string with no beginning or end."

"I've always told you that you trusted

people too much," she said. I could almost hear the soft smile in her voice. "Take a break. Come up for Thanksgiving. My folks are going to my sister's house in Duluth, and Les has something going on out of town with his buddies. We'll have tamales and posole and all the fine tequila we can drink."

"I'll try."

"Promise, love."

"All right, I promise," I said, the promise like a blade in my throat.

"And thanks for giving Les a break from the calls," she said. "He's almost home here now. I've found him another counselor. One almost as good as Mac."

I wanted to scream: you took my kid to see Mac! That lying son of a bitch. But I kept my mouth shut, saying only, "Adios."

Then I called Ron to see if he had had any luck with the money in escrow.

"Not yet," he admitted. "But it'll happen. They're on shaky ground. So I went by your place to pick up your mail from the house sitters. They say the cats are real pains in the ass. But I'll have my secretary pay the bills."

"Thanks," I said. "This shit's getting expensive."

"Why don't you make your partner pay some of the bills," he said, chuckling. "As a learning experience. She's got more money than she can spend in a lifetime. According to Butch, who is whining all over town. Your other pal, though, Johnny Raymond, has gone fishing."

"What for?"

"Probably your ass," he said. "Word is that he's not working out. And Lorna is running through nurses like snot rags and insisting that Mac is alive. She's driving me nuts. Be glad you're not in town. She thinks you're looking for Mac." Then he paused. "What exactly are you doing?"

"I'm not exactly sure," I admitted. "But every rock I turn over, I find something that stinks. The only lead I've got is the old Landry case."

"That's old news, Dog. What does that have to do with anything?" he said. "You make any connections?"

"Nothing I understand," I said. "Somebody paid the lab guy a cool three million to lose the blood and tissue work," I said and thought, *and a bit of stove wire.* "But why, I don't have a notion. Thanks for dealing with things up there, buddy." Then he said something I didn't understand. "What?"

"Kiowa for 'if you have to eat dog in a hard winter, eat the old ones first,' " he said, then laughed like a shaman, his face painted black as he danced madly around a campfire.

"How did it go?" Claudia asked before I could order a drink.

"Not well," I said, "but thanks for asking. Again. The judge still has the escrow locked up, but Ron's optimistic about getting it released. He suggested we share expenses, that you pay for this learning experience."

She paused, then smiled. "I'm not exactly sure what I've learned, but I'd be happy to help. If there was any hope."

"Hope springs like frogs hop," I said. "He also suggested that we eat the old dogs first."

"What?"

"Some kind of Kiowa mojo, I guess," I said. "He's paying the bills right now, so he can say anything he wants."

"What did the Foleys' lawyer tell you?" she asked.

"You can't imagine it," I said. "We might as well eat well, drink, and make merry tonight, love. I've done lies, tomorrow the footwork starts."

I never suspected how many upscale

markets and restaurants dealt in fucking free-range chicken, but I did find out that the Foleys had no set delivery times or dates and insisted on cash on the barrelhead, and they made everybody nervous. I also discovered what the unmarked truck did at night. For fifty bucks, a Mexican dishwasher smoking a cigarette behind a chichi restaurant called Past Tense, a place that specialized in old-style American food with French prices, talked to me. He'd picked up enough English to supplement my playground Spanish to be able to tell me that the crazy old man illegally collected restaurant slops and grease for a third of the cost of the regular garbage company. Which explained why none of the feed stores in town had ever heard of the Foleys.

"*Un hombre malo,* man," the *mojado* said. "He carries a club hangin' off his wrist, a club like something I've never seen. A little handle and a big head wrapped with barbed wire. And his boys say he ain't afraid to use it."

"His boys?"

"He's got a bunch of *cholitos* who work for him," he said, "wetbacks like me," then added, "but young ones. Bad little fuckers, too."

When we switched from days to nights, Claudia complained that footwork had become buttwork, and I offered to send her home, again.

"Be careful, Sughrue," she snapped. "I just might take you up on the offer." But she stopped complaining and settled back into the seat like a woman waiting for something important. The third night, just after three, we found the old man's truck behind Past Tense using its power-lift tailgate to hoist sealed barrels of slops up so the old man and several young boys could wrestle them into the truck. We followed the truck out of town on a secondary road, Highway 94, staying way back with our lights out, all the way up onto the vast, deserted eastern Colorado plateau past a wide spot in the road called Punkin Center. Twenty miles farther up the high lonesome, a place where the cattle stood by the roadside just to watch the cars pass, the truck turned south through a locked gate that led down a dirt track bordering a slight creek. The sun had just risen like a fireball to top the deceptively flat horizon. I knew that the landscape concealed gullies and ridges that could hide a small army.

I stopped, persuaded Claudia to drive back and forth until I made it back to the highway, then crept alongside the road, slipping through the salt brush and scrub until I found the right ridge, just above a catch pond that captured the slight runoff of Little Bijoux Creek. In the arroyo below, just beyond a field of row crops, an installation glowed, more like a small prison than a chicken farm: tin buildings — the largest with a satellite dish — greenhouses, and scrub brush were surrounded by a chain-link fence topped with razor wire; small brown children and chickens wandered everywhere; a large generator throbbed, a windmill squealed, hogs snorted from a pen in the near corner, and the faint shouts of small boys rose into the morning light as they surrounded the truck to unload it. Then they reloaded it with other barrels that looked the same, but were filled with black plastic bags. One *cholito* slipped a *cola* as thick as a mare's tail into his tattered jeans.

That was as close as I wanted to get, all I wanted to know, so I headed back for the road.

"Claudia, my dear," I said. "I think we better look at this in broad daylight. And perhaps heavily armed."

"Make that 'you,' CW," she said, as I

turned the car around. "Doesn't sound like my kind of place. What the hell you think is going on?"

"Nothing good," I said. "But at least we know why the Foleys were so hard to find. And you're right; I'll go alone."

"I'm sorry," she said.

"Don't be," I said. "This is what I do for a living."

"And all this time I thought you did it for fun," she said, but her laughter was hollow.

I drove all the way back to Denver to check the classifieds to find a shotgun, a Remington Wingmaster 12-gauge pump and three boxes of shells, one a double-ought buckshot. A young widow whose husband had died in a car wreck was only too glad to get it out of the house. I turned my cap around, and acted nervous. She was glad to take my cash and get me out of the house.

I picked up a hacksaw, a portable vise, a pair of leather bootlaces, and a battery-powered drill on the way out of town. Back at the motel, I removed the plugs, chopped the stock, and cut the barrel at eighteen and a quarter inches, in the vain hope that I might skate a federal beef. It hung perfectly under my windbreaker.

Claudia watched me carefully, then said, "How many laws have you broken this afternoon, Sughrue?"

"Until I walk out that door," I said, "probably not a one."

"I can't tell you how happy I am about that," she said. "What now?"

"A good night's sleep and an early morning's start."

"You're just going to drive up to the gate in broad daylight, are you?"

"Actually, I'm going to leave the pickup at the ridge, then spend an hour or so looking things over with a spotting scope, then walk up to the gate."

"Jesus," she said, "I'll close my eyes and wait in the pickup."

"No," I said.

"At least let me buy you a drink," she said.

I couldn't deny her that.

This time I picked the lock, so I could drive to the place in the plain Jane with government plates I had stolen from long-term parking at the airport lot, then I stopped beyond the ridge, watching through the spotting scope. The young boys dumped another barrel of slops into a trough shared by hogs and chickens alike. It seemed that the second chore of the day was hog butchering. A dozen young brown-skinned boys turned on a gas ring under a large steel tub with a chain hoist on a tripod over it. But nothing could have prepared me for the size of Edgar Foley. He must have been six ten, perhaps three hundred pounds. His gray, matted beard looked as large as my chest, the cigar stuck in his black-rooted teeth looked like a Virginia Slim between his giant fingers, a fifth of Four Roses whiskey filled his back pocket. It made me wish I had loaded the Remington with deer slugs instead of double-ought buckshot, and I reconsidered my approach. The club hanging off his wrist looked like a small tree. When he strode out of the largest tin building, the only one with air-conditioning units hanging like warts from the windows, the *cholitos* scattered like chickens, then fell in behind him. He paid them no mind, marching to the hog pen, where he opened the gate, kicked gelts out of the way until he found one he liked. Then he killed it with a single stroke to the back of the head. The pig's feet splayed and it hit the ground dead, without even a quiver.

I had been to hog killings in my country

youth. Usually it was a 10-gauge shotgun to the head, then in later more modern days, a .22 long-rifle cartridge driving a flat disc into the hog's forehead. Edgar Foley looked like a man who liked doing it himself and only stopped killing his hogs because of economic concerns. The gang of *cholitos* threw lines around the legs and snout of the gelt, sliced his throat with a stunningly sharp linoleum knife, then like a band of barbarians, the young boys dragged the dead gelt to the pit, gutting it along the way, trailing pig's blood and guts, a trail subject to an immediate and frenzied attack by the chickens. I wished I had a video camera to capture the scene for all the free-range chicken-eating dotcom white-shoe yuppies in the world.

Then it got crazier. Boys came out of one of the tin buildings scattering earthworms and crickets to the chickens. It wasn't hard to believe that the chicken is the evolutionary spawn of dinosaurs.

But the final act was yet to appear. Della Foley, with hair like a storm cloud, came around the corner of the largest tin building, riding on her hips in a custom-made pony cart pulled by a bedraggled donkey. She had an old-fashioned buggy whip in her hand with a long stiff handle, topped by a limber whip that ended in a metal-spiked popper. At least, I assumed it had steel bits in the popper because the first thing she did was pop the head off the nearest rooster, cutting him off in mid crow. Then she cut a piece of the shirt off the back of the nearest young boy, and screamed at him to pick and clean the carcass. He hopped to it. Back at the boiling pit, the boys had chained the hog to the endless chain hoist, and dipped the body into the boiling water.

I knew what was coming next, so I slipped back down the ridge and walked back to my ride. Whatever plan I might have had to confront the Foleys became as vague as a distant dust devil.

"What happened?" Claudia asked as she slipped onto the barstool beside me.

I was two drinks ahead, and after I told her, she asked, "What are you going to do now?"

"Actually, I think I'll pick up the cats," I said, "and see if I can find a job as a security guard in Minneapolis."

"That would last about ten minutes," she said. "And what about Mac?"

"Are these legal or personal questions?"

"Yes."

"Fuck," I said. "I'll fake some INS documents tomorrow, leave the shotgun here, and see what they say."

"I've got a legal Smith & Wesson LadySmith .38 in my bag," she said. "But it's in your safe."

"Thanks," I said, "but if I pointed it at Edgar, he'd probably eat it, then I'd be beat to death by a crippled woman. Bitch is probably Ukrainian."

"Are you ever going to get over that?"

"I'm not sure," I admitted.

"Listen, you asshole," she hissed. "When I was the lead cheerleader at Butte High, we'd just won the state championship against Hellgate High, and I was kissing the fullback. When they turned out the lights, the son of a bitch drugged me under the stands and raped me. I wasn't exactly a virgin, but I'd never been raped. It's a somewhat different experience, asshole."

"Shit, what'd you do?"

"I lived with it," she said softly. "My father could have had him killed — just because he's a tailor, don't think he's not connected — I could have killed him myself. But I just lived with it. Forgave myself and lived with it. So give it a rest. What happened to you was entirely different from what happens to a woman being raped. The next time you mention it or feel sorry for yourself, I'm going to coldcock you."

As Claudia lectured me, her coal black hair and white wings tumbled around her striking face, her cheeks inflamed with anger. I kissed her because I couldn't help myself. She kissed me back; sitting there at the motel bar, we nearly came to it. But we stopped, sighed, then laughed mightily.

"We've got a lot of shit to work out," she said. "Let's not do that again."

"Okay," I said. "But I ain't gonna apologize."

"And I ain't gonna ask you to," she said, then took off, boots thumping, Wranglers swinging, fringed jacket stirring like the wind before a warm, soft rain.

I kept my place, assuming a hangover might make tomorrow's chore easier.

I was amazed how tiny and fierce the *cholitos* were when they met me at the gate the next morning. I didn't show them the shotgun or any faked INS papers, I just said, "La Migra," and they looked at the plain-brown-wrapper Chevy and scuttled away to the big house. After a few minutes, the giant stalked down the front steps and walked toward me, blood in his eye and the club swinging from his thick wrist. I was just as happy that he hadn't bothered to open the gate between us.

"You're not Pacheco," he rumbled. "And it's the wrong day."

"Pacheco's gone," I said. "He gave me the key. I want twice what he was getting and twice as often."

If his wild laughter hadn't made me step back, his breath would have. It smelled like a wild boar's fart, fetid with corruption, rotten as an ancient swamp. His cigar stank like smoked guts.

"Fool!" he shouted, and raised the club to the empty sky. "You from those foul imps, the twins? Tell those . . . those god-less abominations that they've stolen the last of my money. The very last. And the next time they come sneaking around," he added, "I'll call heaven's fire down on them, just as I did on their slut of a mother. And you . . ." he paused, then smiled, "you, my friend, I'll fry and feed to the pigs. One lousy ungodly piece at a time, you devil's scum." As if to make his point, he slammed the club down on a large switch on a gray box attached to one of the inner gate posts. The fence began to hum a deadly song of electricity.

I wouldn't have been surprised if a bolt of lightning had come out of the bare sky, even less surprised if I'd swung up the 12-gauge and put five rounds of buckshot into the evil old bastard.

"You haven't seen the last of me," I said, probably because this whole case had either made me crazy or stupid. "Not by a little bit, you bastard!"

He raised his club again, turned his face to the clear blue heavens, and bellowed, "I pray to God to make it so! I pray!"

I climbed back in the stolen car, "the twins?" ringing in my ears. It was all there in my investigative notes that I had worked out before the injunction. It had to be them: the softball player who had given me the box of matches with the bug in the Depot; the painting crew who had killed Charity Ritter; the tall Girl Scouts who were in the Northwest Hotel just before Carrie Fraizer fell from the balcony; the metal-studded punk rockers who left the bar moments after Ellen, just before she cut off her hands. They were good; they could be boys or girls, shadows, whatever they wanted. I knew all those things even before the restraining order. But I couldn't do anything, even now, not without the fucking twins. Wherever they might be. I drove back to Denver to see what Mr. Pacheco had to say for himself.

We found an interesting and quiet place to have lunch. After we ordered, Claudia looked at me and said, "You can't tell me that you're going to kill somebody, CW. That's going too far. I'm still an officer of the court, and I may be half in love with you, but I'll call the police in a heartbeat."

"Okay," I said. "I'm not going to kill the old bastard. But I'm going to bring him down. Legally. He's got some INS guy named Pacheco on the payroll. I've got him for illegal garbage collection, and nobody knows how many health violations, not to mention the greenhouses. Besides, he probably set fire to his wife." Then I paused for effect, to make the lie more convincing, "Trust me, I'll be as legal as the law allows."

She looked dubious, but stuck out her hand. "Shake on it?"

Ah, you got to love those Butte girls. I put as much honesty as I could into the handshake.

"Where did you get the other car?"

"Rented it."

"I hope so," she said, but I don't think she believed me.

★ ★ ★

I spent the rest of the afternoon tracking down Pacheco and working my way past various INS functionaries. He turned out to be a midlevel pencil-necked bureaucrat, but he must have had enough clout to keep field agents from checking out the Foley place. He had a long, pale brown Spanish face with oddly dark eyes, soft long fingers bound with several rings, and the paunch of a deskbound man. His expensively cut hair was as black as his eyes. He couldn't have looked more corrupt if he'd tried. I suspected the Foleys weren't his only clients. There was so much money in illegal aliens that sometimes even the best men in the Border Patrol went bad. Most agents were noted for their honesty, and few gave in to temptation. But so many hungry eyes stared across the desert toward the USA, and so many came, trudging in plastic sandals and cheap cowboy boots, carrying their plastic jugs of water that always ran out, robbed and killed by the coyotes who had promised freedom. They would not and could not be stopped, and the sorry truth was that the American economy would founder like a horse bloated with green grain without the *mojado* population to do our shitwork.

And there had to be some DEA connection, too. But I hoped to avoid that. Any number of them would be pleased to put a round up my ass for all the times I'd stepped on their polished loafers.

"Mr. Grubenko," Pacheco said without a trace of an accent, "what can I do for you?"

"Tell me how to get into the Foley place."

"I don't know what you're talking about," he murmured, unmoved.

"You want to play it that way, fine," I said, standing. "I've got a friend on the *Post* who would just love this story, and you know that Foley is so damned crazy he'll give you up in a second."

"Who the hell are you?"

"Just somebody who needs inside the Foley place," I said. "It shouldn't interfere with your business arrangements."

"If he catches you, he'll kill you," he said.

"And feed me to the hogs."

"You can count on that," he said.

"Thanks," I said.

"*Por nada,*" he answered. "Crazy as she is, I'd rather do business with the old woman."

"I don't reckon cell phones work out

there in the high lonesome," I said, and he shook his head sadly. "I'd hate to find a reception committee waiting."

"No problem," he said. "No problem at all."

As I drove back to the motel, a slow-moving cold front slipped south over the Cheyenne Ridge, and the light rain and cool breeze made Denver's air almost invisible, moving out the smog that usually filled the depression of the Mile High City. I stopped at the bar and called Claudia in the room. The phone was busy, but finally I got through and told her to come down. We had to talk. She wasn't going to like it, but we had to talk.

I was right; she didn't like it that I refused to tell her what was going to happen.

The glow from the compound bounced off the low, flat clouds as I parked the government ride. The rain had turned to desert mist, as much damp air as water, and it felt great on my face as I slipped down the ridge. My nose filled with the childhood smell of a screen door just before thunder storms — a faint, dusty, almost electric odor. I was as invisible and as clean as I could get: black new running shoes and coveralls I could burn later, latex gloves on my hands, and the shotgun covered with ArmorAll to fox the finger- prints. America is a beautiful place, right? Dynamite is as easy to buy as bad drugs. And you can prime the sticks with fire- crackers and kitchen timers. I buried two sticks on either side of the catch pond spillway, then slipped down by the fence with my bolt cutters.

The small explosions emptied the pond, and the small flood shorted out the gener- ator as I slid through the mud to the com- pound. The hogs didn't seem too disturbed by the small explosions or the sudden rush of muddy water. So I snipped through the chain link, then climbed over the side of the stout wooden pen to steal among the stirring animals.

Only the glint of light off the wire that bound the head of the club and the stench of his cigar saved my life. I should have known Pacheco had been too easy. Foley's club grazed my left arm hard enough to al- most break it. The arm felt dead as I rolled among the squirming, roiling animals, the pig shit, and the sheet of muddy water as Foley followed me, kicking the pigs aside as easily as if they were small dogs, slam- ming the club into their stolid backs, sending them squealing into the night or dropping them as dead as rotten logs. I couldn't let him get close, but he finally cornered me, trapped on my knees. He raised the club to heaven, his eyes full of fire and blood in the iron gray shadows. I had no choice. I lifted the shotgun from under my windbreaker. I just had time not to kill him. But at that range the double-ought round took his arm off at the elbow, the club spinning away with his forearm.

He still came, though, kicking madly and screaming like one of the pigs until I butt-stroked him in the nuts. When he went down, finally, I kicked him behind the ear to keep him down.

In the misty gloom, I spotted Pacheco directing the *cholitos* gathering around the pen. I could almost hear their blades — linoleum knives, cheap switchblades searching the dark air for my blood. I fired two rounds over their heads, and they scattered like chickens through the gate. I heard it open, and the sound of running feet. The boys faded into the night. But Pacheco didn't make it. He reached for his Glock, but without a safety, he shot himself in the groin. I put a round of buckshot that raised a small cloud of muddy water at his feet, and he fell screaming. I struggled to reload the shotgun, then grabbed Foley by the collar to drag him out of the pen so the hogs wouldn't eat him, then I tied off his bloody stump with the rawhide thong off his club. I splashed over to a whining Pacheco, stomped his Glock into the muddy sand, kicked him under the chin to shut him up, then knelt to pull his face out of the water. A couple of disturbed rattlesnakes slithered by his body. I let them go.

As I stood up and tried to shake the paralysis off my left arm, I heard the soft trot of the little donkey. The old woman, her hair wild in the mist, her hand on the whip, firm on the cane handle, came toward me out of the odd gloom.

"Hold it," I said. "And put that whip down or I'll kill your fucking donkey."

"Is the old bastard dead?" she asked in an oddly calm voice.

"He's bad hurt but he ain't dead."

"We can't leave him," she said. "The children will come back to kill him. He was so mean to the children."

"Lady, I watched you with the whip," I said.

"True," she said quietly, talking to herself more than me. "Mean is contagious. And I caught it from him, I guess."

"Has the old man ever been to Montana?"

"What?"

"Montana? The old man ever been there?"

"No. We've never been anywhere but here since we left Georgia in sixty-six," she snorted.

"What about the twins?"

"We don't see the twins," she said. "Not since they got smart, stole one of his precious suitcases, and ran away."

"Where did they go?"

"I don't reckon that's any of your business, mister," she said. "I don't know anyway and I wouldn't tell you no how, not even if you was to shoot me in the foot." Then she waved a stump of a leg at me and cackled insanely at her joke.

"Ronnie was such a brave boy," she continued when she'd caught her breath. "He kept the old bastard off Sarrie May. He took her beatings. They're good people, now, and they're doing good things with our bloody money."

"Good things, right," I grunted, "like killing half a dozen people this summer."

"I wouldn't know nothin' about that," she said calmly. "That doesn't sound like my children," she said, then paused and asked, "I don't suppose you'd carry the old bastard to the hospital?"

"No, but I'll carry you into the house," I said as the generator overrode its short, then chugged back to life. The lights came on. Wet chickens scattered everywhere, fighting over the dead ones. The hogs had less trouble dividing their spoils — first come, first served, and the dead quickly dispatched in a frenzy of grunts and squeals.

Della was the oddest burden I'd ever carried, heavy but light, without resistance, alive but also dead. Her wild hair seemed heavier than her mangled body. I kicked in a door, found the lights, kicked my way through tangled furniture, then dumped her on a bed. The floodlights outside had washed the color from her skin, but under the inside lights, the deep dusky color of her skin glowed. That mixture of Native American — Cherokee, perhaps — black, Spanish, and English sometimes found in the Deep South.

The room was full of computer equipment — screens and towers and keyboards. It looked like an office in Silicon Valley. I was still covered with pig shit and wanted to kill somebody, anybody. If you've never felt that fire, you don't know what it's like:

like an orgasm that never stops, like a moment when everything is right.

"You know," she said as if nothing had happened, as she picked up the family Bible on the night table and clutched it to her chest, "I had Dougie after the old bastard figured out that Dougie didn't belong to him. He burned my legs off, did it on purpose, you know."

I scanned the pictures on the bookshelf across from her bed. The first was a shot of a convoy: two remodeled school buses, two dump trucks, and a three-quarter-ton army surplus vehicle. Group shots of men in religiously enormous beards, women in bonnets and long dresses, children as slight as sprites, fewer people in each picture. Among the photos, as an afterthought, rested a plaque: Della Mae Starrett Foley, Ph.D. in agriculture from Mississippi State. With honors.

"Who the hell are you?" she finally asked.

"You've heard of the crack of dawn, ma'am," I said. "Well, I'm the crack of vengeance."

"You've come to take us down? You'll never find the money," she blustered.

"So what the hell are you white trash doing all the way out here?"

She ignored the insult with a slight sneer, then started to tell me the story.

"When Edgar was stationed at Fort Carson —"

"Edgar is too big and too dumb to have been in the army."

"He joined at seventeen," she said, "before he got his growth . . ." Then she paused. "I don't know if you've ever spent any time in South Georgia, buddy? It's wet. He came up here with a buddy whose daddy worked for one of these big outfits, and he loved it," she said. "It's the most beautiful place in the world, the high plains. You can't believe the dawn light, or sunset, or what it might have been like filled with buffalo." She stopped, pointed to her degree. "I majored in dry-ground farming, drip irrigation, all the things we should have learned from the Jews. And we came out for a new Eden in a place where nobody would ever look."

This time she paused a long time, rubbed one of her stumps, then reached into the nightstand drawer for papers and a squib of smoke.

When she fired it up, the raucous stink of great smoke filled the room.

"It's an old story, Mr. Crack of Justice," she said, then paused as if she'd suddenly remembered something. "You've got to get the old man out of the yard. Please. The *cholitos* will carve him up. He treated them so badly."

"Will you stay put, ma'am?" I said. "And tell me what's going on?"

"I promise," she said, but I didn't exactly know what else to do.

When I finished my chore, stashing the old man on the front porch — I couldn't drag him any farther — I came back inside, and she sighed, then said, "When we came here we believed in the glory of the Goddess of the Herb. Some of our parents had been snake handlers and lye drinkers. But we smoked herb. Then Edgar started drinking, which was against the rules. Then he bought himself an air conditioner and his own computer. He'd spend forever in that room," she said, nodding toward a locked door beyond the bed, "drinking and fiddling with himself after he lost the . . . ability to make love."

I blew the door off with the 12-gauge. Without asking.

"The money's not there," she whined.

Nothing but high-end computers and sexual video tapes.

"He should have bought another windmill," she said. "Saved us thousands in batteries and fuel."

"Lady," I said. "I have nothing but sympathy for your life. You people are fucking idiots. Hell, I'm a white-trash hippie myself. I'm here for one thing. I want to know where the fucking twins are."

"The *twins?*" she said.

I jerked the Bible out of her grasp. A single blue sheet drifted out.

I read it with my heart cracking.

Mommy, Dougy, We're safe in a small town in Montana, Meriwether. We're going to school, and remembering everything that Mommy told us.
> Love,
> Ronnie and Sarrie May.

No date, no address, no worthwhile information.

"What does that mean, 'We're remembering everything Mommy taught us'?"

"I homeschooled them. We learned to hack together. Just for fun, at first. Then we got mean. They use computers like swords," she said. "And they can kill you with a sharp fingernail. I taught them that, too. Before I lost my legs, I was a ninth degree tae kwon do," she said proudly. "And I've never lost a handicapped match since then."

"I'm into gun do," I said as I popped her in the forehead with the butt of the shotgun. I made sure her hard, rough hands were tied together before she got her senses back.

When her eyes cleared, she said, "Cut me loose, you asshole, and I'll take you on straight." Then she got hold of herself and whined, "What kinda asshole would hit a crippled woman?"

"I thought about shooting you," I said. "Until I found this." It had been heat sealed into the cover of her Bible.

If you can ever run away from the old bastard, Mom, we're just south of Chama, New Mexico, an unmarked cattle guard just to the east of the Rio Arriba estates turnoff. There's a cut in the mountains that you can see from the road. Head there. The school, Los Almas Perdidas, is at the base of the break. You'll be safe with us.

At least I knew where to look now; maybe even find out what had sent them on their rampage in Meriwether.

"What happened to all the other people?" I asked.

"Their children disappeared," she said. "Wandered off into the desert, died of snakebite, heatstroke . . ."

"Or fed to the hogs?"

She had no answer for that.

"Is there something I can do for you?" I asked.

"Haven't you done enough?" she said without irony. "Put me back in the buggy, you bastard, and leave me the shotgun. Maybe I can keep the *cholitos* off him. Until help arrives," she added, then became coquettish. "I could tell you where the suitcases are hidden. If I wanted."

I didn't say anything, just picked her up, carried her out to the buggy, and left the unloaded sawed-off and five rounds in her lap.

"Good luck," seemed to be all I could say.

But she didn't say thanks.

I had a good idea what was going to happen after I left, but I didn't think about it.

I was over the ridge before I heard the first shot, the second quickly behind it. Pacheco, then the old man. She took a little longer to make up her mind about the third round — I suspected that the old donkey had been just about her only

338

friend — but the fourth came without hesitation a moment later. I was as clean as I was going to get in Colorado.

Fourteen

After I tossed my outer clothes in various Dumpsters on the edge of town, I put the stolen car back into the airport parking space where I had left the pickup; went back to the hotel and patched my arm as best I could; loaded a sleepy, disgruntled, and angry Claudia with her goods into the truck; then checked out in the middle of the night. I had seen and done things that were never going to go away, but I pushed on. Even leaving just past midnight, it still took two hard days — the last climbing out of the valley of the Rio Conejos and over two ten-thousand-foot passes down into Chama. I knew Chama from the old days. High-mountain fall nights colder than reindeer assholes and great Mexican food that could melt the fillings in your teeth. But like so many small, isolated towns, it had been infected with minimansions around the edges, whereas almost everything downtown sported a FOR SALE sign in front.

In spite of the lovely scenery, it hadn't been what you might call an easy trip.

When Claudia stopped bitching, she slept a long while as I gobbled enough speed to keep moving, but when she woke up she went after me again.

"What happened out at the Foley place?" she demanded.

"Nothing you want to know about, lady," I said. "Absolutely nothing."

"You son of a bitch!" she shouted.

"Someday you'll forgive me," I said. "You might be one of my lawyers, but you'll never hear what happened. Never. And don't ask again, please. If that's not good enough, I'll drop you at the next god-damned town."

She thought about it for what seemed a long time, then said, "Don't ever leave me behind again. No matter what, okay?"

"That's too tough," I said. "I'm on my way to talk to two killers, both of them probably massively insane. I don't think you should go along."

"Sughrue, I don't give a rat's ass what you think," she said. "From now on, buddy, where you go, I go."

"No," I said. "That's final. Alamosa is just down the road. I'll drop you there."

"You do that," she said, "and I'll call Johnny Raymond, and he'll get the FBI to issue a fugitive warrant."

I thought that was an odd thing for her to say, but I didn't know how to stop her. "Okay, lady, but you do what I say and nothing else," I said. "That's the only way it might work."

She nodded, but I wasn't sure that it was in agreement. I had to hope that I could find an ad in the local paper and pick up a piece. Almost anything would do, I thought; then the memory of the old woman with my shotgun blotted everything else out. I could only hope that the *cholitos* would feed the bodies to the pigs and then go back to business as usual, instead of fleeing across that empty, scrub plain into the arms of men who didn't have their best interests at heart.

"Where the hell have you gone?" Claudia asked in her best lawyer voice, that hard voice that made witnesses squirt in their shorts. "You look like a man who has seen a ghost."

"Leave it alone," I said. "Leave it the fuck alone."

For once, she did; then we pushed on toward Chama, topping the Cumbres Pass in the late afternoon sun. The grassy alpine meadows spread out before us, cut by a winding creek and the old narrow-gauge railroad. It looked like a place where a good man could settle with his woman, sledding hay to his cattle through the hard winters, pulling calves in the brief spring, his best friends a gentle mare and an old vaquero, his face a map of the brutal winters and the high-altitude sun of midsummer. But it was just a dream, and I was a fool for even dreaming it.

"You've gone away again," Claudia said, gently this time, her soft fingers briefly crossing my cheek.

We found a decent motel with an empty room with two double beds. But no bar. The nearest bar, something called the High Country, was down the street, a sort of fake western place but with a real western ambience. A few drinks, a bait of enchiladas, and some easy conversation with the bartender, talking about changes. Minimansions and horse pastures among pockets of real dirt-poor people. We borrowed the telephone book to look for Realtors, and as we went down the list, I wrote down the number of the one whose name brought an unbidden frown to the bartender's face.

Back at the motel, I tried to keep Claudia from seeing my left arm as we undressed for bed, but it didn't work. A long ragged gouge ran along a streak of blue-black bruise from my shoulder to my elbow. Badly cut butterfly bandages tried to hold it together.

"Jesus fucking Christ, Sughrue," she said as she cleaned the wound and cut more and neater butterflies to pull the edges tighter.

"How the hell do you know it's not broken?" she asked when she finished.

"Because I can still scratch my ass with it," I said.

"Asshole" passed for good night between us.

The next morning we found a plump, happy woman in a rundown café called Big G's, a place that looked as if it hadn't changed in the thirty years since I'd been in Chama, a place that made green chile huevos rancheros to die for. Then we went back to the room to call the real estate agent, one Earl Dolson, who arrived at our room in fifteen minutes in a crew-cab four-wheel-drive diesel pickup, his version of a cowboy Cadillac. His banker's Stetson had never seen sweat, his beady eyes hadn't seen his oversized belt buckle beneath his gut in years, and his exotic boots squeaked like endangered species on his dainty feet.

We endured the morning, then a lunch

at a downtown hotel, where I popped the question.

"Earl," I said, "we've got a couple of teenagers, and I understand that there's a private school around here."

"That's sure enough true," he chuckled, "but it ain't for folks like us. It's called the School of Lost Souls, or something like that, run by a couple of half-breeds, brother and sister, and they bring in a busload of Meskin preteen troublemakers from Espanola on Monday morning and keep them until Friday night. It ain't no place for decent people."

After lunch, we looked at a couple of places south of town. The turnoff and the break in the mountains to the east came into view as clear as the mountain air. We suffered through a couple more houses, then several drinks before we finally excused ourselves.

Later we went back to the High Country for drinks and some take-out chicken. The bartender had a completely different version of the school. I knew that Espanola had gone from being one of the last great Mexican outposts left in New Mexico and a great town for *vatos*, low riders, but then had degenerated into the capital of Mexican brown tar heroin, a place where even some of the drug counselors were discovered to be addicts. Now it was clear: there was one boy and one girl. The lady bartender, a displaced Texan, thought the De la Hoz's school, run by Elena and Rico De la Hoz, did great work with kids. They had tried to restore both their cultures — Mexican and Indian — made them handle the chores of managing small herds of sheep and goats and a handful of riding stock, and had kept them clean, polite, and hopeful. Having seen the twins' father, though, I had to wonder.

Of course, Claudia wanted to know what was going on. All I said was that we were going calling on Sunday. She went into a deep sulk, pounded a couple of tequilas, then stormed down to the room to call her mother, no matter how much I objected. I had a handful of drinks, then climbed into the pickup to drift slowly through clear high-altitude night sky, berserk with stars.

Claudia faked sleep nearly as well as I did, but her first stuttering snores finally put me past all that.

The next morning we checked out of the motel, breakfasted on huevos rancheros again, then headed toward Santa Fe. We were halfway there before Claudia said a word. "Giving it up, cowboy?"

"No," I said, "but now that we've got their new names, I thought we'd best see what we're getting into."

"Start with death records, right?" she said. "Then pick up the paper trail."

"Something like that," I said. "When I can pick up something again."

The unusual name, De la Hoz, made it almost too easy. Two days in a Holiday Inn on the computer and the telephones. The twins could have taken different names, surely, and made themselves almost impossible to trace, but they had to find a set of boy and girl twins who had died on the same day. In this case, in a truck wreck south of Socorro. Elena and Enrico, as they now called themselves, had faked high school transcripts — probably with a computer and a printer — and enrolled as seniors at Academy del Sol in Alamogordo to finish high school, then attended Mountain States University and graduated with degrees in education. He majored in phys ed and computer science, and she majored in English and theater arts.

They must have had the school in mind all the time, and somehow they had picked up the art of washing cash, an art they probably learned at their father's knee. Lots of phony real estate transactions between various corporations they owned behind various shells. They might be psychopaths, but they had the clever, sharp minds of the truly insane. Their last deal had been to buy the old lodge that had become the school. By the time they opened, all their paperwork was in order, fake foundations in place to pay the bills. A retired principal from Espanola was in charge until he died a few years later, by which time the twins had gotten their master's degrees in administration by going to summer school.

In fact, until Dougie's death, they had spent their summers in various colleges and universities, picking up courses and extra degrees. Afterward, though, perhaps they had spent their days just brooding among their goat herd and contemplating the lovely countryside, until the desire for revenge overcame any good intentions they might have held at the beginning.

"What now?" Claudia wanted to know.

"We wait until Sunday," I said. "Then we're going to school. And I'd really appreciate it if you stayed at the motel."

"Not a chance," she said. "Perhaps if I'd

gone with you out to the Foley place, you'd be able to lift a fork with your left hand."

The bruise had spread down to the wrinkles on my wrist and around the nails of my left hand, and my shoulder made funny sounds when I lifted it over my head.

"Still . . ."

"You don't plan on committing any crimes, do you?"

"I don't plan on anything," I said. "But shit happens."

"Around you, CW, it storms."

"Well, I'm going to the bar to get out of it," I said.

"Have fun," she said, but I don't think she meant it.

As much as I hated to go visiting without a piece, coming up with one turned out to be too much of a chore. I settled for dark glasses, a John Deere cap, a roll of quarters, and a slather of mud on the Montana plates. Late Sunday afternoon we went calling.

The school seemed built of peeled native logs: a small dormitory, a cluster of what looked like classrooms, a small place in the center that looked like the headquarters, and a large barn next to pole corrals. The place was clean and well maintained with neatly raked gravel walks, freshly painted door and window frames, and a sense of extreme order. Very extreme. Maybe even hysterical.

We parked in front of the center building between a battered school bus and an old Blazer, not in much better shape. Nobody showed up, nothing happened, and the last thing I told Claudia was to get in the driver's seat, keep the engine running in case she needed to run, and, goddamn it, stay in the truck.

When I sauntered around the main building, the twins were in the goat pen. Rico was finishing milking an old Nubian. They looked so much alike they might have come from the same egg instead of the same womb. Classic features produced by Mexican, Indian, and redneck genes; clear, lovely skin with a slightly dusky cast beneath. Strong and lean, long-legged, high-waisted dancers' bodies visible even in overalls and T-shirts. For a moment, as I leaned on the fence rail of the goat pen, I doubted that everything I had discovered led to these two lovely people.

The doubt disappeared when Elena turned, her eyes sparkling with recognition as she unrolled a blacksnake whip off her shoulder — unlike her mother, she had gone for the real thing — and from fifteen feet away hit me on the bridge of the nose between my eyes with the leaded popper. The sunglasses and cap flew off, and I could see my nose as it bloomed bloody and painful out of my face. Elena didn't give me much time to register the pain before she crossed the pen, hurdled the fence, and clubbed me behind the ear with the handle of the whip.

I remember thinking for an instant that I was going to spend my declining years, should I have any, getting the shit knocked out of me by various women, then it all went away in a black, bloody mess as I reconsidered my cheap disguise.

When I came back, everything was different. I seemed to be hanging high on a wall of the small gym inside the barn, half naked, my hands cuffed above my head and hooked to a peg, my bare toes barely touching the oak floor. Down at the bottom of my vision, two tiny figures in black karate gear were running and tumbling on a long pad, striking at each other, but stopping an instant before the blow landed. A thousand miles down the building beneath a basketball goal, Claudia was naked, tied over a vaulting horse. Even from this distance, the bruises and cuts from the whip covered her buttocks and back. A trickle of blood crept down the inside of her right leg. Goddamned woman. She hadn't run like I'd told her.

Then I looked back at the tiny figures, dancing in and out of throws and blows, something sexual in the dance, but I didn't know what. I closed my eyes, sucked in a silent breath, and realized that I had enough LSD in my system to drive a normal man insane. Something in me still remembered the San Francisco years, dropping acid and misbehaving between jobs chasing down runaway kids. I could deal with this, I told myself, goddamnit; I could find that spark of sanity below the surges of the drug if I could just get my fillings to stop singing, make the walls stop stretching in and out, and keep my aching face from slipping off my skull bones. I focused on the pain, on the blood trickling down my chest from my nose and random whip cuts.

The wrestling dolls became people, the twins, working out as if this were an ordinary day. Beside the flickering hair of sanity, a burning glow of hatred simmered. Somehow I croaked Rico's name, and they both came to stand in front of me, smiling.

"Well, look who's back," Elena said. "How's it feel, jerk-off? Got it all worked out? Or are you going crazy?"

"I love trippin'," I grunted. "Just love it."

Elena looked briefly concerned, then shook it off. Rico's jacket was half open, his chest cinched by a tight elastic tube top. Elena put her hand on his shoulder as if to exhibit his beauty, then tugged down the elastic band to expose well-formed women's breasts nestled on his chest. Trinidad, Colorado, the transsexual capital of America, wasn't that far away.

I must have looked confused because Elena fondled her brother's silicone breasts, saying, "You should have heard your shrink buddy's wife moan when she saw these babies." Rico actually seemed embarrassed, as if having breasts hadn't been his idea. Then she paused, pulled down Rico's pants, and grabbed his enormous but misshaped penis. "And, boy, did she scream when she saw this beauty." It had a strange bend to it, and seemed mottled and marred with scar tissue as if it had been dipped in lye or boiling water, then burned with a cigar. This time I was sure he was embarrassed because he blushed. It made me wonder what the old man had done to him as a child. She slammed it against the side of his thigh like a small club. "Think how your girl friend's going to squeal when he sticks it up her ass. And you, what are you going to say when he sticks it up yours, you asshole."

"What the hell?" I sputtered, watching the red spray echo my words.

Elena seemed to be in charge because she spit out the words. "Your fucking doctor friend," she said, "he wrote all those books about how it's somebody else's fault. It's never the fault of the asshole who did the shit! And he got that bastard, the one who killed Dougie, out of jail. You don't know what our mother went through to have Dougie!" She was almost screaming now as her brother fondled his oddly flaccid penis. "Well, we showed him whose fault it was. We watched his face as you told him about how his patients died. You made a great witness. We knew he'd call you when Rico broke into the files. It worked like a dream. We would have gotten them all, your wife and all the rest, but we ran out of time. Next summer. We'll finish next summer."

"What I did on my summer vacation," I said. I was almost calm now. Except for the blue flashes and the trailers flickering behind every movement. "Why the fuck didn't you just kill him when you killed the stripper?" I asked him, but Elena answered.

"The stripper?" Elena answered, honestly confused as far as I could tell. "We were saving her."

Rico slapped his dick against his leg again, speaking for the first time, his voice strikingly effeminate, "We wanted him to suffer like our mother did. We wanted to watch him lose everything."

"Guess you left town a little early," I said, my lips rubbery. "He's lost everything. Somebody killed him."

"No!" Rico screamed. "That was for last. That was for me."

"We wanted all of them to suffer," Elena said.

"Suffer," Rico hissed.

"Is that the only thing that makes your fucking ugly horse cock straighten out?" I asked as loudly as I could. "Suffering?"

Boy, was that the wrong question. Or perhaps the right one. He was on me like a snake, his long, slender fingers at my throat. I'd have been dead in seconds, but he made a small mistake. His grip lifted me just enough for me to slip my hands off the peg that held them in the air. I was still handcuffed but free. Except from the stinging slices of Elena's whip popping flesh off my ribs.

However, nothing I did — smash his nose, tear an ear, try to gouge an eye, try to wedge his arms apart — had any effect on his iron grip. From somewhere out of my dim, now wavering and quickly disappearing, past life, I remembered something that an old marine had told me about choke holds. "Break their fuckin' fingers one at a time, son, one at a time."

When his first little finger snapped, Rico grunted, and Elena moved toward Claudia. When the second one snapped, she reversed the whip in her hand, shouting, "I'll kill the bitch!" He still held on, though, through one ring finger, but he started to falter when I cracked the second ring finger. Elena had her whip around Claudia's neck, screaming something very much like bloody murder, when Rico went into shock, released my throat, and flopped senseless to the floor.

I didn't know if I could make it to Claudia in time. But as it turned out, I didn't have to make the trip. Johnny Raymond in full combat gear stepped through the gym door and put a three-round burst of M16 fire over Elena's head, then another, then a third. It was like being trapped in a steel drum with a Chinese New Year's celebration. Then he darted over to Elena and slammed the rifle barrel against the side of her head. Too hard, I thought. Deafened by the gunfire, I couldn't hear the squishy sound as her skull collapsed, but I could see it.

Where the hell had he come from? Then it was almost clear in my drugged mind. He was Claudia's source in the police department, and she hadn't been calling her mother all those times.

He held her to him, screaming something I couldn't hear. Then it came through the echoes, "Flat tire! Flat tire!"

It took a bit to sort things out. To hose me down and slap gauze pads over the worst of the bleeding cuts, to find my clothes and the handcuff keys, to pump an ampule of morphine into Claudia, and wrap her unconscious body in a blanket and stash her in my pickup. When I seemed about to lose it, Johnny brought me back by setting my broken nose with his hands. That flash of pain was very real. He used my cuffs on Rico, set and splinted his fingers as best he could, then dragged him to his rig. Elena was another deal. I suspected that without medical attention, she would be dead meat very shortly.

"I'll take care of it," he finally said. Standing next to my pickup, he was sweating, almost white with fear and excitement. As far as I could tell, he was as crazy as the twins. "I broke into your office, stole all your case files, and copied them as if they were mine," he said, his voice quivering with something akin to pride. "As far as anybody knows, I broke this case."

Shit, man, I thought, *you must really want this fucking job.* "What about all this mess?" I asked. "There's blood and fingerprints everywhere."

"Don't worry about it," he said, plunging another morphine hypo into Claudia's butt. "Just get Claudia over to Angel Fire. East of Taos. Shadow Mountain Condos, number forty-six. Can you do that for me, Sughrue? Take care of her, okay? She's the heart of me. Get out of here. Run. Call me in two weeks. I'll take care of these assholes. I'm sure the bastards kept souvenirs. I'll turn them up before I leave. When I get to Chama, I'll call in a dust off for the girl and turn the guy over to the locals. I'm sure this place is reeking with evidence. But you go the other way. And go now. You never saw me." Then he added seriously, "Remember. Give me two weeks."

When we shook hands, his hand was

firm and solid with love and care for Claudia, but quivering with madness. Fuck me, I was just the stalking horse in this quagmire and, oddly enough, perhaps the only sane person in sight.

I couldn't believe it, but it was still daylight when we crossed the divide beyond the Brazos Cliffs. For hours as we fled the scene, I was still tripping like crazy. The highway seemed to suck at my tires, the curves changed when I was in them, and deadly beasts lurked in the forest shadows. Coming down the pass, I stopped at a turnout to pee and grab a beer before I realized that I had been weeping as much as bleeding. Chances are that if I hadn't been a flake, I would have died or gone mad, either in the gym or on the road. I gobbled a few pain pills and gunned the beer, hoping to come down a little bit. At least, it had stopped raining down my face.

Claudia stayed deeply drugged all the way to where Johnny had an old SEAL buddy from the Mekong Delta, an ex-Albuquerque cop who handled security at the ski area east of Taos. He was waiting in the parking slot of number 46, a two-story condo with a hot tub and stocked with food and drink. He gave me the keys, asked no questions, just helped me carry a naked woman in a Navajo blanket into one of the bedrooms.

"Does she need a doctor?" he asked. "We've got a guy on call at the lodge."

"I'll know tomorrow," I said. "Right now see if you can come up with some pain pills, some tranquilizers, and some antibiotics."

"Already in the first-aid kit under the sink," he said. "What about you, man? You look like shit."

"Worry about Johnny," I said. "He's over the edge. See if you can get hold of him."

"Shit," he muttered. "We did two tours in the same hooch. He's a dangerous son of a bitch, and I owe him my life, but I don't think I want to know what this is about. I know he's a chief of detectives now, but when he came by to set this up, he was as crazy as a kid on his first night ambush. Decked out for war. Weapons, a load of C4, and a case of willy peter grenades in the backseat. He's still a commander in the reserves. I didn't want to know what he was doing, so I didn't say anything. He called in an old debt, so I left it alone."

"I guess we're both in his debt," I said.

"Stay as long as you need," he said. "It's mine. My name is Paul Mendoza. Your

360

name is John Bridges. The pantry's full. What's mine is yours. If you need anything else, charge it to the condo account. I'm going fishing. Deep sea fishing in Florida, maybe."

Then he shook my hand. "For Johnny," he said, "wherever he is. I don't think I want to know what happens next."

"You got it," I said. "Thanks."

He faded into the night, and I suddenly felt calm. Fucked over, misused, and drenched with lies. Sad but calm. I didn't know why, but whatever it was, I took it into Claudia's room and finished it, holding her through the long night.

Except for occasional flashbacks, my trip was over by the next morning, but Claudia's seemed to go forever. She flinched when a cloud crossed the sun or when somewhere in the building a door closed too loudly. When a late fall thunderstorm rattled the peaks above us, she started crying, then wouldn't stop until she passed out from exhaustion. She couldn't stand the feel of clothes on her skin, then couldn't stand to be naked. And she couldn't stand to be alone. I had to carry her to the bathroom and hold her hand while she sat on the toilet weeping. I got as much hot soup into her as I could, and the occasional sleeping pill and Vicodin so she could at least sleep a few hours without the horrors coming back. I tended her wounds and bruises as best I could. And settled her in the hot tub when she could stand it. The wounds seemed mostly superficial, but I knew they cut deep. And from what I saw on the muted television, they were bound to be deeper soon.

Through all this, two things kept coming back: Elena had said they were saving the stripper for next summer and that my wife was on their list. I didn't know what to think about either of those things.

Finally, two or three days after we arrived, I fell asleep, a long, dreamless sleep, and woke to the smell of bacon and eggs frying, the sputtering of a coffee pot, and the popping jerk of a toaster. Claudia stood in the compact kitchen, wrapped in her robe, her hair washed and combed straight back, moving slowly, but moving.

"If you're half as hungry as I am," she said, "you're awake now."

"Do I have time for a shower?"

"Hurry, or it will be all gone."

As it turned out, we had to do it all over again because the first breakfast disappeared so quickly. We even found a bottle of whiskey to pump up the second pot of coffee, all of this without another word passing between us. I dug a pack of cigarettes out of my duffle, lit one for her and one for me. We smoked.

"I've got a few questions," she said calmly, "but no apologies." Her cigarette trembled in her hands. I just nodded. "Acid?" I nodded again. "How long am I going to be crazy?"

"Stay fairly sober, work out a little harder," I said, "and in a few weeks you'll be fine."

"I thought I was going to die, CW," she said. "I thought that if I didn't go insane, I was going to die."

"Not an uncommon reaction to such a heavy dose," I said. "You're tough. You'll be fine. Trust me."

"I do trust you," she said, "but how can you trust me, ever again?"

"You were in love," I said.

"Fuck, no. He was in love," she said. "Crazy in love. And I got caught between the rock and the hard place, between a madman's ambition and his misplaced love. Maybe it was my fault. I used him all these years; then he used me. The moment I dumped Butch, Johnny was all over me with this insane notion of leading you to Guilder. Then he threatened to rat me out — he'd leaked things to me over the years that might cost me my ticket, even buy me some jail time." She paused, then said, "Christ, we never even slept together. I suspect he hadn't slept with a woman in years."

I didn't much like the idea that I had to tell her he never would now. "I think he went a little bit mad. He could have done what I did if he hadn't been hamstrung by the law," I lied. "He gets the credit now anyway. He takes it to the grave with him."

"What?" she said, stubbing out one cigarette, then lighting another.

"His Explorer went off a switchback going down Conejos Pass," I said. "Johnny and the twins were killed." There seemed no point in telling her that Johnny hadn't turned Rico over to the local law or called for a dust off for Elena or that the gym had burned to the ground, a fire so hot that only white phosphorus grenades and C4 could have caused it, as they did the fire in the Explorer.

"My God," she said, "all this for nothing —"

"Not for nothing," I said. "The locals found half a dozen graves under the goat pen and lots of gruesome souvenirs in a stash in Rico's cabin. I don't think the girl knew. He's the one who drove the bus back and forth, and I guess he couldn't survive his bad blood."

"That's so terrible," she said, tears breaking like a fresh spring from her dark blue eyes, and I reached to comfort her.

I won't make any excuses for what happened next. At first we fucked for comfort, and having found comfort, we went at each other like rabid teenagers — we didn't have enough holes in our bodies or enough things to stick in them; even our wounds seemed to need each other, our skin one single burning scar — then we made love like veterans of some distant, inconclusive war. Then like clichés, we stood on the balcony, smoking in the twilight as if nothing had happened.

"You were in the war, weren't you?" she asked softly. "You've got more scars than a practice corpse. How did you survive?"

"Luck and geography," I said, smiling now at the memory of Nacho's giant trigger finger in the hole in my fatigues jacket pocket all those years ago. "That's all there is."

"Which was this?" she asked, her mouth against mine.

"All of the above," I said, "and a bit more."

"Well, I hope it worked," she said. "Because I did it for you, CW."

"What?"

"Small payment for all the lies," she said, then she kissed me in that soft and easy way that says good-bye better than a thousand words. "And I guess I needed it, too. Thanks. Johnny would never have worked it out. Two deaths made to look like suicides, an accidental one, then the mess in Mac's office —"

"I was just lucky," I said. "And nobody's sure what happened in Mac's office. I can't work it out."

Then she suddenly turned serious and said, "Speaking of working it out, CW. If you don't tell Whitney, I will."

"Thanks," I said, unsure if I actually meant it.

"What are you going to do about it?" she asked, touching my face lightly.

"Leave it alone," I said. "Nothing else to do."

"No, you idiot," she said. "About your nose."

"You don't want to know," I said.

"You're probably right," she said, then turned away, heading back inside where the television rumbled with strange cheers.

So we left it there among cheapjack condos, odd temporary monuments to greed and empty thrills, nestled below ancient mountain slopes, rosy and pink as raw flesh in the alpenglow. They seemed to almost touch the dark blue sky above, as a lover's hand almost touches the cheek of the lost loved one in passing.

At that terrible moment, thinking of Whit, I realized that the cheering behind me was a football game, a Thanksgiving football game.

Fifteen

As usual, though, the bad news wasn't even beginning to be over. I put Claudia on her flight home from the Colorado Springs airport — she didn't linger over our good-byes; she couldn't get away fast enough. I took myself to an ER, and had my fucking nose rebroken, then reset, before I drove up to Evergreen to talk to the woman who owned the rottweiler that ate rocks. If this was a circle, I wanted to complete it. I suspected my meeting with Lonnie Howell in her driveway hadn't been an accident.

Another winter was about to come to the Colorado Rockies. The aspen leaves fluttered one last silvery salute, then drifted like frail broken china toward the rocks and pine needles below, but the air was still high and dry, the prospect of snow still an empty threat. Denver huddled in its hole, the shield of smog waiting to be pierced by ice.

The woman had washed the silver threads out of her hair, and her jersey dress held the shape of a much younger woman. She might have been her own daughter, but there had been something childless about her and the house the first time we met. Her eyes still sparkled with silent amusement when she answered the door, but they quickly grew round and serious, frightened into a deeper brown, almost as dark as her dyed hair when she recognized my face beyond the splinted nose and the raccoon eyes.

"Oh, my god," she moaned, then burst into tears. She fled down the small entryway, then darted into the living room, and dove onto a rich leather couch, her face buried into the placid flank of her dog, unmuzzled now.

I took a single hesitant step over the threshold, and the large dog raised a hairy eyeball at me. The rott didn't growl exactly, but she rumbled like a distant avalanche, so I stopped dead still. In my present condition, I couldn't have protected myself against a decrepit Chihuahua. I stood in the doorway like an idiot, watching her heaving shoulders for a long time.

"Ma'am," I said as gently as I could when there seemed a pause in the sobbing, "I don't know what I did, but I'm sorry."

"You don't know what you did?" she said, raising her ruined face to look at me.

Her makeup had smudged between the dog and the tears. She looked twenty years older and very unhappy. "You don't know what happened to Lonnie?" she blubbered. "They burned off his poor sweet face with a blow torch," she said, "then dumped his body out by the airport. God, he was my last contact with Mac."

"They?"

"Probably some of Mac's hired hands," she sputtered. "Probably somebody like you."

"Ma'am," I said softly. "Can we sit down and have a cup of coffee or a drink or something? I don't have any idea what you're talking about."

She sat all the way up, glared at me, shouting, "You work for Dr. William Mac-Kinderick, right?"

"I did once," I lied. "You know he's dead or missing and a suspect in a murder?"

I could have sworn she said, "Pshaw." Then she added, "That cowardly son of a bitch wouldn't have the guts to kill himself. Or anybody else for that matter. Now get out of my house before I set Lilly on you."

Lilly raised her giant head and seemed to smile at me in a very unfriendly manner. I closed the door very quietly on my way out. This time I read the name on the mailbox. Ms. Helen Truley. But I suspected that at one time it had been Mrs. Helen MacKinderick.

I wanted to go home, to sleep until spring, to try to explain to Whit what I'd been through. I strongly suspected that she wouldn't be all that interested. Our single conversation since New Mexico had been brief and to the point.

"Enjoyed your Thanksgiving visit," she said, without preamble. "And thanks for calling to let us know you weren't coming, you son of a bitch."

I started to say I was sorry, then I started to explain, then I decided to hell with it. "In the old days, Whit, you would have known that something terrible had happened," I said.

"Something terrible did happen," she said. "You want Musselwhite to do the divorce, or should I have one of the partners here do it? In spite of the way you are, sonny, let's be civilized about this. I'll come out to get the rest of my things soon. I've found a little house down the street from my folks."

"Can we talk?"

"You've got to be kidding."

There's no answer to that.

When I called my son, his cell phone number had been changed and unlisted.

After I slipped out of Evergreen, glancing over my shoulder now and again to check for the baying of a dog bad enough to eat rocks, I went down to the Denver library to see what I could find out about Lonnie Howell. His death bothered me. Two days after he got home from Montana, while he was packing for his trip to Mexico, a person or persons unknown had broken into his apartment, drugged him, and taken him out to one of the unfinished developments southwest of the airport where he had been tortured at some length, then shot in the head several times with a .22 pistol. Because he had been abducted in Denver, then killed in Arapaho County, there was a question of jurisdiction, so the whole thing passed over to the state boys, then just passed over. Nobody in the Denver Police Department, the Arapaho County Sheriff's office, or the CBI seemed to remember Lonnie Howell.

I went back over the mountains to Delta to see Lonnie's uncle, who had led me to him in the first place. Mr. Howell was still drunk, living in his recliner on TV dinners and pints of Four Roses, and bitching about how long it was taking to settle Lonnie's estate without a will. I asked if he was going to spruce up his place, but he said hell, no. He was going to take Lonnie's money, by god, and retire to Mexico and buy a nice little place on the beach.

For a hundred dollars he let me rummage through Lonnie's crap scattered around a small bedroom in the back of the carless garage. I didn't much like what I found. An eight-by-ten of a young, bone-thin Lonnie with a squad outside a burning village. Two of the men looked like Nung mercenaries. The squad's tiger-striped fatigues were conspicuously devoid of marks of rank, unit, or even nationality, and none of their weapons were U.S. government issue. Their eyes were miles past the thousand-yard stare — dark and hollow, sad and deadly. Those kinds of pictures usually meant Operation Phoenix or some other phantom group of terrorists and assassins usually sponsored by the CIA or some other off-the-record outfit. That was bad enough, but when I dug up a photocopy of Lonnie's orders for the general discharge, a name leaped off the page at me. They had been signed by Captain William MacKinderick. I was suddenly very sick at heart.

When I showed the photograph to Mr. Howell and asked if Lonnie had stayed in touch with any of the guys, he laughed, cheap whiskey breath filling the fetid room. "Any of those boys look like fellas you'd stay in touch with, Bud?"

"He ever mention any names?"

"Naw. He just said the outfit was called the Phenix City Jammers," he said. "You know, Phenix City, Alabama, 'cross the border from Fort Benning. Guess the officer was from there. I took basic there before Korea," he said. "Bad, bad town, and the fuckin' army's fulla pussies anyway. That's why I told him to join the Corps."

"Which one's the officer?" I asked.

"The only one smilin', I'd wager," he said, pointing to a tall, bald man with a smile that reminded me of Lilly's, all teeth and bad news. He had a jaw like a stone sledgehammer, cheekbones that looked as if they had been chipped from flint, and his left ear looked as if it had been half chewed away. "Reckon you'd buy a used car from this guy?" the old man asked, chuckling.

"I think I did," I said.

"Oh," he said. "Sorry."

"The same time," I said, "but a different war. I was just a bored RA lifer looking for excitement."

"Find any?"

"Didn't we all?"

Old man Howell didn't say anything, just lifted his pants enough to show me his artificial leg. "Some of us a little more than we wanted," he said. "Keep the picture," he added, then asked, "You gonna find out what happened to my nephew?"

"I'm afraid so," I said, then handed Mr. Howell one of my cards.

"I wasn't kidding about the used car thing, though," he said.

"What?"

"Yeah, I see his ads on the TV all the time," he said. "Smiling Jack's. Over in Greeley."

"Thanks, Mr. Howell," I said. Greeley wasn't that far out of my way. Hell, nowhere was out of my way now.

Smiling Jack's smile had disappeared behind eighty pounds of hard fat and expensively capped teeth, but his eyes hadn't changed. The look he gave me when he found out I had bluffed my way into his office to toss the photograph on his desk would have killed a rattlesnake at close range.

"What the hell you want, buddy?" he asked without preamble.

"I want to know about this kid," I said, pointing at Lonnie.

"I'm in business, buddy," he said. "What's it worth to you?"

"Name your price," I said.

"Five hundred?"

"Deal," I said, then paid him.

"What's to know?" he said after he had carefully counted the money, folded it into his money clip, then stuck it into his pocket. "Just another fuck-up who chose to join my operation instead doing a long stretch in the brig."

"What for?"

"Nobody ever asked," he said. "No need to know."

"Why did he get a general discharge?"

"He burned out quicker than most kids," he said. "It was the quickest way to get him back to the states and keep him quiet."

"Burned out at what?"

"Interrogation," he said simply.

"How long did it take you to burn out?" I asked, but his only answer was a smile as thin as the edge on a straight razor. "You know, I'll bet you own a junkyard, too."

"I might," he said, confused for the moment. "Why?"

"And a chop shop?"

"Get the fuck out of my office, you asshole, before you wear out your welcome," he said, standing quickly.

"You know a guy named Bobby Chenoworth?" I said. "Down in El Paso?" Bobby was an old bandito half-breed who had several junkyards and a reputation for survival.

"I might."

"Next time you talk to him, tell him CW said hello," I said.

" 'CW' who?"

"He'll know," I said. Bobby owed me a large favor for finding his runaway teenaged son, lost among criminal yuppies down in Mazatlan.

"You want your money back?"

"Not after it's been in your pocket, partner," I said, then walked out.

I drifted back to Meriwether, in no hurry to face the mess I suspected I'd find at home or deal with these revelations about my friend, Mac, be he dead or alive. I suppose in the back of my mind, I had secretly suspected that he was alive. But that would mean that I would have to accept the idea that he had bludgeoned Sheila Miller. And I couldn't get my mind around that notion.

Mostly, I just made myself stop thinking

about it. I caught the tag end of a long, lazy Indian summer. Or perhaps the beginning of another open winter, another in the long seasons of drought we'd suffered lately, harsh dry spells that seemed to come along more often these past few years.

Everything else seemed almost fine, though. Everybody seemed to have bought Johnny Raymond's version of the events leading up to his death. He'd solved the murders, tracked down the perpetrators, and died trying to bring them in. Or if the cops didn't buy it, they'd kept their mouths shut, and Johnny had been buried with proper honors. The charges against Arno Biddle had been dropped for lack of evidence because of my photo, and he had moved back east to be closer to his daddy's sugar tit. The judge had released Mac's money, so Musselwhite and I had settled up. I paid off my expenses, socked a pile of money in the bank, sent Les some kicking-around money and put a down payment on Whitney's house in escrow, the first move toward our property settlement. She still wouldn't talk to me, but her lawyer seemed to be a kind, rational person. I had the pickup serviced, then stashed it in the rear of the garage. After all those hard-sprung noisy road miles in the truck, my Outback felt as comfortable as old man Howell's rocking lounger. Over the days, I had a few drinks, spent a couple of afternoons drifting down the Meriwether River in an old raft, bothering the occasional trout, but usually watching the fish eagles embarrass me. Mostly though, I sat on the front porch of Whit's house drinking slow beers, enjoying the gift of the lowering sun, playing with the cats, watching them bring me trophies — voles and sparrows, garter snakes and bits of trash out of Whit's moldering compost heap — wearing my Walther PPK/S .22 under my arm because the Browning seemed too much firepower — too heavy for whatever trouble came my way — and waiting for the other boot to drop.

But when it dropped it wasn't a boot, it was a trainload.

It began with a call from Lorna one Saturday morning. I seemed to have reached that point in life when women no longer felt inclined to say Hello or How are you? or How's it hanging, buddy?

"Sughrue," she said quickly when I answered, "I'm selling the house and all Dr. MacKinderick's things to an investment group. Tomorrow. They're planning to turn it into a high-end bed and breakfast. If you'd like something to remember him by, a memento, so to speak, you best get here this morning before the inventory starts." Then just as quickly she hung up the telephone.

So I went over to the house. Lorna had dressed down in her version of widow's casual — black designer jeans, a gray cashmere sweatshirt, tiny Italian backless pumps, and a small gold chain around her neck holding what I suspected was a single three-carat diamond — and kept her makeup subdued. She seemed perfectly normal, or in completely hysterical control. She also kept her sunglasses on so I wouldn't see her drugged eyes. She kept conversation at a minimum, too. She almost said something when I picked one of Mac's Hebrides paintings, the one with the shingled beach and the crofter's cottage, but she stopped for a moment, then her complaint slipped out.

"Why don't you take one of Carrie Fraizer's *little* pieces?" she said, then covered her mouth quickly. "Or take them all."

"You don't want me to have this one?"

"Oh, hell," she muttered between her fingers. "Go ahead." Then she clicked down the hallway on her tiny heels, something angry in the switch of her hips, something insane in the stiffness of her back.

"So you've decided that he's dead?" I said to her retreating figure, but she ignored me. So I stepped into the den to pick up a half-empty bottle of Lagavulin.

When I got to my house — I had to start thinking of it as my house — I had visitors. A moving van was parked in the alley, a Hertz rental car behind it. *Whit has flown out,* I thought as I pulled into the driveway in front, stashed Mac's things in the office, grabbed a beer, then resumed my seat on the front steps. But before I could crack the can, the storm door opened, and running footsteps crossed the porch. I feinted right, then turned left, catching the kid under the arm and tossing him over my shoulder. He rolled to his feet in an instant, then met me halfway across the yard. He'd picked up some new moves from karate class, but I blocked them, then stung his cheeks with quick jabs. He switched to a new style, probably karate, and tried an ax kick to my chest, but I caught his foot with both hands, flipped him, then pinned him in a pile of leaves and kissed his grinning face until he shouted in embarrassment, "Dad!" Looking over my shoulder. I heard a car pull up in front.

Lester and I stood up, brushing leaves off and smiling. The kid was tall for twelve with long and lean muscles like his dead father, but he had his mother's sweet face.

"You've let the boxing lessons go," I said.

"Mom says it's a barbaric sport."

"And the martial arts aren't?" I said.

"Mom says they teach self-confidence and respect for life."

"She's right," I said as I heard car doors slam behind me. "Respect her judgment," I added. "Always. It kept me alive once or twice."

"Sorry about the cell phone stuff, Pop," he said. "Can I call you?"

"We'll set up a time on e-mail, okay?"

"Sounds good," he said, punching me on the shoulder. "Mind if I run over to Scooter's house to shoot some hoops?"

"Ask your mom," I said, then he turned and dashed toward the house. Through the briefly open storm door I could see Whitney directing two burly guys in green khakis. She gave me a flat, empty glance.

"Sughrue," somebody said behind me. "Why don't you rake your leaves?"

"They're Mother Nature's debris," I said to Agent Morrow. "Let her rake them."

"We have a few questions," she said.

"Sure," I said as I walked back to my beer, Morrow and Cunningham on my heels. I cracked the can and sat down.

"You mind not drinking that right now?" Morrow said. "It's not even noon."

"It's my breakfast," I said, took a long pull on the beer, then asked her, "What can I do for you guys?" Cunningham blushed, and I could tell that Pammie didn't know about the tape, and he didn't know about her earlier part. I had them by the nuts, so to speak, but that was no reason not to be polite.

"You moving?" Morrow said.

"My wife's truck," I said.

"We understand you've been out of town?" she said. "You mind if we ask where?"

"You mind if I ask why?"

"You know the drill," she said.

"Sure," I said. "First, you guys show me your IDs, then I turn into a quivering mass of confessional jelly, right? But not today, okay? I haven't seen my son in months. So I'd appreciate it if you came around later. And then let me know why you're in my front yard."

"Have you been in contact with Dr. MacKinderick?"

"I thought he was dead," I said.

"There's been some activity in his bank account," she said. "A large payment to you, for instance, through your lawyer."

"All properly billed and arranged long before his disappearance," I said.

"Have you been looking into the murders of his patients' partners?"

"Talk to my lawyer," I said. "I'm sure you know about the injunction. And call before you come back, okay? I'm sure you'll be in town for a few days."

"Why don't we come back later?" Cunningham said, opening his mouth for the first time. Morrow nodded slowly. "Thanks for your time," he added almost gratefully.

As they drove away, I pulled out a cigarette. I could have their jobs, but they could make my life hell on the way out.

I sat on the steps, set fire to the cigarette, and ignored the girls scratching to get out. Then I heard the storm door open, but not shut.

"You're smoking again," Whit said behind me.

"Be glad I'm not shooting smack," I said angrily, without turning around.

"You don't have any right to be angry with me," she hissed.

"Not you," I said, "them." Her anger seemed to click up a notch every time I talked to her. I didn't understand it.

"What was the FBI doing here? What the hell have you gotten yourself involved in?"

"The fucking idiots think I know something about Mac," I said. "What happened to his money, where he is, all that shit."

"Do you?"

"I found out a lot of things about Mac," I said. "None of them particularly good. But the rest of it, no, I don't know a thing."

"Will the FBI be back?"

"I've got a tape of them behaving badly," I said. "They won't be back."

"They're an odd couple to be behaving badly," Whit said. "How'd you get the tape?"

"I've got a suspicious mind," I said, then stubbed out the butt and stood up to face her. She stood over me in jeans and a sweatshirt, a streak of dust across her cheek, holding the door half open or half shut, but still just as lovely as she'd been years ago when I was living in Lawyer Rainbolt's basement, and she'd come down the stairs carrying messages from the boss of the firm. "Why didn't you let me know when you were coming out?"

"Why didn't you call about Thanksgiving?" she asked. "And what happened to your nose?"

"You don't really care what happened to my nose," I said. "If you did, this wouldn't be happening. I fucked up badly, and Thanksgiving Day I was holed up with a woman down in New Mexico, trying to put myself back together —"

"Her?" she asked, looking over my shoulder, then slipping back inside. "She looks like she could put you back together."

When I turned around, Larise Grubenko was stepping out of the backseat of the only limo in Meriwether, a restored 1975 Cadillac stretch limo, wearing her traveling clothes — an Irish green suit with a reasonably long skirt, black stockings, and matching pumps with only four-inch heels, her mane of yellow hair gathered into a fancy ponytail that poured like a golden stream from a round bun. My hand darted reflexively under my armpit. Larise saw the move, took off her sunglasses, spread her arms, then smiled as harmlessly as a child as she strode up the walk toward the porch. I met her halfway.

"What the fuck are you doing here?" I asked. I suspect that I was flushed with shame more than anger. "How the hell did you find me?"

"Mr. Sughrue, you are not the only private detective in the world," she said. "My husband flew his little toy airplane into the side of the hangar — I think he wanted to destroy the money but it was safe with me — but my citizenship is in question. I'm going to Canada, where it's not so complex. Edmonton, where I have family, where I have a chance to invest in my brother's business —"

"A strip bar with hookers, I assume."

"You've had a taste of what it's like to be a woman," she said. "We make our lives how we can."

"I think I already knew that," I said, "but thanks for the reminder. Once again, what the fuck are you doing here?"

"My poor husband remembered something he didn't tell you," she said. "Shooting his airplane was very cruel. It confused him —"

"Perhaps I should have shot you?"

"Perhaps he would have thanked you," she said, her smile growing wide across her capped teeth. "But he told me something I thought you might like to know."

"What?"

"The woman who gave him the money had red hair under her wig," she said, "dark red hair." Then she reached out to shake my hand. I almost refused. "I'm sorry," she said. "Women are what men make them," she added, "and if anybody comes asking about me, please lie. My brothers aren't as nice as I am." She gave me another wolfish smile, then went back to the limo, raising her hand in a small wave through the darkened window.

Red hair. Lorna. But why? I didn't want to think about it.

I didn't know what to feel. Still angry, sure, but confused, too. I went back into the office for another beer. The two moving guys were carrying the couch out the back door. As I sat on the porch steps with another beer and another cigarette, the storm door opened again. But didn't shut.

"It's not even noon," she said, "and you're on your second beer."

"You have any cocaine?" I said.

"Was that her?" she said. "She was a beautiful woman, but obviously feckless. Just your type."

"Just a guy I met on a case," I said over

my shoulder. "Sex change worked."

"So who's that?" she asked as Claudia's Jag stopped in front of the house. I heard the door close behind me.

Chickens coming home to roost? No, I felt like roadkill, eagles feasting on my guts as I took forever to die. So I didn't bother to meet her halfway. Just sat there waiting for the worst day of my life to end.

"I just stopped to say good-bye," Claudia said, "and I'm sorry. I'm off to Butte and another life."

"You got your car back," I said. "That's good. Somebody told me recently that women are what men make them, so you don't have to say you're sorry." I stood up, gave her a hug, then added, "Please take care of yourself. You're a fine woman."

Then she spotted the moving van in the alley. "You don't deserve this," she said.

"Nobody deserves anything," I said. "I told you: it's always luck, and grandfather eats old gray rats and paints houses yellow."

She paused, stepped back, her hands still on my shoulders, then she kissed me like a brother, hard and fast, driving a spark of pain from my nose to my knees, and said, "What about love and courage and kindness?"

"Requirements," I suggested. "Benefits."

"Are you going to be okay?"

"I'll figure something out," I said. "Don't worry. And good luck." As I said that I realized that it extended to Larise, too.

Claudia went back to her gleaming Jag, and I went back to the porch steps and my beer. Within moments I heard the door open, but once again not close. The girls slipped out and wandered off to frolic among the dead leaves that covered the front yard like a tattered rag rug.

"That was her?" Whit said. "You slept with Claudia? Christ, it would be easier to forgive you for fucking the transsexual."

"Well, shit, I lied about that," I said. "To salve your feelings. She's a Ukrainian whore, but I couldn't afford her. She gave me a freebie. I guess we're kind of friends."

"And Claudia?"

"That's different," I said. "None of this involves you. Except this." I reached into my shirt pocket to extract one of the cats' bits of trashy debris. The green silver-foil remains of two condom wrappers. Mac's shamrock rubbers. "Look what the cats drug in," I said. "You sleep with that bastard?"

Whitney's blushing face said it all.

"Either come out or go back inside. But stop this halfway shit."

"Oh, shit," she said. Then she came all the way out the door and sat beside me. "I'm not going to say 'I'm sorry,'" she murmured.

"There's a lot of that going around," I said. "But I'll break the mold; I'll say it: I am sorry as hell, sorry enough for all of us. Someday I'll tell you about it. If I live long enough."

"That doesn't change anything."

"Didn't expect it would, love," I said.

She went back in the house without another word. And it was over.

Darkness came early, as it always did in late fall, but I sat on the porch steps until full dark, surviving on beer, deer sausage, rat cheese, and an almost animal silence, broken only by a brief farewell to my son. I may have grunted in pain when the moving van pulled out, followed by Whitney's rental, but I wasn't sure. I was fairly sure that when my cell phone rang in my pocket, that it wasn't good news.

Sixteen

At ten the next morning, by driving through my hangover like a crazy man — I'd spent the night sipping Scotch and rewiring my cell — I was waiting on the Melita Island dock on Flathead Lake. Just as George Paul had suggested, unarmed and docile. I didn't know what sort of madness I was facing, but after everything I'd learned about my friend, MacKinderick, I wasn't about to take any chances. A big guy was waiting on the dock. He looked oddly familiar.

"Hey, didn't I see you at The Phone Booth?" I said.

"Maybe."

He'd been one of the guys with Georgie Paul at The Phone Booth when I was tracking Sheila Miller. I lose names sometimes but never faces. Sometimes it keeps you alive. He patted me down carelessly, almost taking my word that the rewired stun gun was a satellite cell phone as we climbed into a Boston Whaler and headed for Wild Horse Island in the middle of the huge lake. As soon as it became apparent which dock we were heading toward, I said to him, "Hey, you don't believe it's a cell phone, call your girl friend."

"Don't have one right now."

"Call your mother."

"In Portland?"

"It's on me."

He dialed, pushed Send, then put the cell phone to his ear. The shock almost knocked him out of the boat. I nearly let him fall overboard, but I wasn't completely sure that he was one of the guys who had done Lonnie Howell, so I slipped the .357 Smith & Wesson from under his Carhartt tin-cloth coat, and when I pulled in down shore from the dock, I left him barefoot, bound in the dock line, and his dirty sock in his mouth. I popped him with another charge just for fun. It took the better part of an hour to circle through the lodgepole pines, dead falls, and occasional stately ponderosa to come steeply downslope to the back door of the cabin. I guess I shouldn't have been surprised at the crowd sitting around a poker table in the middle of the main room of the cabin: Georgie Paul, of course, and Charlie Marshall; Elwood Studer and Ken Forbes; but Angie Cole, she was a surprise. The other truck driver from The Phone Booth was walking down to the dock.

"One of you idiot bastards move," I said as I stepped through the back door, "I've got a round apiece for all six of you." You could have stirred the silence with a stick. "Georgie, call that guy back from the dock." He didn't hesitate a second, just hurried to the door, and shouted, "Eddie!" Then sat back down as I moved beside the door. Eddie got the shock of his life right in the ear when he came inside. He went down like a wet paper towel.

"Everybody," I growled, now that I had two .357 revolvers to go with my bad temper, "empty your pockets and purses on the table, take your shoes off, and go sit on the couches in the corner. Sit on your hands and cross your feet. And be fucking quick about it. I've got a hangover that would kill a normal man; I've been lied to, fucked over, and damn near killed. I've lost my wife, my best friend, and any hope for the future existence of the human race. So be goddamned quick." They must have believed me because they moved at the speed of the guilty. Of what, I didn't know yet, but surely guilty of something. "So what's going on?" I said.

They all tried to answer at once. The only clear thing in the babble was that it had been my good buddy's idea.

"Shut up!" I shouted. "One at a time." The thick silence again, broken only by Elwood's weeping. I stirred through the mess on the table. Cell phones, keys, a couple of Swiss Army Knives, wallets, bills, and change. And a Polaroid shot of Whitney dropping off Lester, who wore a blazer and a tie, in front of a stolid brick building.

"This is bad, boys and girls," I said as I picked up the picture. "Really bad and perfectly stupid. If you'd threatened my family twenty years ago, I'd have gutted you fuckers without another word, filled your body cavities with rocks, wrapped you in duct tape, dropped you in the lake, and burned the cabin down. Thank your lucky stars that I'm now a semi-adult and able to hire out the wet work." Then I grabbed a cell phone at random off the table, dialed a dead drop number that my ex-partner and I had used for years, and left a message. I rattled off their names — Georgie, Charlie, Ken, Elwood, and Angie — then added, "Those Tongalese tree trimmers we used to know down in Long Beach. They still around? Good. Anything happens to Whitney or Lester, anything at all, I want these fuckers fed feet first and alive into the chipper." Elwood broke into a wail, and Angie started to weep silently. "Georgie, I want you to slap Elwood until he shuts the fuck up," I said as I cut off the call. I knew Georgie would take pleasure in slapping the helpless fat boy. "Elwood," I said quietly, "where's your mother?"

"She fell down," he blubbered softly.

"So we can add murder to the list of your sins," I said, and nobody disagreed. "Charlie, you tell me what the fuck's going on."

He blushed and stuttered but finally got it out. "Medicare fraud," he said, almost ashamed.

"Medicare fraud?" I said before I could stop myself, quite simply amazed. You could have knocked me over with an onion-skin carbon copy of a doctor's bill. "What the hell's this about?"

Nobody answered at first, then Ken, the lawyer who couldn't stop himself, shifted before he said, "About two or three hundred million dollars."

"You fuckers are all rich and you're stealing from the government," I said. Only Charlie and Elwood managed to look ashamed.

"It was such a perfect plan," Georgie said proudly, "and your best buddy is the one who worked it out. We overbilled Medicare claims by nickels and dimes and the occasional dollar. It's an invisible worm of a program."

"Three hundred twenty-six hospitals, nursing homes, and mental health clinics," Ken said, also almost proudly. "The loose change funneled automatically into an off-shore account. Elwood and Landry set up that part. But Mac came up with the lock."

"The lock?"

"We can't access the account without all eight keys," Charlie said softly.

"Keys?"

"Fucking box scores of baseball games," Angie said, then wiped her face. With her makeup gone she was no longer the poor little rich girl. Now she looked like her father when he'd bullied the city council into approving another of his shitty particle board developments. "Goddamned box scores, players' names, and game numbers."

"Foolproof," Elwood muttered. "The NSA couldn't break into our system."

"Until that idiot Landry went off the deep end," Georgie complained, "and fucked up. Then we were locked out."

"But Mac said he could get Landry's key," Ron said. "But he didn't. Then the damned lawsuit screwed everything all up."

"My guess is that you all chipped in to pay off the lab guy," I said, and they all nodded sadly. "And sent me after Lonnie Howell? Who the Doc knew from Vietnam?"

"Top-of-the-line interrogators don't come around every day," Charlie said, as if it were very important information.

"But he didn't come up with the key, did he?" I said. "He got sick of the business when Landry killed the kid. Then he faked Landry's suicide," I said. "Well, boys and girls, I've got some bad news for you. He did get the key, and when he was safe, he was going to sell it to you. But you cheap bastards couldn't wait. You killed him before he could tell you. Skinny little bastard with mismatched snowboots and a hole in his stocking was nine times as tough as your hired help."

They all nodded sadly, as if the money had been one of their favorite children, sent away to never come back. "So what the hell do you fucking idiots want with me now?" I asked.

They all looked at each other until Georgie finally let it out. "Well, the FBI is asking questions we can't afford to answer, so we wanted to hire you to find Mac."

"What makes you think he's alive?"

"Somebody's been trying to get into the account," Elwood said.

"And what makes you think I might look for him?" I asked. "What could you offer that would interest me? I've got you by the short hairs now. I can retire to someplace warm and pleasant on your stupidity. I wouldn't look for Mac for love or money. Revenge maybe, but that's between me and my worthless conscience."

"He said you were in love with his wife," Angie said, as if accusing me of murder.

"She knew about the scam," Charlie said quietly. "He said you'd never let her go to prison."

I had nothing to say about that. I just laughed. They blossomed with nervous grins, which faded as my laughter became more and more insane.

"I'm in love with his wife?" I chuffed between laughs as I settled down. "I'd eat buzzard guts before I'd fuck Lorna," I said.

And speaking of buzzards, Mac could charm one off its roadkill, I guess, and we were all his victims in some way. For the first time, I really hoped he was dead. For his sake. As Whit had said a long time ago: I had piss-poor judgment about people for a guy in my line of work, but I had never looked for anybody I didn't find. It was a gift or a curse, I had never decided which.

"Okay," I said when the crazy laughter finally died like the last ember in a wood-stove, said almost without thought, "you fucking jerk-offs. If he's alive, I'll find him. Before I start, I want a million dollars — five hundred grand up front in my offshore account, five hundred grand in escrow, and three corporate credit cards with no limit for expenses. And I want your box score keys." They looked at each other again. I wrote down the three names, DOBs, and addresses of my three best fake identities. "I can tell that you rich, cheap bastards have to talk it over. Whose place is this?" Charlie nodded. "Get me a pillow case," I said. He was up and back like a shot. I loaded it with shoes, cell phones, car keys, and revolvers. "I'll leave this shit with your boy on the other side," I said. "He'll come around eventually, I hope, then you better hope he's got the guts to come back over to get you. And tell your boys that if I ever see either one of them again, I'll kill them on the spot without another word. Then I'll start on you bastards. You'll be amazed how far down the line I'll get before they stop me." As I headed toward the door, I paused, turned around, and added, "And don't forget what it's going to feel like sliding feet first and alive into a wood chipper." Fucking white collar criminals with faces as white as death. They made me sorry to belong to the same species.

So I went back to my perch on the porch in the afternoons in front of the empty house behind me. I worked out in the late mornings, sweating out yesterday's slow beers. A front moved in from the east, a hard, cold snowless wind pushing over the divide, shifting Mother Nature's debris into my neighbors' yards. I got some hard looks, but nobody bothered me. They all knew I wasn't exactly a good citizen, which was probably why my wife had left. At night the girls and I watched old movies on the satellite television until I fell asleep in the chair. I could tell they'd never endured a Montana winter outdoors because as the temperature fell they spent more time sleeping on me and less time hunting. At some point I rented a houseful of furniture so the house sitters wouldn't have to sleep in an empty house. But I stayed outside most days.

And tried to work it all out again. Mac must have hired Lonnie Howell to interrogate Landry for his key to the system, but then the burned-out kid lost his nerve, panicked when Landry killed Doug Foley, then set up Landry's phony suicide. I hadn't been listening closely enough when Guilder told me what he'd dropped into the lake. *Blood and tissue samples, and a bit of stove wire* that probably had triggered the revolver as Lonnie drove away. And chances were that he had loosened the propane connection, too, but the explosion was larger than he had expected, which is how he lost the rear fender of his pickup truck. But Lonnie got greedy, which cost him his life. The scam seemed as solid as a lawyer, computer geek, and an accountant could make it, planning, I assumed, to use Angie Cole's dad's real estate business to give their dirty money a final rinse.

I could see the twins breaking into Mac's computer for his patient list, information to hurt his patients, sure, but I believed Elena's denial that they hadn't killed Sheila Miller, and they had no reason to steal Mac's hard drives and backup disks. Mac was worried that the scam might be mentioned on one of the disks. Well, I couldn't work out everything just thinking about it. In fact, every time I thought about it too long, my thoughts dissolved into a picture of a gutshot Mac in the middle of a long, painful humiliating death, crawling around as coyotes chewed on his intestinal loops. I tried to talk to Lorna, but she had disappeared, as had Marcy Miller. I called Lindsey Porter to suggest a gathering of Mac's ex-wives, but she said they weren't interested unless I could find out where his money had gone. She said she would talk to me, though, but she didn't know any more now than she had a few weeks ago. She just wanted to talk.

I kept sitting there as the weather changed, moving off the steps and up on the porch couch, bundled like a duck hunter in a blind, watching the weather as if the answers to all my questions were written on the light snow or the misty wind. I took the tape and splint off my nose as the bruises faded. Agents Morrow and Cunningham came by for another visit. Morrow was grumpy and frustrated at her failure to come up with anything more about Mac's disappearance and my refusal to invite them inside out of the cold wind. She knew his patients were lying, she said, but they wouldn't break their silence. Cunningham was as awkward and jumpy as a frog on ice cubes, but I stayed polite, avoiding their questions as nicely as I legally could until Pammie gave up, leaving with a promise to *see* me again.

Georgie Paul showed up at dusk the day

the first real snow fell, large drifting flakes. He wanted me to know that his group had come up with the first five hundred grand and had deposited it in my offshore account. He seemed proud of the fact that he recited my account number from memory, unaware that the five-hundred-grand figure automatically triggered a move into five other accounts set up by my ex-partner, who had retired to Belize some years ago. Then he handed me the credit cards and a list of baseball games.

"Don't you feel like a whore or something?" he said, shivering in the chill wind. "Taking money to look for your former friend?"

"Be careful," I said, watching a 7 Series black BMW pull up behind Paul's Navigator. "You assholes make whores seem like respectable citizens." Two blocky men in suits, overcoats, and fur hats stepped out of the car and stomped across three inches of wet snow in floppy galoshes, their hands in their pockets.

"Who are those guys?" Georgie asked nervously.

"Whatever happens," I said, "don't make any sudden movements."

One of the guys had a sloppy mustache, the other a unibrow. They didn't waste any time on pleasantries as they stopped at the bottom of the steps. The one with the mustache growled, "Larise Grubenko, you have seen her?" I didn't say anything. "She is our sister." I still didn't say anything.

"We will pay you," Mr. Unibrow said. "Five hundred dollars."

"Or break your knees," Mr. Mustache said, pulling a Smith & Wesson hammerless .38 with a potato-sized silencer clamped to its short barrel, a silencer nearly as big as the revolver itself. He pulled it out of his pocket slowly for effect.

"You guys don't even look like brothers," I said, "any more than the guys behind you." They didn't turn but paused long enough for me to pull out my piece. The short-barreled Walther PPK/S wasn't known for its long-range accuracy but I got lucky and popped Mr. Mustache in the eye and put the other six .22 rounds into Mr. Unibrow's face. The war and the rest of life had taught me that the first punch usually wins the fight. The .22 rounds bounced around inside their skulls like marbles in a urinal, whipping their already minimal brain tissue into bloody jelly slopping over the edge of their brain pans. They fell like sides of beef; splashes of wet snow outlined the heap of their bodies.

"Jesus fucking Christ!" Georgie said.

"Shut up and give me a hand," I hissed. The neighborhood hadn't moved, the .22 rounds muffled by the heavy snow. The Christmas decorations blinked and glowed in the whirling flakes, but no doors opened, no curious faces appeared at the windows, no careless caroler roamed the streets. Holiday fireworks had been rattling around Meriwether for days. Georgie Paul shook like a dog shitting peach seeds, as my dad used to say, but I bullied him into helping me drag the bodies into the backseat of the Beemer. I took the pickup out of the garage, put the dead guys' beautiful car into its place, then stuffed Georgie into the La-Z-Boy in my office and gave him a glass of Mac's Scotch. And checked the front yard.

There was almost no blood, and the drag marks were already filling with snow, but I scuffed them out anyway, searched the porch until I found all my brass, then went back into the office to get my camera and the fingerprint kit. The girls were avoiding Georgie as if he were a bad dog. They squatted in the far corners, growling under their purrs. I poured myself a glass of whiskey, too, and quickly replaced the barrel and reloaded the Walther as calmly as I could. I hadn't killed anybody in a long time. I had thought I was through with that shit. But I pushed it to the back of my mind with the Scotch, and did my job. I snapped several head shots of the bodies and a set of prints for Agent Cunningham before I dumped the lumps into the trunk. Maybe he could keep their buddies from showing up at my house. Then I sat down at my desk to call El Paso.

Disposal was going to be expensive: two guys and a flatbed wrecker all the way to Montana, then back down with the Beemer and its ugly cargo under a nylon shroud, headed south toward a terrible accident in the crusher. Somebody would melt the Walther's barrel for me. I locked the garage door and taped the key inside a loose corner piece.

"Can you use my computer to transfer twenty-five grand into another account?" I asked Paul as I went back inside to pick up my whiskey.

"What?"

"You can't stand the heat on this any more than I can, buddy," I told him. "Put that in the front of your mind. The best you can hope for is twenty-five to life."

"I didn't do anything," he whined.

"That's the crime, jerk-off," I said. "Can

you move the money?"

"I guess so," he said. "But why do I have to pay for this shit?"

"Because I don't want to," I said. "So fucking do it now," I demanded, then gave him the account number. "Remember, you could be taking a ride, too. Three bodies are the same price as two."

"What's my excuse?" he asked, resigned.

"There's no fucking excuse for you, Georgie," I said, "but you'll get some stock in a perfectly legal imported car dealership on the border, which will go bankrupt sometime in the near future, then you can claim a tax loss."

"I guess I've got no choice," he grumped, then sat down at my desk. "Sughrue," he added quietly, "I'd really appreciate it, though, if you wouldn't call me Georgie."

"No choice, Georgie," I said. "None at all."

He went to work at the keyboard without another word. Even with trembling fingers, it didn't take him very long. Modern technology has made crime a gentler proposition. I tried to feel bad about the dead guys, but I didn't feel much of anything. Fucking Mac had started this snowball rolling, and I was left standing in front of the avalanche of lies, more lies, and dead bodies. I let myself sink into the lounger, face-to-face with Mac's painting. An expensively restored crofter's cottage set above a shingled beach at the head of a hook-shaped bay. I had to admit that he wasn't a bad painter. The bay looked dangerously dark and deep, the beach rough, the hills beyond smooth and ancient, crossed with tumbled-down rock fences, filled with soft bogs between the dangerous crags, the tiny cottage with its wisp of peat smoke a place of safety in a harsh, unforgiving world.

Finished, Paul stood up, stretched sleepily as the adrenaline sifted out of his system. He even yawned as I asked, "Is your wife at home?"

"What?" he said, yawning again.

"Your wife," I said. "Is she at home?"

"Visiting her fucking mother in Indiana," he muttered, barely able to keep himself awake.

"Call her," I said. "Tell her you've got business in Seattle for the next week or so."

"What kind of business?" he asked rubbing his eyes like a small child.

"The business of staying alive. You fuck up, I'll dump your ass off a ferry into the

Sound," I said. "And we've got to give ourselves some semblance of an alibi in case something goes wrong."

"Alibi?" he repeated dumbly

"Go get in your rig, man," I said, "and wait for me to pull up behind you. Then I'll follow you home. You can grab a bag, then climb into my pickup, and I'll drive you to Seattle." Paul moved like a zombie, but he moved. I tore open a bag of dry food for the girls, left some cash for the house sitters, grabbed my traveling gear out of the Subaru, and tossed it in the pickup.

At his house, Georgie packed like a broken robot, his limbs without strength or direction. I stacked him and his bag in the pickup cab, filled him with downers, which worked as well as handcuffs, and headed west. The storm slowed us, but by midnight we were crossing the pass into Idaho. At the bottom, the snow turned to rain. I took another dose of amphetamines, and pushed the truck harder. We hit Seattle at dawn. I called my house sitters, claimed that the storm had caught me on the coast, and arranged for them to stay a week.

The only connecting rooms I could find at that time of day were in a suite at the Four Seasons. I put Paul in his bedroom, still drowsy from the road miles and the Mexican Valium, then I lost it. It all came to a terrible head inside, all the lies and greed and stupidity — some of it mine.

I beat him senseless. One shot under the chin to get his attention, then I worked over his guts, ribs, and kidneys until he was weeping like a child, begging me to stop. But I seemed to be taking out weeks of frustration and lies on the helpless man. It's a pure wonder that I didn't kill him. When my arms finally wore out, I threw him on one of the beds, dumped an ice bucket of cold water over him, then another, and another until he came around.

"I think you've broken something, man," he whimpered.

"You remember what that thug's eyeball looked like when the round popped it, the way the fluid splashed out on his cheek, the way his face suddenly collapsed on that side," I said. "Think about a knife blade in your eye, Georgie. If you leave this room while I'm gone, if you make a call to anyplace but room service, I can promise you that I will break you in half just before I cut your fucking eyes out."

"My God," he said. "You're insane."

"You better fucking believe it."

I hope he believed it. For his sake.

★ ★ ★

I put the DO NOT DISTURB sign on the suite's door, informed the front desk that my partner had the flu and shouldn't be bothered until we checked out. Then I took a cab down to First Street to work my way from dive to dive, slamming shots and beers with my people — winos, petty criminals, low-level drug dealers. Indian people drinking themselves into extinction, cheap whores, and clots of men whose failures reeked with anger and resentment. I couldn't manage to get drunk, couldn't even get high smoking crack with a half-breed Umatilla behind a bush down on the zigzags, couldn't even find a fistfight. Hell, I couldn't even get arrested. But sitting on a bench down on Alaskan Way, down where Mac and I had talked that afternoon shortly after Ellen Marshall had committed suicide in such a bloody, horrible fashion, her hands tumbling off the saw, I realized something. I should have thought about it at the time, but I was still wobbly, coming down from the quick shot of acid one of the twins had jabbed into the back of my neck a couple of nights before, and thanks to the massive dose Elena had given me, it came to me: a realization, a flashback, and bitter knowledge: I knew how to

412

find Mac. All I had to do was sober up and call my favorite perverts, Cunningham and Morrow. The sobering-up part consumed the better part of two days. I took pity on Paul, let him into my stash of Vicodin for the pain. But I wouldn't take him to the emergency room, not even when he begged. It was all I could do not to kill him. The Ukrainian Mafia guys had released something ugly inside me. Years ago I'd found some kind of sanity in the blood-drenched defense of my family. Now it was different; I wasn't on the run this time. I was on a rampage, calm and stupidly mean, ready to kill the first person who crossed me, but somehow without anger, which confused me. I drugged myself into sleep. When I woke at dusk two days later, I ate a room-service steak like a starving man, drank two beers, checked on Georgie Paul, who hadn't died but looked like a dead man, recently exhumed. Then I called Lindsey Porter to see if my truth matched hers.

She looked even better than the last time when she opened the door before I could ring the bell, looked as if she might have dressed for my visit, her lush body boldly naked under a pale blue jumper and dark blue turtleneck that matched her eyes, her feet seductively bare with pink painted nails. I couldn't see her makeup, but I could smell it.

"I'm glad you could make it," she said. "I know the ferry is a problem this time of night."

"Thanks for letting me come out on such short notice," I said. "I didn't know I was going to be in town."

She ushered me to the breakfast bar, saying, "You strike me as a man who prefers a bar stool more than a couch. And kitchens more than living rooms."

"Either is a good guess," I said as I sat down on the stool. "Or a damned good perception. My mother hated couches and living rooms. We were always at the kitchen table when I was a kid. Hell, the television was in the kitchen."

"Mexican beer, shitty Oregon wine, or Lagavulin?" she asked as she moved toward the wet bar.

"How about two fingers of Scotch and a beer back?"

She smiled as if it had been a test, and I had passed with flying colors. "What did your mother do?"

"She was an Avon Lady, among other things," I said. "Waitress, carhop, grocery

414

store checker, and the first female taxi driver in Corpus Christi, Texas."

"And your dad?" she asked as she set both Scotches and both Negra Modelos in front of us.

"My dad?" I said. "Well, mostly he was just a sweet, funny crazy man who spent most of his life going away. He never did anything very long, but he did lots of things very well. Cowboy, bartender, roughneck, hayhand, welder, short-order cook. But what he did best was drift away."

"My parents were born, raised, and buried within shouting distance of the Sound," she said. "I suspect that will be my fate, too."

"In the summers, I visited my old man in every state west of the Mississippi from Mexico to Canada," I said. "Drifting around, too."

"And women loved him?"

"It looked that way," I said. "He made them laugh."

"And you?"

"Wrong question," I said. "Wrong time."

"Sorry," she said, then we clicked glasses. "You said you had some questions."

"Honeymoons?" I said. "You're in touch with most of Mac's ex-wives. I need to know where you all went."

"The San Juans, St. Thomas, Tahiti, the Canaries," she said. "And, I guess, the Hebrides with this last wife."

"When we were on the bench that day," I said to myself, "he wasn't looking at the fucking water, he was looking at the islands."

"What?"

"Nothing," I said. "Just thinking out loud."

"You're thinking that he's alive?"

"Maybe."

"And you're going to look for him?"

"I don't know," I said. "I just don't know. But why don't we just let it alone for now."

"Fine," she said. "This is about you and me, Mr. Sughrue."

"You can call me CW," I said.

"And you can call me anytime."

So that's how we spent the evening. Telling stories, rustling up snacks, and drinking too much, laughing and becoming friends. At some point she moved to the stool next to me, and when we laughed we leaned into each other. When it became apparent that I was too drunk to negotiate the rambling roads, fog, and drifting rain to the ferry landing, we suddenly stopped

416

laughing in the midst of a silly story, the silence glowing between us.

"You can stay the night, you know," she said. "I'd like that."

"Thanks," I said, "but if I do, I'd best sleep on the couch."

"Why?"

"Well, your ex-husband, who used to be my sort-of best friend, fucked my soon-to-be ex-wife at a very bad time in our lives," I said. "She couldn't deal with the guilt, and I couldn't deal with her anger. And I'm afraid that when I find him, I'll kill him. I don't want to sound like John Wayne, but I've never killed anybody who wasn't trying to kill me. But I'm afraid I might shoot Mac like a rabid dog, gutshoot him, and kick him to death before he bleeds out. That might complicate our relationship."

"Or cement it," she said, her smile sweet with revenge, her laughter warm on her mouth as she kissed me.

It felt like a safe place, and who was I to disagree?

The next morning was rife with guilt, apologies, and recriminations over fresh bagels and smoked salmon, but enough of the sweetness and laughter of the night re-

417

mained so we knew, in spite of everything, that whatever happened we weren't through with each other.

My meeting with Agent Cunningham didn't go quite as nicely.

First, we had to find a place where Cunningham was sure he wouldn't be recognized, as if FBI agents were television stars, then a place where we could have lunch. It was impossible to estimate how many calories a day it took for him to keep that huge body running. Finally, we settled on an old bar nestled under the West Seattle bridge.

"This is the deal," I said as he finished his second chili cheeseburger, and I slid the pictures and prints of the dead Ukrainians in front of him. "You find out who these guys are, then get out the word that they were about to roll over on their bosses, and make sure everybody thinks it's a family hit. Then you get the tape back."

"What happened to these guys?"

"Well, buddy, I shot the motherfuckers in my front yard."

"What?"

"It was me or them," I said. "And a story you don't want to hear."

"Jesus, what in God's name did I do to deserve you in my life?" he said.

418

"You fucked that madwoman," I said. "Whatever happened after that, you deserved."

"Did you ever fuck her?"

"I wouldn't touch her with a ten-foot alligator's dick."

"God, she was amazing," he said, shaking his head.

"Was that before or after she stabbed you, kid?"

"Oh, fuck you, Sughrue, I'll do what I can," he said.

"You damn well better," I said. "And there's one more thing."

"Jesus shit."

"He wept, too," I said. "I want this person's passport number tracked. Call me." Then I gave him the kid's name.

"You son of a bitch," he said.

I kicked him in the shin so hard he turned white and nearly lost his cheeseburgers. While his mouth was open with the pain, I slammed the heel of my palm under his chin. And he nearly bit the end of his tongue off.

"I told you not to call me that," I said. "The next time, I'll fucking hurt you. Thank your pissant Kansas god that I'm in a good mood today." Then I stuck him with the check and left.

Seventeen

Dr. William MacKinderick was right where I expected to find him. But he'd left the flat-rock patio out of the painting. And the table where he sat outside drinking tea and smoking a pipe, wrapped in a heavy knit sweater and a canvas coat against the misty weather. Hell, he even had a tweed hat on his head and a bottle of Lagavulin beside the tea cozy. Almost everything else was just the same. The dark, deep bay bound by the ancient hills. The ruined rock walls, the bogs, and the rocky quiraings rising like forgotten fortresses beyond. Down at the edge of the bay, a form in a yellow rain suit and hood fished very hard with a heavy saltwater rig, casting a weighted treble hook with dangling bait that looked like baby eels, then retrieving it quickly, fishing quickly and tirelessly.

The bay hadn't been easy to find. Two weeks on a rented fishing boat out of Uig, stuck with two weathered Scots who almost never spoke, and when they did, their accents escaped me, so I had to guess at what the words meant. Even their hand gestures held a relentless economy. And when we shared my Scotch, their sips were so tiny they should have been tasteless. Midway through the first week, I realized I should have hired a pilot and a plane, but I knew I could never explain it to the captain or bear his disfavor. I'd eaten so much smoked fish, I didn't bother to smoke. But the occasional langostino saved my life.

I'd taken the long way to the Isle of Skye — Hong Kong, Singapore, Rome, then London — wasted round trip tickets under different names each time, then made the long drive on the wrong side of the road up to Scotland and across to the island, then over to Uig to rent a boat.

I parked my rented Volkswagen on the gravel beside a new Land Rover in front of the cottage, then walked quietly around the house. But not quietly enough.

"Well, it took you long enough," he said without turning.

"I guess I'm not too smart," I said. "But my wife probably told you that."

"I'm truly sorry for that," he said. "How are things between the two of you?"

"None of your fucking business," I said.

"So what are you doing here?" he said, still not turning as I walked over dry grass and damp stones to the table.

"I thought I came here to kill you," I said. "But you're such a pathetic son of a bitch, I don't have the heart for it. Giving you your life is punishment enough."

"I knew you'd dig it all out, Sughrue," he said. "I guess in some way, I wanted you to know."

"Save your psychobabble, asshole," I said. "You're going to need it in court. What's your key?"

"The game when Gil McDougal hit Herb Score in the eye with a line drive," he said. "Yanks, Indians, 1957."

"I should have guessed that you'd pick a tragedy, a time when real men suffered," I said.

"It's a child's game," he said, "a useless fact now that Landry's dead."

"Kirk Gibson. Dodgers, A's, 1988," I said. "Landry's key."

"How the hell did you know that?"

"Luck and geography, buddy," I said.

"Jesus wept," he said, turning now, a small .32 semiautomatic in his hand. "If you're not going to kill me, my friend, will you have a tot of whiskey with me?"

"Why in the hell would you go to all this trouble to steal that money?" I asked. "Don't you have enough already?"

"It's a lot of money," he said. "And once you've had money, you don't know when enough is enough." He raised the whiskey bottle, then smiled, the little grin he'd sported as he rounded the bases when he'd homered that last summer night when all this had started.

"Shove your tot up your ass," I said, knowing that if I knocked that grin off, I wouldn't stop. "I'm not your friend."

"I'll second that," Lorna said behind me as she came around the corner of the house, followed by Georgie Paul and two other very familiar people.

They must have parked down the lane and stayed off the gravel as they'd walked down to the house. Shit, I was the world's worst private investigator. Somehow they had followed me around the world. But then, of course, they did have the FBI giving them a hand. I never had a chance of losing them.

Lorna had dressed for the weather, glowing in a light gray designer rain suit with a matching tam and wellies. Everybody else looked like rags discarded into an alley in the East End.

"Wonderful," I said. "All is saved. The Feds are here." Morrow and Cunningham didn't even bother to look ashamed, al-

423

though Cunningham did try to hide his parabolic mike behind his leg. "Oh, dear, I guess they've been seduced by big money and bad pussy."

Pammie slapped me so hard I had to sit down in one of the cold metal chairs. When I got my wits about me, I picked up the bottle, slipped the cork, and had a long pull.

"Enjoy it, you asshole," Lorna said. "It's going to be your last." Then she added to Mac, "Why don't you have one, too, honey pie, because you're as dead as he is." Then she shoved Cunningham. "Kill them!" she screamed. "You said you'd kill them when we had the keys."

I suppose cold-blooded murder hadn't been on the training roster at Quantico because Cunningham hesitated. However, Lorna didn't. She grabbed his Glock off his belt holster and let off a round that nearly took his dick off but only grazed the front of his muscular thigh. It was enough to put him down, though, pitching him into Pammie and taking her down with him. As Lorna turned toward her husband, the fisherman on the beach turned, too, her hood flying off, casting her heavy treble hook at Lorna, screaming, "No!" The thick leader took a turn around

Lorna's neck, then the hooks snagged deep into her cheek. When Marcy Miller heaved on the rod, she nearly tore off the left side of Lorna's face. Lorna fired a single round before she collapsed. But that was enough. The .40 caliber round gutted her husband, slicing across his abdominal muscles as neatly as a scalpel. When he lifted his sweater, shiny blue-gray loops of intestine spilled out. He didn't even try to shove them back into his body.

But Marcy Miller did when she rushed up from the beach, weeping and screaming until I pulled his sweater down and put Marcy in a chair. Then I picked up Cunningham's gun and, just in case, lifted Pammie's as she hovered over Lorna. She was calm enough to stop the bleeding, but didn't seem to notice when I took her piece. I threw Mac's shitty little .32 into the bay. I had accounted for all the guns now. Georgie Paul looked as if he wanted to run, but once again the bloodshed had frozen him.

"Come here," I told him. "Come here and sit down." He came as obediently as a child in military school. "I want you to take this young lady back to the States," I said, "and care for her as if your life depended on it. Because it does."

"No," Marcy blubbered, "I killed my mother. I told her not to fuck him. But she didn't listen. I killed her."

I remembered that horrible moment in Mac's office, standing where she must have stood watching through the storeroom grill. I took hold of her shoulders, shook her until she faced me with open eyes, then lied as hard as I could, which was pretty hard by now, then said, "You didn't kill your mother. Believe me, you didn't, and this gentleman here is going to pay for some real therapy until you realize that. It was just a bad dream that Mac gave you. You did not kill your mother. You weren't even there." I couldn't tell if she believed me, but she stopped screaming and trying to gather the slithering guts of Dr. William MacKinderick.

Then I turned to Georgie Paul. "You got it, my friend?" I said. "Be goddamned sure you've got it. And you'll never see me again."

"Look," he said, holding his palms up in surrender. "I pray to God I never see you again."

Then I took out the list of keys. "How many are right?"

"All of them but mine," he said. "Try Barry Bonds' first home-run game. What are you going to do?"

"Well, buddy, I'm going to take the rest of my million dollars," I said. "And I've got a friend who will put your stolen money to good use. He has a history of that sort of behavior. The Red Cross, Doctors Without Borders, and perhaps a few radical groups who'd like to cut your capitalistic nuts off. Is that okay? A bit more attractive than a federal slam for the rest of your life. A small price to pay."

"I guess so," he stammered, "but what do we do about all this shit?"

"Hey, the keys are in the ignition of Mac's Land Rover," I said. "Get Marcy's bag and passport and get the hell out of here. Now. We've got a couple of FBI agents and a dying international fugitive, and if they can't cover their asses, there's no hope for us."

When they were gone, Mac whispered, "Thank you, man. Now why don't you put me out of my misery?"

"Hey, motherfucker," I said. "Just be glad there ain't no coyotes in Scotland." Then I emptied the piece-of-shit Glocks and tossed them on the ground. "I'll send the police," I said to them. "You assholes figure it out. Cover your ass. You're trained for that."

Then I left like a dog in the night, pushing back through the mist that before Glasgow became a rain so hard that sheep were falling down. What the hell, Glasgow had an airport, Hertz could find the Volkswagen, and I could fly someplace warm and sunny where the women were brown and naked, full of laughter, and didn't give a shit if you loved them or not.

But like a bad dog, I went home to a winter as cold as a madman's imagination. I learned to live in Whitney's house and call it mine, sometimes. I saw Lester whenever he had the time to spare. It seemed like only seconds before he was taller than me, as tough as his father but full of his mother's delightful laugh. I knew that someday I'd have to tell him the truth about how he came into the world, how his father forced his mother into whoredom, how she escaped, and how she'd died in an ambush gone wrong. And how I'd killed his father.

Whitney and I went through with the divorce, but we've almost become friends again as we talk about when and what to tell Lester. We're trying to learn to forgive each other, but we walked across too many graves to get here. I've never been able to tell her the truth about Mac and his greedy, rotten heart. Somehow it doesn't seem worth the trouble now. Whit and I are still a bit edgy around each other, and neither of us refers to that last part of our marriage or our lives. We carefully stay away from it.

I see Claudia from time to time. She seems to be filing lawsuits against every company who ever misused Butte, and she seems to be having a great time. After some dancing around it, we slept together again. But we don't talk much about the past. Sometimes, when we're together, the bad times come back, and we do more weeping than fucking, but the connection is still there, like an old rope, frayed but still strong, remarkably strong.

And sometimes I drive to Seattle to see Lindsey Porter. She's the only other person who knows the whole story. Except for Musselwhite, who listened without much comment, just a small threat to drop me off his client list if I didn't behave, then a rib-cracking hug, and some more Kiowa mojo about eating dogs. Lindsey and I have talked about making something more serious of our lives together. But the web of lies and secrets hanging between us is too thick and tangled to stumble through, so mostly we just enjoy what we have, and hope for the best.

I don't know what happened after I left Skye. I don't even know if Mac died, but I suspect he survived. Whatever happened, it didn't make the papers. There was a rumor that he and Lorna were living in seclusion in Switzerland on the last of his money while they tried to put the side of her face back together. But nothing solid ever came of the rumor, so I left it alone. I mailed the tape to Cunningham, and since it didn't come back, I assume he and Pammie are still FBI agents, working for the Yankee dollar. Cops get to be human, after all, learn from their mistakes, like all of us, and I wish them well. I suspect they'll be better people now. At least more careful.

Maybe even the group of greedy whore-dog businessmen are better people, too, for being almost caught. Who knows? Greed is a tapeworm. Shit you can't get out of your body. Whatever Marcy thinks about her mother's death remains locked between the walls of her shrink's office. Thanks to Georgie Paul, that asshole, I do know Marcy is doing well in college. She's got a full scholarship to Wharton and is looking at Harvard Law. Hey, cheap irony. I save her life, she becomes the enemy. That's cool. Life is more important than ideas.

And me? Well, hell, I try to stay home more often playing with the cats and doing the scut work that comes my way — depositions, employee thefts, domestic disasters — but I don't go hunting for lost people much anymore. The women tell me that after all these years I haven't even found myself. Of course, I haven't looked all that hard, yet.

good life is more important than video ...
And that. Well, hell, I try to stay home
more ... playing with the cats and ...
the ... at work that comes myself ... person ... over them, longest answer.
but I don't go hunting for lost people
much anymore. For woman, tell me who
after all these years. I haven't even done
myself. Of course, I have an idea it all her
hand, except

Author's Note

The title of this novel is taken from Richard Hugo's wonderful collection of poetry, *The Right Madness on Skye*. The final stanza is quoted below.

Tell Harry of Nothingham stop and
    have the oxen relax,
I want off at the crossroads. That's as
    far as I go.
I was holding my breath all the time.
    Didn't I fool you?
Come on, admit it — that blue tone I
    faked on my skin —
these eyes I kept closed tight in this
    poem.
Here's the right madness on Skye.
    Take five days
for piper and drum and tell the oxen,
    start dancing.
Mail Harry of Nothingham home to
    his nothing.
Take my word. It's been fun.

About the Author

James Crumley is the author of eleven novels, including one of the most critically acclaimed detective novels, *The Last Good Kiss*. His *The Mexican Tree Duck* won the Dashiell Hammett Award for Best Literary Crime Novel from the International Association of Crime Writers. He lives in Missoula, Montana.

The employees of Thorndike Press hope you have enjoyed this Large Print book. All our Thorndike and Wheeler Large Print titles are designed for easy reading, and all our books are made to last. Other Thorndike Press Large Print books are available at your library, through selected bookstores, or directly from us.

For information about titles, please call:

(800) 223-1244

or visit our Web site at:

www.gale.com/thorndike
www.gale.com/wheeler

To share your comments, please write:

Publisher
Thorndike Press
295 Kennedy Memorial Drive
Waterville, ME   04901